The Dynamic
Marching Band

The Dynamic Marching Band

Printed in the United States of America
©2008 by Wayne Markworth

Interior graphics by Wayne Markworth
Photos by Phil Sinewe and Wayne Markworth
Cover and interior design by Isaac Publishing, Inc.

Distributed by Marching Show Concepts, Inc.
For information regarding special discounts for bulk purchases,
please contact Marching Show Concepts, Inc. at 1.800.356.4381

Accent Publications, Inc.
an imprint of Isaac Publishing, Inc.
P.O. 342
Three Rivers, MI 49093
www.isaacpublishing.com

Library of Congress Control Number: 2008920676
ISBN: 978-0-9787472-3-7

First Printing, January 2008
Second Printing, September 2008

Acknowledgments

I am in grateful appreciation to the many friends, family and colleagues who helped with ideas, concepts, discussions, arguments and late night staff meetings. Without their assistance, inspiration and review, it would have been a short and boring book.

To Sherry Gilmore, for her ongoing guidance, advice, editing, and all things graphic. She has been a tremendous help in completing this book, making it a living and growing resource.

I am especially indebted to my lovely wife, Tami, for her devotion, support, intellectual analysis, critical review and stimulating conversation over the many years. Without her, I would not have been able to complete this project.

Wayne

Andrew Markworth	Band Director, Centerville High School, OH
Kara Markworth	Color Guard Staff, Centerville Jazz Band, OH
Josh Baker	Band Director, Greeneview High School, OH
Brandon Barrometti	Band Director, Centerville High School, OH
Rhett Cox	Band Director, Timber Creek High School, FL
Dave Coleman	Photographer & Trumpet artist, Xenia, OH
Joe Eck	Marching Staff, Centerville Jazz Band, OH and Student, Wright State University
Tim Fairbanks	Percussion Director, Centerville Jazz Band, OH
Jodi Fairbanks	Color Guard Director, Centerville Jazz Band, OH
Dr. Terry Frenz	Band Director, University of Cincinnati
Michael Gaines	Drill Designer
Randy Gilmore	President, Marching Show Concepts
Sherry Gilmore	Graphic Designer, editor, Marching Show Concepts
Scott Hickey	Scott Hickey Impressions, Boulder, CO
Dave Kaiser	Band Director, Wyoming High School, Wyoming, OH
Fran Kick	Creator and presenter of KICK IT IN®
Scott Koter	Former Band Director, Kiski Area High School, PA Program Coordinator, The Cavaliers Drum and Bugle Corps
Ryan Lamb	Percussion Staff, Centerville Jazz Band, OH Grad Student, Wright State University
Dr. Tim Lautzenheiser	Music educator and speaker, Attitude Concepts for Today, Inc.
Mike Maegley	Band Director, Kings High School, OH
Marlene Miller	Vice President and COO, Fred J. Miller, Inc. Uniforms
Greg Mills	Band Director, Kings High School, OH
Phil Sinewe	Photographer, Centerville, OH
Bart Woodley	Visual Coordinator, Centerville Jazz Band, OH

Table of Contents

Foreword

by Dr. Tim Lautzenheiser

Author Wayne Markworth, former Director of Bands (Centerville High School, Centerville, Ohio) is the architect behind the nationally acclaimed Centerville band program. He has dedicated his professional career to creating an exemplary band experience for those fortunate students who have been the benefactors of learning-and-performing in first class concert ensembles, remarkable jazz bands, and an outstanding marching band. The Centerville band program *IS: THE DYNAMIC BAND PROGRAM.*

Thanks to Wayne's ongoing desire to contribute to the world of band education, everyone can now enjoy the *wisdom of master teacher* via this all-encompassing treasury of pragmatic information written so it is applicable to any-and-every music-learning and music-making culture. From "taking attendance" to developing a worthy philosophical foundation—and everything in between—each page offers new insights and valuable suggestions to all who are eager to achieve *excellence* in every facet of *the total band program.*

Because of Mr. Markworth's thoughtful and sequential blueprint, one can use this text as a resource guide, an idea library, an embellishment to the existing curriculum, but—most importantly—it offers the critical road signs to successfully traverse the pathway-of-quality. This is not a book to be read and then put on the shelf, but rather it is one that will serve as an ongoing reference to be tapped time-and-time again; keep it within close reach.

Perhaps there is no way to write an all-inclusive manuscript that offers every bit of information about building *the total band program,* simply because the learning landscape is always evolving with new ideas, new music, new technology, new opportunities, new data, etc. However, the following pages are filled with tried-and-true suggestions that are not only conceptual, but also proven…proven by a *lifelong teacher* who brings a wealth of personal knowledge to the forum. The history of the Centerville bands serves as positive proof of the immeasurable value of the thoughts-and-suggestions shared by Wayne Markworth.

Last, but certainly not least, I have always been, and I will always be a Wayne Markworth fan. He represents the epitome of the ideal blend of *content* and *context.* He is an innately gifted musician, an incredibly sensitive human, a humble man of the highest integrity, and a gifted communicator. His bands thrived because of his commitment and dedication to developing the art form of music to its highest level. Wayne Markworth proves that *one person can make a difference.*

It is a privilege to share these supportive thoughts highlighting *THE DYNAMIC BAND PROGRAM* written by A DYNAMIC BAND DIRECTOR.

Strike up the Band!

Preface

The Dynamic Marching Band is more than just a clever name for a methods book. It is a challenge to band directors to make the marching band a dynamic activity both in terms of musical and visual performance and as a vital and meaningful experience for the students.

The Encarta® World English Dictionary definition for dynamic is:

1. full of energy, enthusiasm, and a sense of purpose and able both to get things going and to get things done

2. characterized by vigorous activity and producing or undergoing change and development

3. involving or relating to energy and forces that produce motion

4. involved in or connected with the study of dynamics

5. relating to or indicating variations in the loudness of musical sounds

6. used to describe any system that changes over time.

These phrases truly describe the best that the marching band of today has to offer to students and the people who work with them. The marching band season, which encompasses many months, literally and figuratively sets the tone for the entire school year in the total band program. This textbook is designed to provide information and stimulate thought and further study on the exciting world of the contemporary high school marching band. The target audience is the college music education major preparing to be a band director and the young director already "in the field." Veteran directors will likely find new information and new ways of thinking about the activity and perhaps get a dose of motivation and renewed vigor.

As the definition states, a dynamic activity is one that changes and evolves and marching band is certainly no exception. That which was "in style" or worked well in a show ten years ago may not work as well today. Communities and students change over the years and the director must be in tune with the situation. The modern band director needs to stay current with trends by attending clinics, workshops, performances of the best marching units in the band activity and most importantly learning from every situation experienced. This is a theme of this text – *learn from every experience*. Music education and band in particular is a career that can never be totally mastered but the challenge is rewarding.

All successful band directors develop and adjust materials over a period of many years to save time and communicate effectively with the band students, staff, parents and administration. A special feature of this book is the supplementary material available at www.dynamicband.com, containing forms, charts and usable materials that can be adapted to fit the band director's situation. These files are in Word, Excel and PDF formats that can be altered as much or little as the director chooses. The intent is to save the young director countless hours of trial and error building up a library of usable materials.

The content of this book equally emphasizes the *music education* and the *life skill development* of the students in the band program. The director must understand that whatever the level of the band program, from the most novice band to the highest level of competitive band in the land, the learning and well being of the student members must come first.

It's all about the kids!

Chapter One

Foundations
of the Marching Band

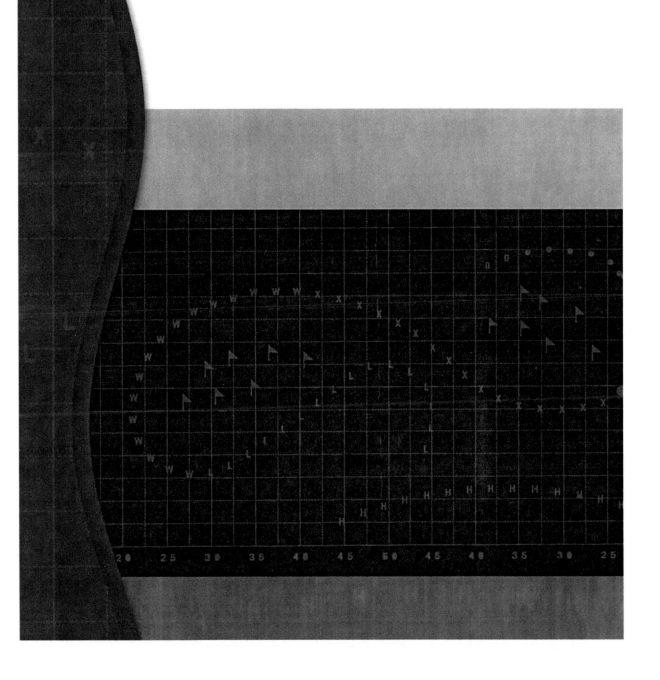

THE TOTAL BAND PROGRAM

The marching band is an integral part of the total band program.

A balanced total band program has the concert band as the heart and foundation. The marching band, however, is a very important element and supports and enhances the goals of the program. Each school is unique with many variations in approach, goals, organization and emphasis. The foundation for all marching band programs needs to be the emphasis on music education and the development of the student members.

Most marching bands function for a substantial part of the school year, with rehearsals frequently beginning in the summer. Therefore the band director needs to approach it with a strong commitment to sound music education goals and not treat the marching band as something to endure until concert season begins.

A graphic representation of a typical total band program follows:

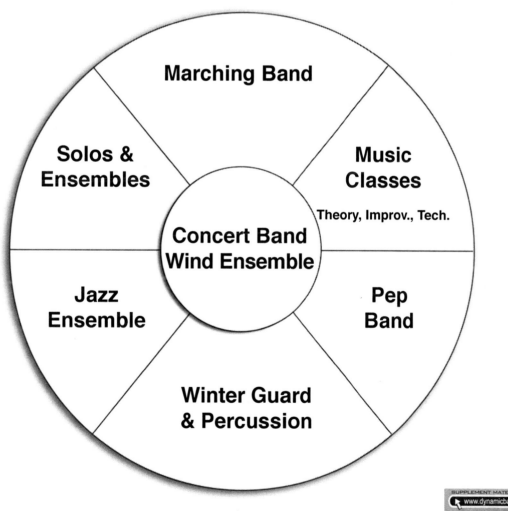

The Beginning of Each and Every Year
The marching band SETS THE TONE for the entire school year.

A substantial amount of time is devoted to the marching band in the fall and often the summer as well. Since it is the first contact with students for the new school year, everything that is done will lay the groundwork for the entire school year. What happens in the marching band, both good and bad, will affect all ensembles, classes and activities in the band program.

Because of the amount of time available to most marching bands, a tremendous foundation can be laid for good musical growth, social skills and leadership development. The marching band is a great vehicle for developing community and parental support for the band program and the entire school. It is the most visible music ensemble in most communities. When most community members think of the high school "band," they are thinking of the marching band.

The Musical Elements

- Tone quality and intonation should be addressed on a daily basis.
- Technique development in addition to the music performed can be stressed.
- Musicality must be developed for successful performances.
- Balance and blend is also essential for good performances.
- Practice skills will be emphasized on an individual and ensemble basis.
- All of these musical elements will carry over into the concert band and jazz program throughout the year.

The Social Skills

- Teamwork is essential for any successful group endeavor.
- A leadership program should be developed for the benefit of the students and group.
- The opportunities for positive social interaction and developing rapport far exceed the typical academic classroom or concert ensemble setting.

The Support Elements

- A successful marching band needs the support of the band parents/boosters organization. This requires parental support and involvement that will carry over to the entire band program. Successful students generally have supportive parents.
- Marching band is relatively easy to generate publicity, which enhances the total band program throughout the school year.
- A supportive school, faculty, and administration are important for a band program. These people can usually understand and support the more visible marching band that will develop into support for the concert and jazz ensembles as well.

The Values of Marching Band Participation

For most members, marching band is the most memorable thing they do in high school.

Participation in a strong marching band is an opportunity for students to grow in many areas – musical, emotional and social. Few other high school activities present such prospects for development. The values of participation are numerous.

- Performance opportunities in exciting venues

- Individual musical development

- Musical enjoyment and appreciation of all kinds of music

- Teamwork

- Commitment

- Responsibility

- Leadership

- Time management

- Goal setting

- Band family atmosphere

- Sense of belonging to an organization

- Confidence and Self-esteem

- Opportunity to experience success and failure

- Development of people skills

- Stress management

- Self-discipline

- Values of intense effort and hard work

- Excellence

- Motivation

- Physical Fitness

From the 50 Yard Line

"More than...50 friends, 50 dreams, 50 futures."

It is difficult for young band directors and music education majors to understand the positive impact that marching band participation can have on students if they did not have the experience of a dynamic and positive marching band themselves. In fact, many high school marching bands are not a great experience and learning laboratory with the values just described. The documentary *From the 50 Yard Line* uses the magic of mixed media to capture some of those values of the marching band experience that mere words cannot begin to express.

The film follows the well-known Centerville Jazz Band from tryouts, to band camp, to practice and finally, to the 2006 Grand National Championships. The documentary also follows the Fairfax High School Band, that was reinstated after 18 years of silence due to lack of funding. The film shows the similarities and differences between these two bands. The documentary showcases the power of music and the impact of the band experience.

The film presents the football field not only as a sports venue but also as a stage for the marching band. The viewer sees the great rewards of disciplined practice, the often-overlooked technical artistry of the group endeavor and the important life changing effects of instrumental music education. Another layer delves into the misconceptions and misunderstandings about marching band, interviewing average people on the street. The film tells the memorable story of music education, complete with the never-before seen emotional aspects of the experience. The students at the schools are wonderful subjects and their personal stories genuine and compelling. Nowhere else do you see hundreds of teenagers working together in such unison and commitment for one common goal. The film is part music video, part reality show, part drama, and full-on entertainment.

Los Angeles based Executive Producer / Director, Doug Lantz, a freelance journalist for ABC News followed the band for 8 months through auditions, band camp, practice, football games, local competitions and the Atlanta and Indianapolis BOA events. Doug is also a Centerville Jazz Band alumnus (1981-1985). *From the 50 Yard Line* highlights the importance of instrumental music in education and the life changing effects for those involved.

For more information about the film, visit *www.fromthe50yardline.com*.

Mission Statement

A Mission Statement should explain the purpose of the band.

The mission statement of the marching band should be a clear representation of why the activity exists, and should explain its purpose, values and nature. It could be read by someone unfamiliar with the program, like a transfer student, and immediately convey the essence of the band.

(A Sample Mission Statement)

Marching Band Mission Statement

The mission of the Central High School Marching Tiger Band is to make a positive difference in the lives of the band members by providing musical and visual experiences and performances, and to assist them in achieving their potential as they develop confidence, cooperation, leadership, responsibility and high standards of excellence and character.

The Goals of the Marching Band

By striving for meaningful goals, students will achieve the many values of participation.

The goals of the marching band should grow from the more general Mission Statement. The goals must be student oriented, achievable and match the values of the band.

(A Sample Goal Statement)

Goals of the Marching Band

The goals of the Central High School Marching Tiger Band:

• Each member will strive for high **standards of excellence.**

Be Your Best

• Each member will develop a sense of **responsibility** for attendance, preparation and each other.

Show Respect
Be Prepared
Be On Time

• Each member will expand his/her **awareness** in rehearsal and performance to enhance the overall individual and ensemble quality.

• Each member will develop **self-discipline** in and out of rehearsals.

7

Marching Band Styles

Marching bands come in all sizes, styles and types.

There are many styles and approaches to take and the band director needs to find the right match depending on the existing band program, the school and the community. It is not like the school's football team, where there are eleven players, there is an offense and a defense and they compete every week. The marching band director new to a school should obviously maintain the type of band he/she inherits. The director will need to decide what direction he/she wishes to take the program or keep it the same. It is very difficult to change a program that is viewed as successful to a very different approach. For example, a band that has been traditionally a show band, non-competitive and a strong program is not going to be interested in changing to a competitive, music program oriented band. (The director should weigh this carefully before accepting a new position.) The adage "Don't change anything your first year" is a wise one (excluding poor playing and behavior).

The most important concept to keep in mind is the band program must be **high quality musically and visually** and a **positive music educational and social experience** for the students. **Excellence** must be the goal of everything the band does. There should be more emphasis on music than marching (60/40 is good) if this is to be a music educational process. The band must play quality music and arrangements that challenge the musicians to learn and perform. Many approaches and scheduling options will be discussed along with pros and cons for each.

Types of Bands

In a nutshell there are only two approaches to marching bands:

- Non-competitive bands that perform at football games, parades, community functions and possibly non-competitive festivals but do not compete.

- Competitive bands that compete as well as performing the typical functions of a school band– football games, parades, and community functions.

A discussion of the values of competition or non-competition is addressed later in the chapter. Within each of these approaches are many styles or types of bands. There also are many variations or combinations of the types presented below.

Non-Competitive Bands
Friday Night Football Band
For lack of a better term, these types of bands mainly function as a football spirit band and perform at pre-game and half-time. There main purpose is to support the football team by creating spirit and excitement for the crowd and team. They often perform 4 – 5 different shows each season. Usually they only appear at home football games (and away in some areas) and pep rallies.

- **Pros**
  - Modest time commitment
  - Many music arrangements can be learned and performed.
  - School support is demonstrated
  - Visual drills are usually simple

- **Cons**
  - Due to the need to do many shows, the music arrangements are often simplistic and not educational.
  - For the same reason, the quality of performance is often not strong.
  - Concert band start-up can be late depending on scheduling.

Parade Band

Some marching bands have parade performance as their main focus. Many parade bands are located in northern climates where fall marching band is impractical after October 1. The parade performance usually involves a street routine, sometimes elaborate, while moving or in front of a reviewing stand. Often the parade season runs from May 1 though October 1 including the summer. Parade bands are often in a competitive circuit. Video clips of parade bands can be found on-line.

- **Pros**
  - The activity is appropriate for the climate.
  - Modest time commitment during school
  - Quality arrangements, since there are few songs needed, can be of higher quality.
  - Concert band can begin early in the school year.
- **Cons**
  - Summer time commitment is usually required.
  - Arrangements sometimes do not have much development because of the moving nature of the performance.
  - Drills are limited because of street width.

Show Band

There are areas in the country where show bands are popular. These can be southern style modeled after the Florida A & M Band and others, or northern style, modeled after the Ohio University 110. They perform at football games and festivals primarily. There are some competitive circuits for show bands and some show band classes within other competition venues.

- **Pros**
  - Entertaining performances with great audience appeal
  - Student members often enjoy the colorful visual aspect of the shows, especially the dancing.
- **Cons**
  - The exaggerated body moves and marching style make it difficult for young members to perform in a musical manner.

Big Ten

The Big Ten style was the model for many of the Midwestern bands for many years, but even the Big Ten schools now seem to use much stylistic variety, having adopted many of the characteristics of the high school competition bands. An exaggerated high knee lift is a feature of the style as is frequent fast tempos. The Ohio State Marching Band is a good example of traditional Big Ten style.

- **Pros**
  - Entertaining performances with good audience appeal
  - Student members take pride in being modeled after a college band especially if it is nearby.

- **Cons**
  - The exaggerated knee lift and marching style make it difficult for young members to perform in a musical manner.
  - Due to the physicality of the style, the music arrangements are often simplistic and not educational.
  - For the same reason and the many shows often performed, the quality of performance is often not strong in young students.

Competitive Bands

Music Style

This approach to marching band focuses on the music as the main element and was formerly referred to as "Drum Corps Style." Many competitive bands have their own identity or personality but the approach is pretty consistent, so there are not separate "types" of bands. Examples of identities would be classical music, contemporary/original composition, theatrical, visual and prop or symphonic band music oriented.

- **Pros**
  - The marching style allows for the best possible music performance, for young members in particular.
  - The amount of time dedicated allows for quality music and arrangements to be utilized.
  - More complex and entertaining drills can be used.
  - More time means more opportunities for life skill development, leadership and building a band family atmosphere.

- **Cons**
  - A large commitment of time and money is required to field an active competitive band.
  - A supportive boosters organization is essential (might be a Pro).
  - Burnout can be a factor.
  - Concert band start-up can be late depending on scheduling.

Rehearsal Schedules

Curricular

This scheduling method utilizes the curricular band class, during the school day, as the marching band rehearsal. The "band" is the marching band in the fall and the concert band following the fall.

- **Pros**
  - No after school time is required for rehearsals. This is particularly important where transportation or work schedules are problematic.
- **Cons**
  - Minimum time is available to produce a quality product using good music arrangements and visual elements.
  - The band members spend only minimal time together developing the important non-performance skills and values.
  - Concert band start-up is late often leaving only ¾ or less of the year for concert season.
  - Rehearsal facilities that do not distract other classes may be a problem.
  - If there is more than one concert band, combining them may be difficult.
  - Scheduling the color guard into the class can be a challenge.

Co-Curricular

With this scheduling method, rehearsals are outside of the normal school day, either after school, evenings or before school. The term "extra-curricular" is often used for outside of school and implies NOT curricular. Since there are so many educational values learned in the marching band, it is important to use the term "co-curricular" whenever possible. It sends a subtle but significant message to parents and school personnel. A program that rehearses totally outside of the school day is usually a volunteer organization (see below).

- **Pros**
  - The concert band program can begin on the first day of school. This adds at least 25% educational time over programs that wait until November to begin.
  - Amount of rehearsal time is flexible.
  - More than one concert band can be combined for the marching band.
  - Color guard availability is not a problem.
- **Cons**
  - Transportation can be a problem.
  - Time commitment can be large.

Combination

Most bands that are not totally after school use a combination of the in-school band class with some additional after school or evening practices. The amount varies from one extra rehearsal to three or four a week.

- **Pros**
  - Gives enough time to achieve better results and use a quality product.
- **Cons**
  - Added time commitment beyond the school day

11

Required Marching Band Membership

This is a band program that requires all members in the concert band program to be in the marching band. There usually are exceptions made for students in fall sports, with disabilities or religious objections. Some districts that have several high schools have a blanket policy regarding marching band membership so that all schools are the same.

- **Pros**
  - An adequate number of marching members is assured or at least all of the possible members of the total band population.
  - All students in the band program are receiving the same benefits musically.
  - There is a consistency in working with all of the various bands knowing they have all received the same musical training.
- **Cons**
  - Some students opt to not be in the band program at all in order to avoid marching band.
  - Students will be in marching band who really do not want to be there or are indifferent. This greatly affects overall attitude and performance.
  - Deciding what to do with the non-marchers (exceptions above) is a problem.

Volunteer Marching Band Membership

Many bands now use the volunteer approach to marching band membership. This is especially true for programs with a large number of students and several concert bands. The rehearsals will be outside the normal school day.

- **Pros**
  - The Pros of the Co-curricular program (above) are the same.
  - All students in the marching band are in it because they want to be, and attitude, work ethic and performance are strong. (Sometimes it is the parents that insist the student is in.)
  - A large time commitment is accepted because it is voluntary.
  - Many programs compare the marching band to an athletic team and justify tryouts and reserve members.
- **Cons**
  - The Cons of the Co-curricular program (above) are the same.
  - Time commitment can become excessive.
  - The marching band members receive much more musical training than the non-marchers in the concert bands creating a disparity.

Any style of high school marching band is justifiable educationally if

High Standards of Excellence

in musicianship and marching are maintained.

Philosophies of Competition and Non-competition

To be or not to be competitive...

One of the most important decisions a band director must make is whether to compete or not. As was stated in the previous section, the marching band director new to a school should obviously maintain the type of band he/she inherits and decide if, how and when to change. It is very important to have a philosophy in writing for either competition or non-competition and it is important to periodically communicate this viewpoint to the students, parents and administration. A good argument can be made for either case, depending on the school situation and the personal philosophies of the band director.

A Sample Case for Competition

Although there are pros and cons to competing, we feel the positive values far outweigh the negatives. We choose to compete in marching band because we feel it is the best motivator for you to excel as individuals and as a group. Our band's motto is "Be Your Best." We strive to achieve this every day and not just in show performances. However, we all tend to prepare better when we know there is a performance approaching, and a competition focuses this even more than a football halftime show or other performance. It is the same with academics—we all tend to study and learn more if there is a test than no test.

We think there is competitiveness **in human nature** that can be either good or bad. When friends get together and shoot baskets, it is not long before they are playing a game. When people go bowling or play a card game, they soon start keeping score because that is part of "playing the game." Band competitions should be *treated as a game* with no more or less emphasis put on it. When used as an enjoyable activity and means to achieving other goals, it can be very rewarding.

We treat competitions as a test or exam and use **the score** as a measurement of our success and improvement from show to show. Of course, there are always variations in scoring since it is a human activity. We will tell you if we think the score was accurate or perhaps too high or low for the particular point in the season. Just like in school our goal is to get 100 points. In band there is no perfect score, but our approach is to *strive for* excellence and perfection. If your goals are to be just pretty good, it is too easily achieved. Since scores start low and improve as the season progresses, we use the score as a benchmark compared to previous contests or seasons. We set goals such as "we hope to break a score of 80" by a certain time in the season. If we reach that score, and we think it is accurate, we have achieved a goal or plateau for the week.

When we rehearse, perform and compete, **we only have control of ourselves**—how well we practice, how well the show works and is written, and how close we come to achieving our potential. We do not have any control over what other bands show up at the contest and how well they are achieving their goals. Other than doing our best, we have no control over how the judges evaluate us. Our goal is to compete in great stadiums and where great bands are competing whenever possible. We want you to be challenged in rehearsing and want you to see the great bands of our activity.

We try to define the terms **winning and losing** in other than placement terms but in life skills terms. We have all seen first place groups that acted like losers and last place groups that were really winners in their behavior and attitude. We expect you to react the same regardless of what place the band receives—congratulate others and be humble if complimented. Human nature being what it is, we all prefer to place higher rather than lower and *that is okay*. The marching band competition scene should be viewed as part of the educational process of our band program. It opens up many opportunities for learning that cannot be duplicated elsewhere.

A Sample Case for Non-Competition

Our high school marching band has developed into a "Performance Band" as opposed to other schools who still have "Competition Bands." Our philosophy is that cooperation is the goal of our music program as opposed to competition. The marching band still focuses on quality performances but concentrates on parades, football games and other community events.

We perform music that is enjoyable and accessible to the average fan in the stands as opposed to esoteric music that many competition bands perform. The students prepare 3-4 shows each season and enjoy the style and variety.

Competition in marching band tends to concentrate on beating the other bands rather than focusing on one's own performance. In band and in society in general, the need to be "Number One" has gotten out of hand and overshadows important values. In our band we strive for cooperation, self-discipline, commitment, leadership and responsibility. All of these qualities are achievable in the Performance Band model.

We believe in performing music for its intrinsic values—learning for its own reward, especially in the field of music education. The extrinsic values—awards and placements—are shallow in a contest and do not have long lasting worth. Being in a Performance Band allows the members to concentrate on their performance and not worry about the judges, awards and contest results. The satisfaction comes from an outstanding performance, achieving *your* best results and not being *the* best.

Because of the focus on local performances, there is a reduced time commitment in the summer. Band Camp is the first summer practice and is held two weeks before school begins. The next week involves morning practices only.

There is also a reduced expense involved with the marching band program and therefore the band fees are about half of what a competition band's fees are. The Band Boosters can reduce the number of fundraisers and the workload involved with them.

Finally and most important, the Concert Band truly becomes the focus of the total band program. More time can be devoted to Concert Band practice in the fall and a late fall concert is scheduled each year. Music sight reading skills are improved because of the greater number of music arrangements performed by the marching band.

The Performance Band is a Win-Win situation for the band members, director, parents and community.

Band Motto

Every director and band program has frequently-used sayings and mottos that appear in conversation and on the band room walls and bulletin boards. It is a good idea to adopt an official band motto that encompasses the overall philosophy of the band program.

Here is one motto that works well:

Be Your Best

Be Your Best is a goal that everyone can achieve. It simply means that–Be **YOUR** best. This is not the same as "Be **THE** Best" which is something that few can achieve. It is all that is expected of you, but it is expected *all of the time*—every minute, every practice, every day and every performance. Further, it is expected that you will Be Your Best *outside* of organized band activities, as well as in rehearsals and performances.

You can measure your success and do not have to wait until someone else, like the director, senior or band judge tells you. You know!

Band Expectations

Show Respect

Respect yourself. Respect others. Respect the band facilities, equipment, and uniforms.

Be Prepared

Band members are responsible for doing their best, working on their individual skills, and practicing. All equipment must be brought to rehearsals as requested.

Be on Time

Students should arrive at the building 15 minutes *before* the rehearsal is scheduled to begin in order to be ready to start on time. If you count on someone else to get a ride to practice, tell him or her the time you have to *be there*, not the time rehearsal begins. With this concept, you will be prepared physically and mentally to begin the rehearsal and not flying in at the last minute or worse–late. You also will have a cushion of safety if there is extra traffic or you are running a couple of minutes behind.

ATTENDANCE POLICY

Every successful organization has guidelines regarding attendance and punctuality.

Every successful marching band has a defined and printed Attendance Policy that is distributed to the band members before the season begins. Because band is a team effort, an absence can affect the performance of a whole section and therefore the whole band. Because of this, the attendance policy must be strict in nature. For a policy to be fair, it must be administered consistently with consequences assigned from the director relative to the severity of the situation.

(A Sample Attendance Policy)

Attendance Policy

Expectations: You have made a commitment to be in the marching band for the fall season. Everyone is counting on you! In order to have successful band rehearsals and performances, it is essential that we have full attendance. **The absence of one person not only affects that person, but also the entire group.** The critical factors of uniformity, balance, spacing and alignment cannot be improved or maintained with absences.

Legitimate Excuses: Legitimate excuses for rehearsal or performance are illness, family vacation, accident, serious illness/death in the family and doctor's appointments. If possible, contact the Band Office at 123-4567 prior to an absence from a performance. **Students must bring an excuse note from parent or guardian following any absence.** A request to be excused from a future rehearsal or performance must be turned in at the earliest possible time and will be considered by the director, pending the legitimacy of the case presented.

Unexcused Absence: Unexcused absence from a performance is unacceptable and may result in dismissal from the marching band. Absences, tardiness or leaving early because of work or homework are **not excused.** Problems with absences, tardiness or leaving early from rehearsal will be given appropriate consequences regarding performance opportunities.

Ask: If you are not sure or have a request, problem, or question, *ask* the band director at the earliest possible time.

Reserve Policy

Reserve members are the extra players on the team.

If the marching band is large enough, it is good to have reserve members or as some bands call them "alternates." Reserve members are marching band members that perform in parades and football pre-game shows but do not have a full time position in the competition show. They attend all performances, trips, rehearsals, and band camp. The Reserve Policy should be printed and distributed to all members before the season begins.

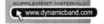

(A Sample Reserve Policy)

Reserve Policy

The CHS Marching Band is a **team** effort, and like any team we need to fill every position without any empty spots. This is critical because of two reasons:

1. The listeners and viewers (whether it is mom and dad or a band fan from another school or a judge at a contest) expect the best possible performance. An empty spot detracts from the performance of everyone on the field.

2. The absence of one person not only affects that person, but also the entire group. The critical factors of uniformity, balance, precision, spacing, and alignment cannot be improved or maintained with absences. Marching band members rely on each other for these things as well as psychological support.

In addition, our roster fluctuates because of illness, accident, and students transferring in and out of CHS. Our competition instrumentation is sent to the drill writer in early spring, and many changes happen between then and Band Camp. Members are re-evaluated for regular and reserve positions at Band Camp as well as throughout the season.

In order to give all members a fair opportunity and still maintain the highest standards of performance, we have established the following **Reserve Policy:**

1. Band members have performance expectations to be met at various deadlines - music memorized, guard routines, marching skills, drill formation positions, etc. These are usually checked by squad leaders and/or staff and called "check-offs."

2. Assuming these skills are learned, **all members march parades and pre-game shows.**

3. In most sections there are a few reserves or alternates that **take turns at performances and rehearsals.** These are usually rookies and occasionally others. If the doublers that share a position are equal in check-offs and ability, they will take turns in performances. If one member is clearly stronger, that person will march the important competitions. Due to the visual nature of the **Color Guard**, doublers are not usually used. Every attempt will be made to include as many performers as possible, pending their level of achievement.

This system has been successful over the years. It has also helped to *motivate* the members to always do their best and stay on target. The marching skills demanded by the contemporary marching band are very complex, and many times the physical coordination of young members does not mature until their sophomore year. Rookies often "pay their dues" their first year and then become a "regular" in succeeding years. No positions are ever "set in concrete" and many changes occur as the season progresses. Every effort to be as fair as possible and have as many members perform as possible will be made.

The Marching Band Staff

Every successful marching band has a staff to assist the band director.

Even the smallest of marching bands needs at least three full time staff members—one for the wind section (usually the band director), one for the percussion section and one for the color guard. The skills of these sections are so diverse that they cannot be taught successfully at the same time in a rehearsal. It is necessary for these sections to frequently rehearse separately and when combined, have the specialist focus on their section. The situation is not different than an academic teacher trying to teach algebra, geometry (both math subjects) and German at the same time. If any significant level of achievement is expected, a separate teacher and space is necessary. It is also very comparable to a high school football team. The vast majority of teams, if not all, have special assistant coaches for offense, defense, special teams, linebackers, etc. This is an analogy that all school administrators will understand, as well as the staff-student ratio.

Funding for at least these positions should be provided by the school district. In cases where this is truly not possible, the band booster organization should fund the extra positions. Providing additional staff support is one of the most important roles of the booster organization. See Chapter 13: The Band Boosters for more information. The band director should make a formal request every year to increase school district support for marching band staff.

The number of full or part time staff should be commensurate with the size of the band. As the size of the band increases, so should the number of instructors. In addition to the instructional considerations, the supervision and safety of the large number of high school students should be paramount to the school administration and the band director. This is especially true if the marching band travels to any event. The director must follow all school policies and procedures in hiring and utilizing marching band instructors even if funded by the boosters.

Design staff – The design or creative staff includes the band director, wind and percussion music arrangers (unless published), the drill writer, percussion and color guard caption heads and the color guard choreographer. See Chapter 7: Show Planning for more information.

Instructional staff – The larger the ratio of qualified staff to students, the better the level of instruction and the quality of band performance. The staff listed for small, medium and large bands in Chapter 12: Band Camp should be utilized once or twice a week for small sectionals. On a daily basis, at least half this number should be in attendance, with a minimum of one staff to 25 students.

Band camp staff – Band camp is the most important time of the season in terms of fundamental instructional time that will affect the entire year. Therefore, it is essential to have an adequate number of staff members teaching at band camp. See the "Instructional Staff" section of Chapter 12: Band Camp for specific staff information.

Evaluating the staff – It is the band director's responsibility to periodically evaluate the performance of staff members and communicate this individually to them. A staff member who is a district faculty member or paid by the school will generally have an official evaluation process that must be adhered to. Problems must be resolved quickly and professionally.

Characteristics of Great Band Directors

Passion/Enthusiasm

The successful director must have a passion for all aspects of the total band program – marching, concert, jazz and winter activities and the well-being of the students. This enthusiasm is always reflected in the band members.

Open Minded/Learning Attitude

One of the strongest characteristics of a great teacher is the willingness to learn from all opportunities. The band director can only come close to mastering the job in a lifetime and only if he/she is constantly learning and growing. The director who "knows it all" and is unwilling to change, will not be successful in the long run.

Confidence

Every successful band director exudes confidence in a humble manner. It is a fine line between confidence and arrogance, and the director must be careful not to cross that line. Everything is new to a young teacher and he/she must sometimes "act" confident. Great teachers are also great actors when they step on the stage (podium).

Energy/Fortitude

To run a successful total band program, the director must have great energy and fortitude. The job entails long hours daily, often 6-7 days a week and sometimes 24 hours a day. Even the daily rehearsals demand high energy to motivate and inspire teenage musicians.

Communication

The great director communicates well with students, staff, administration, parents and the booster organization. This is a characteristic that must be a priority. It is vital for the director to say "please and thank you" frequently. Band directing is a people skills career working with students, parents, administrators, secretaries, custodians and fellow staff members. Appreciation goes a long way in creating support.

Organization

"Organization is the key to success" is an often-quoted phrase that is certainly applicable to the band directing profession. The office work done outside of rehearsal can be overwhelming. It is important to handle paperwork and meet all deadlines.

Knowledge of band pedagogy

A basic foundation of pedagogical skills learned in college, from experience and from master teachers is essential to success. The band director who is enthusiastic, open minded and confident will learn and grow throughout his/her career.

Humility

All the above characteristics would be awe-inspiring but without a dose of humility, would probably be intolerable. It is okay, in fact essential, to say, "I made a mistake" from time to time when it happens. Students usually know anyway! It will make you seem human and students will have more respect for you.

Spiral and Sequential Learning Models

This method book will emphasize the spiral model and sequential learning.

The spiral curriculum uses sequential learning and emphasizes the add-on effect of skill and concept development. The student keeps coming back to the same ideas but at a higher level, in a circular or spiral manner. The students are constantly revisiting a music fundamental, but the quality increases as the students return and become more comfortable with a concept.

The spiral model also addresses the problem of students in an ensemble playing at many levels of ability and achievement at the same time. If the director waits until everyone or nearly everyone has mastered a concept, little progress will be made in the development of total musicianship.

An important aspect of the spiral curriculum model is that the students are motivated to a much higher degree because they are constantly making progress and playing *music*. Without motivation, learning suffers significantly.

A good analogy for using the spiral model for teaching band is a private lesson. A typical 30 minute private lesson (never enough time, just like a band rehearsal) would break the time into areas of concentration:

       5–10 minutes – **Tone** development (airflow, long tones, scales, etc.)

       5–10 minutes – **Lyrical** study or song (applying the tone development to *music*)

       5–10 minutes – **Technical or Scale** studies (maintaining good tone as technique and rhythm are addressed)

       5–10 minutes – **Technical** etude (continuing good tone and applying technical and rhythmic accuracy)

       5–10 minutes – **Solo or excerpts** (all elements of music combined to play *music*)

Here is how spiral learning applies to the private lesson model: 10 minutes of tone development *plus* 10 minutes on lyrical music is *better than* 20 minutes of working on tone alone. The students are more motivated and move the concept into real music sooner. More material is covered as well. In this example, there is only enough time to expand one area to ten minutes or the 30 minute time allotment will be exceeded. Of course when a concept is first introduced, such as characteristic tone at the first lesson, more time is need for initial explanation. As the concept is expanded or spiraled to other areas, less time is needed on that area of focus since it is applied to all areas. In other words, the study of a concept never ends.

The **linear** approach is to work on an area until significant progress is made before moving on to the next. Those who have taught private lessons know that development and improvement occurs at a slow rate. It takes months to develop good tone, technique or vibrato. To overdo the time spent on any one area limits motivation and delays the development of total musicianship.

The second main concept used throughout this book is the **Sequential Learning Concept**. This is teaching all concepts in a progressive and logical fashion and not omitting or skipping anything to get to the end product. There can be no gaps in the instructional process, and the instructor must "touch all the bases in order." A simple example from the marching topic is to teach and rehearse *all* of the fundamental skills in the marching program and then transfer the skills to the drill or show. One would not expect good results if *only* forward march was practiced and then a complex drill was rehearsed.

The **spiral** and **sequential learning models** work in concert to achieve great results.

Chapter Two

The Wind Section

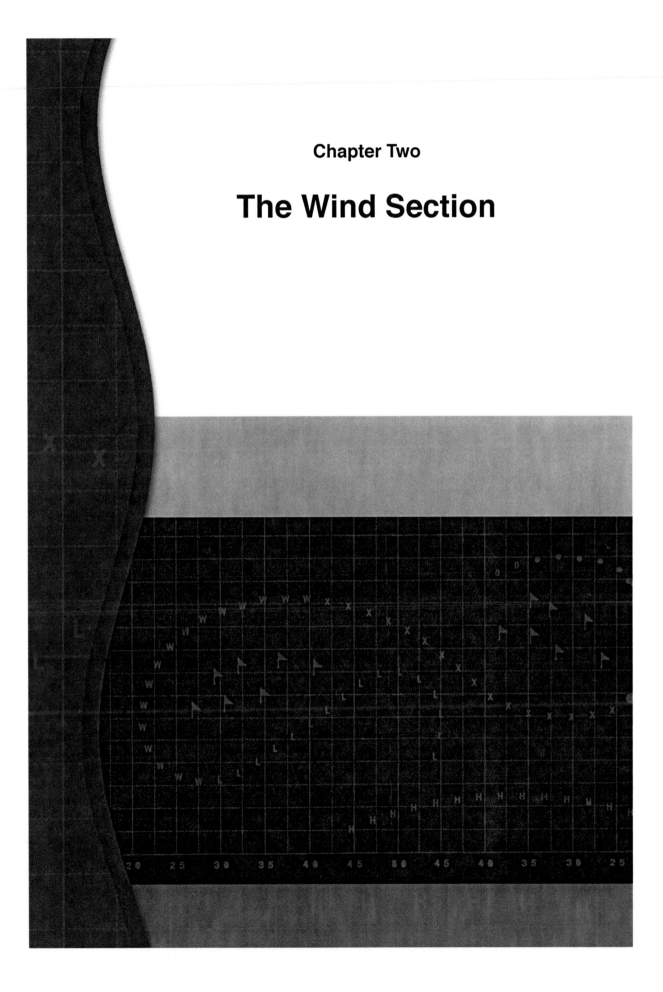

Concert Approach—Indoors or Outdoors

Good tone and technique is good tone and technique regardless of the setting.

Taking a concert band approach to brass and woodwind playing produces the best possible music performance for the marching band and assures that marching band music instruction reinforces what is taught in the concert bands, jazz ensembles, solos and ensembles. All of the ensembles in the band program are constantly reinforcing the skills and concepts taught in the other groups.

The days of "blood and guts" marching band playing are thankfully gone. That approach is no longer acceptable in competition, parade or football performances. A concert approach to wind playing will produce the most favorable results and advance the development of the individual players. Directors are urged to model the finest woodwind and brass playing from concert bands, orchestras, soloists and small ensembles.

Specific rehearsal concepts are discussed in Chapter 6: Rehearsal Techniques.

Several concepts for the wind section are important:

- A daily warm-up that emphasizes tone quality and technique must be used **daily**.

- Good tone and technique should be insisted on at all times.

- Quality arrangements that support good music education principles should be used.

- Music rehearsals, without percussion if possible, should be held both indoors and outdoors trying to achieve the same musical results.

All of the elements of good musicianship **must** be emphasized in fundamentals **daily**.

Quality of sound—Tone, Balance, Blend, Intonation

Technique—Scales, Rhythms, Lip slurs, Articulations, Range development

Musicianship—Phrasing, Style, Dynamics (full range), Expression

Warm-up circle—Winds

23

Tone Quality and Airflow

Tone quality is the foundation of all good ensembles.

An ensemble that has great technique and poor tone quality is not impressive. Most listeners will forgive minor technical problems if the ensemble's tone quality is beautiful. The elements of balance, blend and intonation go hand in hand with good tone quality. The basis for good tone quality on all wind instruments is a relaxed airflow. This is created with a large volume of air propelled through the instrument with minimal tension in the throat and upper chest.

The role of the diaphragm and its importance is often confusing to young musicians. The diaphragm is a curved muscular membrane that separates the chest cavity from the abdominal cavity. When the lungs are filled, it goes down and then relaxes by returning to the up, concave position as the air is forced out. A musician cannot *make* the diaphragm work other than by filling the lungs with air; it then works automatically. The phrases "use your diaphragm" or "push from the diaphragm" **should be avoided** because they usually produce tension in the stomach, chest and neck. Simply remind the students to "take in more air" or "fill your lungs with air" and "relax."

Cool Air vs. Warm Air Philosophies

Although highly revered in some circles, the Warm Air Philosophy *does not work* when playing a wind instrument, or at least it is usually misinterpreted. Experiment: Hold your hand 6 inches from your mouth and blow warm air "hah." You can just barely feel the air. Now hold your hand an arm's length from your mouth and blow warm air. The air does not reach your hand nor will it make it through the column of any wind instrument! Now do the same experiment with cool air and you can feel the air. The correct concept should be—blow warm air and feel the relaxation in the throat, neck and chest. Now while maintaining that relaxed feeling, blow cool air through your instrument.

Relaxed airflow is the key to good tone quality and tension is the enemy!

Breathing exercises are excellent to use prior to a warm-up. There are many good methods.

A simple but effective breathing exercise:

1. Stand with good posture.
2. Relax shoulders, throat and upper chest.
3. Fill lungs from bottom to middle to top (stomach rises).
4. Exhale all air through mouth—no tension—using *cool air*.
5. Four counts in, four counts out, five counts in, five counts out, etc.
6. Other exercises are similar but vary the number of counts in and out.
7. While the exercise is in progress, verbalize reminders to students:
   a. Relax shoulders, chest and throat.
   b. Inhale more air.
   c. Feel like you are filling your stomach with air.
   d. Exhale like you are blowing out a candle—cool air—fast air stream.

See *The Breathing Gym* by Sam Pilafian and Patrick Sheridan for further exercises (see Appendix) Of course, good tone quality is not possible without quality instruments, reeds and mouthpieces. These should be checked and corrected frequently.

Intonation

Good intonation is a direct result of good tone quality and airflow.

There are many approaches to developing good intonation and veteran directors are often adamant in insisting their method is the only way it should be taught. In reality, based on multiple learning styles and the spiral model, many methods of tuning should be utilized. Playing with good intonation is a learned skill that progresses through stages. It is a waste of time to spend time tuning when good sounds are not being produced with good airflow.

The admonition to "listen" has little effect on young developing musicians. What do you listen for? A discussion and demonstration of intonation beats and how to reduce and eliminate them is important. There are three levels of listening:

- Level One – listen to yourself

- Level Two – listen to those on either side of you

- Level Three – listen to the entire ensemble

It is absolutely essential that any tuning takes place **after** a careful warm-up has been played. Tuning before the warm-up will only insure that the instruments will go out of tune after the instrument temperature rises and the embouchure adjusts to playing.

Instrument tuning slides, barrels, etc. should be pulled to a standard length and adjustments made from there. Every player has different physical characteristics of the mouth and lips, as well as varying instrument quality, so placement will not be identical. Extreme variations are a sign of poor embouchure, bad reed, incorrect mouth cavity or dirty or poor quality instrument. The instrument should be adjusted to get the player in tune and gradually correct any problems over a longer period of time.

Several tuning methods should be utilized on different days to use the spiral learning method:

- Long tone unison exercises (see Daily Warm-up)

- "F" across the band starting with the tubas

- Visual tuning using an electronic tuner or computer (let students look at the meter)

- Using an Intonation CD to match pitches and eliminate beats (highly recommended)

- Each student should individually tune using one of the methods several times a week and before each performance.

Private Lessons

The fastest path to improvement for musicians and therefore the band is private lessons.

Private lessons are an excellent opportunity for student musicians to improve their skills and make the most possible musical progress. Interaction between a young musician and a skilled teacher provides a wealth of motivation and knowledge that can only be achieved through private instruction. A private lesson program should be developed, within the school if possible.

Private lessons work well with all levels of students:

- Advanced musician—advanced techniques and extra challenges are possible

- Average level—focus on the musical needs and progressive skills of the student

- Basic level—extra help or "catch up" with progress of band class or grade level

There is much research that shows that participation in band or other music ensembles greatly increases learning in other areas as well as scores on standardized tests. The academic increases are even more dramatic for students taking private lessons for several years.

Articulation Definitions for All Ensembles

The same approach to articulation is taken in all band ensembles.

There is no such thing as marching band or jazz articulation. The same concert approach should be taken regardless of the setting.

There are degrees of interpretation in articulation styles just as in any element of music. "Let's use a lighter articulation in this British band march" for example. Accents in music by Gustav Holst are much different than in music by Michael Daugherty. However the fundamental approach should be standard, and variations can be based on these general rules.

The concept of relaxed airflow and good tone quality needs to be maintained throughout all articulation patterns and ranges of the instrument. *The articulation syllables presented below are misleading because in reality, no one should say or sing a syllable when they tongue. The syllables are approximations of the cool airflow sound with a slight touch of the tongue at the start. Occasionally a student will get a growl in their throat because they are actually using the vocal chords. This must be remedied.

Articulation concepts:
1. There are three parts to each articulated note:
   a. Beginning (avoid the term "Attack" as it denotes too strong a start)
   b. Duration or length
   c. Release or ending

2. Articulation syllables* used to start the note:
   a. "TOO" for general playing and accents
   b. "DOO" for legato and staccato (saxophones use "THOO")
   c. Some clarinet specialists think "TEE" should be the basic articulation for clarinet be-cause of the mouth cavity formation and the affect on the characteristic tone. As the air is released, it must still utilize cool airflow "OO."
   There is little difference in "TOO" or "DOO" on clarinet.
   d. These syllables are the most natural and do not interrupt the airflow or affect intonation.

3. **Avoid** the following syllables:
   a. "TAH" or "DAH" – the jaw drops and intonation scoops, tone is affected.
   b. "TEE" or "DEE" – the throat closes restricting air flow (see 1.c above) and creates a c. nasal tonal quality.
   c. "DAHT" or "DOT" – this is often used in jazz styles but affects air flow and note release. It should only be used by advanced jazz musicians – college or older. It should NOT be used in marching band just to gain some precision on the release, because it creates an unmusical sound.
   d. "TOH" or "DOH" is good to open and relax the throat but air does not flow past a few inches.

4. Note lengths should be standardized:
    a. Legato – full length
    b. Staccato – ½ normal length
    c. Avoid the word "short"
    d. Use "light" and "half value"
    e. A staccato note is the same approach as legato but shorter

Accent – ¾ normal length and one dynamic level louder

Marcato (jazz, "treetop") accent – ½ normal length and one dynamic level louder

Long accent (accent with legato mark) – full length and one dynamic level louder

5. Note ending should be a breath release; simply stop the air. Avoid tongued releases or closing the throat as this gives an abrupt, unmusical release. A tapered breath release is musical and leaves a ring to the end of the note.

6. Instructors should always *sing correct syllables* when demonstrating, and students should sing parts with correct syllables as an exercise. Without playing and having to worry about fingerings and notes, the students can concentrate on correct articulations and rhythms. Once this becomes automatic, correct articulations in performance will be achieved.

SUMMARY
Articulation Syllables for ALL Ensembles

Articulation	Symbol	*Syllable	Length
Legato	-	DOO	Full
Staccato	.	DOO	½
Accent	>	TOO	¾
Marcato	^	TOO	½
Long accent	>	TOO or DOO	Full

Remember:
Airflow
Only use "TOO" or "DOO"
*(*Saxophones "TOO" or "THOO")*

The Daily Warm-up
"We don't have enough time to warm-up properly"
"We don't have enough time to NOT warm-up!"

The overwhelming amount of material to rehearse in an always limited amount of time tempts band directors to get to the music or marching problems as quickly as possible. The rehearsal too frequently begins with no warm-up or a quick run through the Bb concert scale. **It is a simple fact that an individual musician or an ensemble will make only minimal progress without proper daily warm-up at the beginning of a practice session.** However, a group or individual who does warm-up religiously will develop and improve at a much faster rate. A director often hears a student say, "I'm just not getting any better even though I practice every day." Ask the student about his daily warm-up, and the answer will usually reveal a minimum warm-up or none at all. Of course, a student may have other poor practice habits and still not improve.

Playing a band instrument is a very muscular activity. No one would think of running a race without carefully stretching and warming up. Severe muscle damage can occur if the muscles have not been properly prepared. Playing an instrument, especially brass, is also very dependent on carefully preparing the muscles for a vigorous workout. Therefore, a daily warm-up is essential to properly prepare the muscles and to avoid physical damage. The percussion section should warm-up separately if another instructor is available. The percussion and wind warm-ups should fit together so they can be played together when necessary.

Secondly, the music that must be played in any situation is of course based on a solid foundation of tone, intonation, balance, blend and technique. The warm-up period is the perfect time to focus on these aspects of good musicianship. When these become automatic in every note and phrase that is played, then good tone, intonation, etc. will be present in everything performed - a chorale to a rock tune. Conversely, it is very difficult to develop a good **foundation** when the first music played is rhythmical and needs a focus on technique and rhythm.

Finally, the warm-up at the beginning of the rehearsal establishes a **focused attitude**. It starts the rehearsal off in an atmosphere of concentration and relaxation. Self-discipline is also more likely to occur by beginning in this mood.

There is no warm-up that fits every situation, but there are some common characteristics in the approach taken by most professional brass performers. The brass warm-up is probably the most critical and the other sections can benefit from a good symphonic brass approach. The first step should be a few simple **breathing exercises.** (See sample Breathing Exercise on page 24.)

The remainder of the warm-up should contain exercises that develop tone, technique, articulation, rhythm, intonation, and dynamics. This is based on a spiral curriculum. An exercise will incorporate several of these areas of concentration. A successful approach is to work **progressively** from long tones to faster rhythms, from slurs to legato to shorter articulations, from a comfortable *mezzo forte* volume expanding to soft and loud gradually, from unison to harmony, and most importantly from low to high range gradually. The warm-up can be divided into three sections that can be interspersed with stretching exercises or warm-up marching maneuvers to maintain interest.

There are many quality warm-ups in use in successful band programs and most are similar. The following refers to *Daily Warm-up* (See page 30). It is based on a fundamental low Bb concert as the "home base" for a relaxed natural brass tone. Most school brass players who use F concert as "home base" tend to pinch, especially trumpet players. Low Bb is the most relaxed fundamental tone. The first two sections should be played at a full **mf** level as this creates the most natural, relaxed tone quality.

SECTION ONE

1. Low chromatic long tones, slurred, moving gradually from low Bb concert up an octave.

2. Bb concert scale in half notes, repeat as quarter notes, then eighth notes—slurred.

3. Legato quarter notes up the scale, eighth notes down the scale. "Etc. to" means continue the pattern up or down the scale until reaching the next written measure.

4. Simple lip slurs in a comfortable range. These are great for woodwind fingers as well.

SECTION TWO

5. Eb concert scale, slurred, half, quarter, and eighth notes. Try to imitate the relaxed feeling and sound as in Bb concert.

6. Legato triplets followed by staccato quarter notes. Try to imitate the relaxed tongue action of the legato when playing staccato. Play staccato notes half length and not short.

7. Interval tuning exercise, starting on Bb, down a half step, back up, down a whole step, back up etc. This is followed by a Bb unison, to a third, to a dominant seventh chord and tonic chord in Eb. The musicians then begin to work on harmonic tuning as well as balance and blend. This adds the first use of crescendo and **f** and can be followed by #1 measure one to refocus sound quality and relaxation.

SECTION THREE

8. F concert scale, slurred, in half, quarter, eighth, *and sixteenth* notes.

9. Rhythms on the F concert scale, or choose two rhythms from the music to be performed, one up the scale and the other coming down.

10. Half step tuning/Dynamics - whole note half steps moving up chromatically, each half step combination is played at a different dynamic level (**pp** to **ff**). This is followed by A to Bb major triads at gradually increasing dynamics.

11. Simple chorale chord progression going from soft to loud to soft.

12. A more complex chord progression, or choose something from the music to be performed, going from soft to very loud. Follow with #1 again to refocus sound quality.

This type of warm-up will prepare the players for the rehearsal as well as improve their basic playing skills. If used **religiously**, these skills will automatically carry over into the music being rehearsed. Even though fifteen to twenty minutes will be needed, once it is learned, the time will be worth every second as the overall quality will improve over a period of weeks at a much greater rate than if little or no warm-up is used. For those bands that have concert band in the school day and marching band after school, it works very well to play part of the warm-up in each session. Generally a thorough warm-up will last a player throughout the day. When a period of time elapses without playing, four or five exercises will generally be all that is needed to get the muscles ready.

"You don't have enough time to NOT warm-up."

Daily Warm-up with full score and parts is available for purchase from Marching Show Concepts; 1.800.356.4381, www.msconcepts.com.

Trumpet

Daily Warm-up

Wayne Markworth

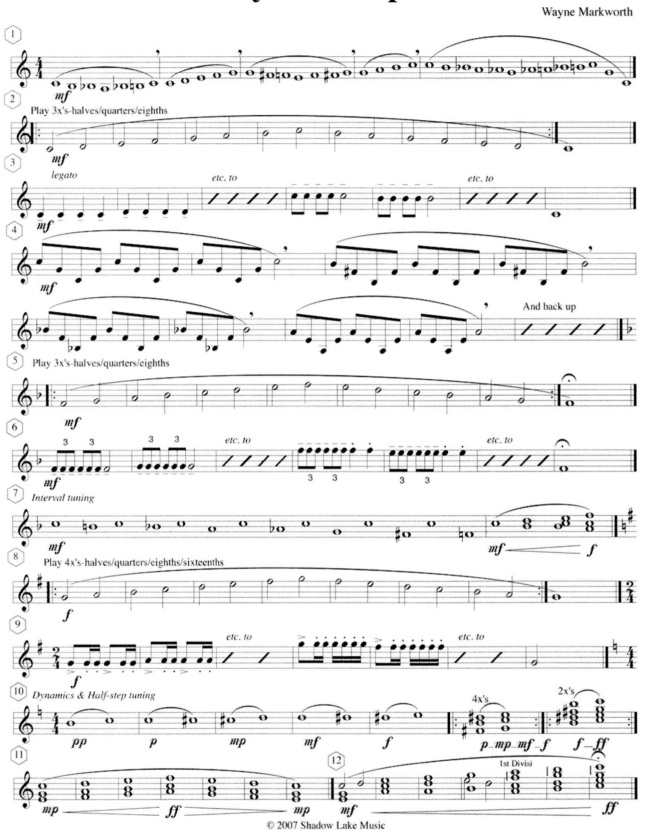

Daily Warm-up Two

This is a more advanced warm-up for further development.

Daily Warm-up Two (see pages 32 & 33) is designed to work on more advanced techniques and concepts. It works well when a second warm-up is needed, e.g. *Daily Warm-up* for morning rehearsal and *Daily Warm-up Two* for evening rehearsal. Concepts outlined earlier in the chapter are similar with expanded technique and range. Number 10 is purposefully left blank to be used as a chorale/lyrical study from an appropriate selection from the music being performed. The *Daily Warm-up* series works equally well with concert bands and jazz ensembles.

Daily Warm-up Two with full score and parts is available for purchase from Marching Show Concepts; 1.800.356.4381, www.msconcepts.com.

Range Builder

This is a simple but effective exercise for developing range for woodwinds and brass.

Range Builder (see page 30) will help musicians achieve expanded range facility with a good tone quality. Woodwinds need to concentrate on fingerings and brass on airflow and embouchure. This is a progressive exercise that should be approached with patience. Range development occurs over a period of time and not quickly. Play only number one until it sounds good and is played with ease, then add a line. There is always an array of maturity in any ensemble, and all players should not be expected to play at the same level. A few concepts are essential:

1. Play with full tone quality and relaxed airflow and observe the dynamic levels.

2. Play with minimum amount of tension in embouchure. Most range problems come from too much tension causing the lips to stop vibrating, rather than not enough pressure.

3. Keep fingers relaxed. This is frequently a woodwind problem.

4. Breathe only where marked. Many young brass players try to reset their embouchures to play high notes. This inevitably leads to a pinched sound. Observing the breath marks will lead to an open sound.

5. Do not try to play higher than can be played with a good tone. While the range must be pushed gradually, muscle damage can occur if too much pressure is used. It is a fine line and students need to understand that they should stop playing before pain occurs.

6. The exercises need to be memorized so that the students can focus on airflow. Improved technique and scale/arpeggio study is an obvious bonus. Students often show more interest in developing their range than practicing scales!

When more scales are memorized, they should be inserted, e.g. Gb concert between 4 & 5, A natural concert between 6 & 7, etc. A chromatic scale without an arpeggio is also a good exercise. Three octave scales and arpeggios can be added for woodwinds when appropriate.

Understanding that rehearsal time is usually limited, try to use the *Range Builder* once or twice a week and encourage at home practice on other days. It is also effective in a jazz ensemble rehearsal.

Range Builder with full score and parts is available for purchase from Marching Show Concepts; 1.800.356.4381, www.msconcepts.com.

Trumpet

Daily Warm-up Two

Wayne Markworth

Daily Warm-up Two - Trumpet

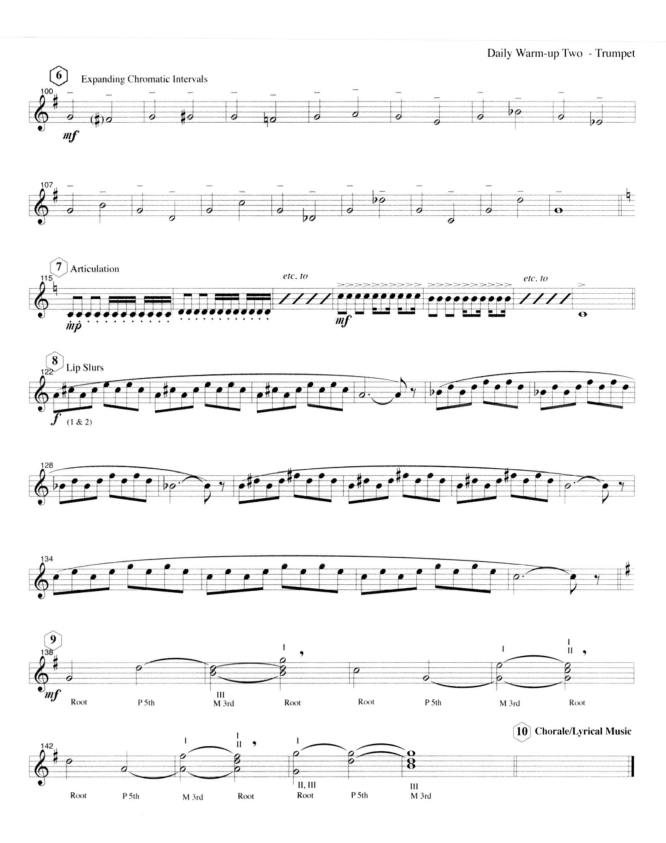

Trumpet

Range Builder

1. Play with full tone quality & air flow
2. Play with minimum tension
3. Breath only where marked
4. Add Ab, B and Db when ready

Balanced Instrumentation Goals

Having a balanced instrumentation in the wind section should be a goal of all bands.

A balanced instrumentation will always make an ensemble sound better. An unbalanced ensemble can make it difficult, if not impossible, to achieve a truly musical performance level. Successful band directors have many opinions about what constitutes balanced ensemble, but the chart on page 45 offers a good starting point for various sized groups. The "pyramid of sound" with a full low range, medium mid-range and less high, is the basis of these suggested numbers taking into account the typical instrument choices of most school musicians. There is also a consideration of geometric numbers for drill aspects of the visual program.

Although achieving a balanced instrumentation is often the "eternal quest" for most directors, the closer the ensemble comes to good balance, the better are the performance results. Creative arranging, staging and rehearsal techniques can help improve a balanced effect.

Some goals for a balanced instrumentation (refer to the chart):

1. Woodwinds should out-number brass.

2. One piccolo *only* should be utilized for flute sections of 8 or more.

3. Sections of one or two players should be avoided by switching to similar instruments, e.g. one mellophone is difficult to blend with other brasses. Switch the player to trumpet or low brass until at least three can be fielded.

4. Bass clarinets are used by many successful bands but are often not effective until four can be fielded. Adjust the other woodwind numbers to include bass clarinets.

5. To avoid only one or two players in a trombone or baritone section, using only baritones is an effective solution. However with eight players, four trombones and four baritones should be fielded. The trend in some bands to use only baritones limits the true tonal sound spectrum of the band. The trombone is an essential voice of the band sound and should not be eliminated for visual reasons or to emulate a drum corps sound.

6. Using groups of fours is very helpful for the drill writer as well as consideration of symmetrical geometric forms, e.g. 64 can be an eight by eight block.

7. Some marching bands have used flugelhorns successfully for more depth of the bottom trumpet parts or as an alternative to mellophones.

8. The percussion numbers should be in balance with the wind numbers and will be addressed in the next chapter.

9. The question of using over-the-shoulder tubas or sousaphones is a matter of personal preference and priority. Both types are available in quality models with concert bores. The marching tubas can be unwieldy for smaller students but have the advantage of converting to a concert band instrument. Some directors do not like the visual appearance of the sousaphone, as it is unlike all other brass instruments.

Balanced Instrumentation Goals
Marching Band

Total marching musician members:	32	48	68	96	132
Woodwinds	**12**	**24**	**32**	**48**	**64**
Flutes	4	8*	10*	18*	24*
Clarinets	4	8	12	18	24
Saxophones	4	8	10	12	16
(* includes one piccolo)					
Brass	**12**	**16**	**24**	**32**	**48**
Trumpets	6	8	9	12	18
Mellophones	0	0	3	4	6
Trombones	0	3 (0)	4	6	8
Baritones	4	2 (5)	4	5	8
Tubas	2	3	4	5	8
Battery	**6**	**8**	**12**	**16**	**20**
Snare Drums	2	3	4	5	7
Tenor Drums	1	1	2	3	3
Bass Drums	3	4	4	5	5
Cymbals	0	0	2	3	5
Front Ensemble	**3**	**4**	**6**	**8**	**11**
Marimba	2	2	3	3	4
Vibraphone	1	2	2	3	4
Auxiliary Perc.	0	0	1	2	3
Color Guard	**8**	**12**	**16**	**24**	**36**
TOTAL	**43**	**64**	**90**	**128**	**179**

Chapter Three

The
Percussion Section

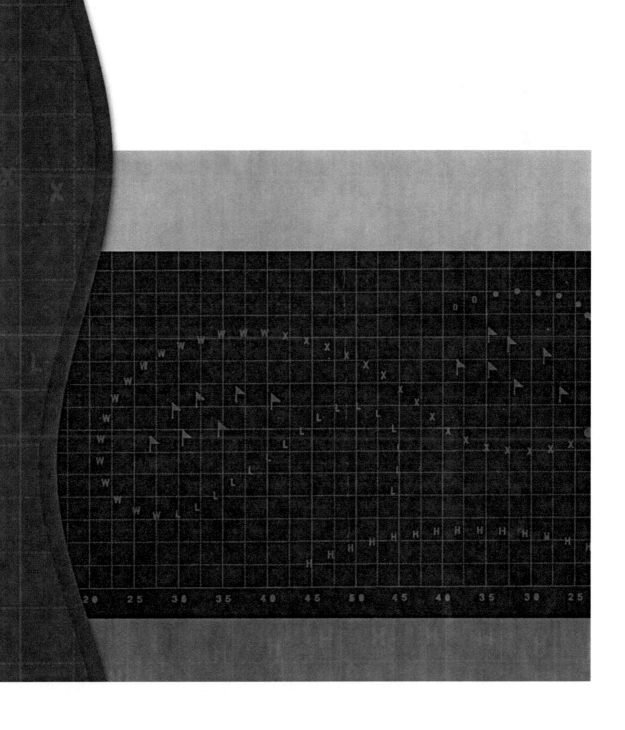

The Percussion Section

The topic of the percussion section in the marching band cannot be covered in one brief chapter in a book on marching band. There are, in fact, books and DVD's devoted entirely to this subject. In the contemporary marching band, the skills demanded by the percussion section are very specialized and ever developing.

As was mentioned in the first chapter, it is essential for any sized band, whether novice or advanced, to have a percussion specialist on the staff. The drumline, as the percussion section is frequently referred to, needs time devoted entirely to their needs and education. Further, the skills and musicianship learned in marching band will continue through the total band program.

This chapter will therefore be an overview of the marching band percussion section and lay a foundation for further study. It will cover what the band director needs to know to oversee the percussion program or if necessary, teach the percussion section at a basic level.

The diverse needs of the marching percussion instruments (the battery) and the front ensemble (sometimes called the pit) will be approached as separate skills and needs. The educational approach to percussion presented here should be utilized regardless of the type of marching band program—competitive or non-competitive.

Percussion Staff

As the percussion section grows in size and ability, so should the staff.

The lead teaching role in the percussion staff ideally should be a full time percussion teacher. In a large school this might be the assistant band director. In other situations, it might be a part-time instructor who just teaches the marching band as a supplemental contract holder or is paid by the band boosters. There are often percussionists in a community who perform, teach private lessons and would be available to teach the high school drumline. In a smaller setting, there might be an advanced college percussionist who could fill this role. Experience in a DCI drum corps is very helpful as a marching percussion instructor.

As the section grows, the first instructor to add would be for the front ensemble. A young adult percussionist can often fill this role. Next to add would be a second person for the battery, so one person could work with the snares and quads (tenor drums) and one could work with the bass drums and cymbals. For band camp and extended rehearsals with a large section, it is ideal to have one instructor for each sub-section.

Since percussion technique is so specialized, it is important for the percussion section to rehearse separately form the winds. This is only possible with a dedicated percussion instructor. At the beginning of the season, the percussion should practice 50% or more of the time apart from the winds. If the front ensemble has an instructor, they should rehearse separately from the battery at least 50% of the time. Some of the time, the front ensemble should rehearse with the winds (without the battery) since their parts are usually supportive and intermeshed. This is the time for learning the parts and developing technique and ensemble precision. Later in the season, the band focus is more on ensemble skills and less separate sectionals are needed.

Instrumentation - Battery and Front Ensemble

Every good music ensemble needs a balance of voices.

There are many considerations in trying to maintain an ideal balance from percussion to wind instruments and within the percussion section. If there are too many percussionists, they will overwhelm the wind section even with careful attention to dynamics. (There never seem to be too few percussionists relative to winds!) Attention to balance needs to start with the beginning band and addressed each year, striving for a good concert band balance. This will help resolve problems before they get to the high school when students are "entrenched" on their favorite instrument. Also, as the percussion section becomes accomplished, they will gain a lot of recognition in the school furthering the desire of many students to play drums.

Within the percussion section, it is important to have a balance of voices just as one would in the brass section – highs, middles and lows. Different skills and levels are demanded of the various instruments so care needs to be taken to match the players and instruments. There also needs to be a balance of battery to front ensemble players. Because of the growth of the indoor winter percussion activity, there is great interest in the development of mallet players and equipment in high school band programs. Many students are becoming mallet specialists in their interest and talent level. Of course all high school percussionists should be total percussionists, well versed in snare drum, mallets, timpani and drum set. These trends have been very good for the quality of percussion education in the schools.

Starting with bass drums (BD) as the foundation of the section, it is ideal to have five BD but four can work well. In a small section, three can be used, however the effect and variety is reduced considerably. The technical demands of the bass drummers are not near that of the snares or quads, but the timing aspect can be a real challenge. When the selection process or audition is in progress, a careful explanation of the skills needed for each section should be explained. Gone are the days when the best students played snare and the worst played bass drum or cymbals. Strong sections are now developing "specialists" who want to play bass drum, for example, for four years.

Within the battery, there should be more snare drums (SD) than quads (Q) (toms, tenor drums, etc.) generally 2:1. The number of cymbals (C), if any, in the battery is flexible. With few drummers, the front ensemble can handle the cymbal duties. If there are a great number of total drummers, many players can be in the cymbal section and with careful writing and technique, not overpower the wind section as much as many snares or quads would. Many students can then have the opportunity to march and develop those skills for future seasons.

Suggested Percussion Instrumentation					
Winds	**Snares**	**Quads**	**Bass**	**Cymbals**	**Front Ensemble**
to 40	2	1	3	0	3
40-55	3	1	4	0	4
56-79	4	2	4	2	6
80-109	5	3	5	3	8
110 +	7	3	5	5	10

The battery sub-sections use the concept of "listening in." The section leader/strongest player is placed in the center and the next two strongest players on either side of him/her, etc. The idea is for the outside players to match the timing and volume of the section leader. The section leader is usually called the "center snare," for example. The leader's instructions or count-off's can also be heard better if placed in the center. Odd numbered sections are preferable to place the lead player in the middle, but the concept works with even numbers as well.

The front ensemble's primary instrument is the marimba with the secondary instrument being the vibraphone. The ratio should be 1:1 and if uneven, more marimbas should be used. All other instruments including bells, xylophone, cymbals and any possible auxiliary percussion instruments are color instruments.

The **no battery–all front ensemble** instrumentation is an option for smaller bands. It is difficult to get a sense of cohesion and musical percussive effect with a battery of fewer than six members. As soloists or duets rather than sections, the ensemble result is not very strong. With all of the students in the front ensemble (which can be placed anywhere on the field) a concert band percussion approach is taken in writing, rehearsal and performance. Another option is to march the small battery section for just the opener and/or closer. This will create some variety of textures and sounds and also give the students an opportunity to develop marching skills for the future. A third option is to use every percussionist in the battery. This allows for a fuller section rather than two "thin" sections. The drawbacks are the missing mallet voice in arrangements and the lack of mallet training for future growth of the section.

A few competitive bands have chosen to use this concert percussion approach, using only a front percussion ensemble, even with large sections and have achieved successful results. The section then functions purely as a concert band percussion section and is effective especially with a more symphonic or concert band type repertoire. It very much changes the overall sound, tradition and effect of the total marching band. It should be noted that there are adjudicators who, while appreciating the creativity and artistry, will not give this approach full credit because of the lower level of demand in simultaneous responsibility. Although generally there are no contest rules prohibiting this, some view it the same as if the entire clarinet section was seated on the front sideline. ("Sure they sound great, but they are not marching!")

Percussion Equipment

The world of percussion equipment is very complex and often foreign to the young band director who is not a percussionist.

Percussion equipment is expensive and gets a lot of wear and tear in an active band program. Care needs to be taken to purchase quality equipment for good musical results and for longevity. The same equipment serves many purposes throughout the year in the total band program and with proper care and maintenance; it can last for many years.

There are several quality percussion companies that manufacture battery and mallet instruments and accessory equipment. Percussion specialists usually have their preferences of certain brands, and this is an important consideration. The top bands and DCI percussion sections should be observed to see which companies are currently making first rate instruments. Of course budget is always an issue, but it is not financially prudent to buy poorly made equipment that will have to be replaced frequently and sounds inferior. It is better to gradually purchase instruments over a period of years and then have a long-range replacement plan. Percussion instruments, if properly cared for and maintained, can last 5–8 years or longer.

Music store representatives and company websites can be helpful in determining the proper purchases for a program's needs. When there are several quality choices, go for the best price.

Battery Instruments

Most battery percussion instruments are made with maple shells (6 or 8 ply) and metal hardware of various weights. Many colors and finishes are available. A choice must be made between two or three levels of quality and construction. Some companies' drums are heavier than others. This could be an important consideration if the players are frequently young and smaller.

Snare drums - (first number is head size and second is drum depth in inches)

- 14 x 12 – for the competitive, mature marching band with many performances
- 13 x 11 – for the developing and younger drum line
- Indoor Drums (13 x 9 or 14 x 10) can be effective in the marching band especially if major competitions are in domed arenas.

Quads are recommended with four toms and sometimes a fifth and sixth small "spock" drum as an option. Three drum marching toms are not recommended for high school level groups because of the more awkward sticking patterns and smaller sound spectrum.

- 10, 12, 13, 14 – for the competitive, mature marching band with many performances
- 8, 10, 12, 13 – for the developing and younger drum line

Bass drums – five is ideal and four is workable.

- 18, 20, 22, 24, 28 – for the competitive, mature marching band with many performances
- 18, 20, 22, 26 – for the developing and younger drum line – use lighter drums

Cymbals

- 18" Medium heavy - for the competitive, mature marching band with many performances
- 16" Medium heavy – for the developing and younger drum line

Drumheads

It is important to budget an amount for drumheads every season. Depending on the frequency of the rehearsal and performance schedule, several sets of drum heads for the entire battery should be used. New heads lose their resiliency and sound "dead" after a period of time, so it is more than replacing broken heads. If the students are allowed to play with poor technique (especially at football games!), many drumheads will be needed. Do not allow this to happen!

Recommended seasonal sets of drumheads for the competitive, mature percussion section:

- **Snares** – One set for every 3 weeks of rehearsals and performances, new set for final week of season
- **Quads** – Small drums same as snares, low drums every 5 weeks
- **Basses** – One set at beginning of season, new set for final 3 weeks

For the developing and younger drum line:

- **Snares** – One set at beginning of season if Kevlar (and broken heads)
- **Quads** – One set at beginning of season, new set mid-season (and broken heads)
- **Basses** – One set at beginning of season (and broken heads)

Depending on the type of snare drums used, either a plastic dotted batter (top) head or a Kevlar batter head should be used. For the bottom snare head, a plastic or Kevlar head should be used. Plastic batter heads produce a more traditional sound. Kevlar have a crisper sound and allow for more precision. They are much more durable and are more cost effective, especially for young students. Do not over tighten and get a very high and non-resonant sound. Fortunately the days of the "pop corn" snares that sounded like a drumstick on a kitchen countertop are long gone! The marching snare drums should sound like a snare drum and not a bongo with snares. Pinstripe heads without dots are recommended for quads. Smooth white heads are recommended for bass drums. They need to be muffled to prevent excess "boom." Bass drum heads can be purchased pre-muffled or it can be done with foam weather-stripping.

If possible, change heads after practice and bring to approximate pitch and let them sit overnight. Then tune them before the next rehearsal begins. In regards to which company to use, if there is no staff percussion specialist, refer to what the major DCI and marching bands are using.

Carriers

It is important for the students to have quality carriers for their health and ease of playing. A quality carrier is well worth the extra expense. The tube carriers have the best characteristics of proper support, lightweight, durability and completely adjustable for various sized players. The snare and quad carriers should be worn under the uniforms for the best look if at all possible. Fit the uniform jackets for these players with the carriers on. Bass carriers and any part of the carrier that is showing should be painted to match the uniform. Make sure the carriers are compatible with the design of the drums.

Stands

If it is feasible financially, stands should be purchased for snares, quads and bass drums to be used during lengthy, standing rehearsals. This saves a lot of physical strain on the young students in particular. Make sure the drums are at the same height as with the carriers. This should not be over-used as students will need to develop the muscles and skills to carry the drums.

Mallet Instruments

The front ensemble has developed into an important section on its own in the competitive marching percussion arena. This has been positively influenced by the winter percussion activity. Quality equipment is important and also expensive. Care should be taken to purchase good sounding instruments that are also durable and transportable. Sturdy marching frames with wheels are essential, as is adjustable height to accommodate various players.

Instrumentation will depend on the preferences of the band director and percussion specialist but there are some general guidelines to use. A young, developing front ensemble program should be concerned with building technique and musicianship, which will carry over to the concert band program and build for the future as well. Generally the developing programs have a smaller number of percussionists so the instrumentation will be based on number of players.

Front Ensemble	Marimbas	Vibraphones	Aux. Perc.*
3	2	1	0
4	2	2	0
6	3	2	1
8	3	3	2
11	4	4	3

* The number of auxiliary percussion will depend on how many percussionists there are who are "not real strong" yet–musically or visually. Rather than marching in the battery, they can be placed on auxiliary percussion instruments with parts to match their capabilities and develop their musicianship gradually.

Of course, the instrumentation must match the band's available inventory. Xylophone and bells are color instruments, which should be used sparingly and played by any of the pit members. Suspended cymbals are frequently mounted on the marimbas and vibes.

Marimbas - The true characteristic marimba sound comes from rosewood bars. However, rosewood instruments are very expensive and not durable for outdoor use. The synthetic bars that are currently being used are quite sufficient for the marching band activity.

- 4 1/3 octaves is the standard size for high school marching band programs (two players can play on this instrument if two marimbas are not available)
- 3 1/2 octaves "junior" marimba is usable for the developing and younger section if price is a serious concern. However this instrument will not be very satisfactory for high school concert band and indoor winter percussion.

Vibraphones are the secondary front ensemble instrument.

- 3 octaves is the standard size for high school percussion programs.
- A motor should be included to use as an occasional color effect, although it costs more.

Xylophones should be quality instruments and mounted on transportable frames. The mini-xylophone is usually quite suitable for marching band use but not for concert band.

Concert bells and mini-xylophones can be mounted on the marimbas or vibraphones or on a separate table stand.

44

Auxiliary Percussion

All concert percussion instruments can be utilized for the front ensemble, such as concert toms, cymbals, hand drums, gongs, etc. These instruments should be well organized on trap tables or stands and transportable on carts or frames with large wheels.

Timpani

The timpani, if appropriate and demanded by the music to be performed, can be utilized in the front ensemble to good effect. It demands an excellent player, especially in regard to tuning, and should not be used without one. A sturdy cart needs to be utilized for transporting the timpani.

Sticks and Mallets

Sticks for snares and quads and mallets for bass drums and mallet instruments are a very personal choice of the percussion instructor to create the desired sound and technique. If no percussion instructor is available, the top marching band percussion sections should be studied to see what is currently being used the most. The players' level of development will be a determining factor as well. Purchasing of replacements can be handled in a number of ways. Students can purchase their own, just as woodwind players have to purchase their own reeds. This will lead to better care and storage. The band or school can purchase the initial pair, and students can be charged for replacements. A good inventory of replacements should always be available. A sturdy toolbox with a lock works well for this. Put one responsible student in charge of the stick box and bring it to all performances, as well as replacement heads.

Stick and mallet bags should be attached to the instruments in an inconspicuous place to allow for a variety of sounds and back up sticks in case one is dropped on the field.

For visual, weight and durability reasons, sticks are usually taped from just past the bead to the hand grip position with white electrical tape.

Front Ensemble players should have a wide variety of mallets available to use of varying degrees of hardness. A set of older or rubber mallets should be available for the inevitable rainy day.

Amplification of the Front Ensemble

Many marching bands are using microphones and amplifying the mallet and other percussion instruments in the front ensemble, mimicking the trend in drum corps. The intent is to allow the mallets to be played with correct concert technique and be able to compete with the volume of a strong brass section.

Warning: Do so at great risk to the balance of the total ensemble! Although there are the two "pros" to the argument mentioned above, the "cons" far outweigh them. Most marching bands do not have the volume created by a large and mature brass section as in a drum corps. The problem occurs when the woodwinds and mallets are playing together. Most often, even with volumes set low, the mallet instruments overwhelm the sound of the woodwinds placed farther away from the audience. Further problems include the limitation of tone color variety and dynamic shaping that is washed out through amplification. Additionally, the transparency of the staccato style is lost as a texture. Bars closer to the mics speak louder than those farther away.

Correct concert technique should be utilized regardless, and the outdoor marching activity simply demands 10% more stroke than indoor performance.

Occasionally front ensembles are placed on the field in various locations. In this instance, *judicious* amplification is needed to deliver the sound to the audience. The goal should be to imitate an acoustic sound.

Tuning

Tuning is an important aspect of the percussion section, and instruments should always be in good tune prior to starting a rehearsal. A good quality of sound is just as important in the percussion section as in the wind section, and playing and listening characteristics change as tuning is adjusted. Therefore it needs to be consistent and a daily concern.

Tuning does not always mean tightening. Find the most resonant sound for the instrument and match the others in the section. Percussion specialists have their preferences, but the band director should monitor to make sure the pitch level matches his/her musical tastes.

Snares should be tightened a uniform amount to produce a nice crisp articulation. Do not over tighten. The drum should still sound like a snare drum. Tighten the bottom head slightly less, so that it can resonate and create the snare sound.

Quads - Find the most resonant sound starting with the highest drum and tune down in minor thirds.

Basses - Find the most resonant sound starting with the lowest drum. Tune ascending using the following intervals Perfect 5th, Perfect 4th, Major 3rd and minor 3rd. Bass drums get very "boomy" unless they are muffled with a foam strip around the circumference of the drum near the rim or purchased pre-muffled.

Tuning procedure - Tighten each rod with fingers until a pitch is produced. With a drum key, use criss-cross tuning (clockwise for Kevlar) tightening each rod ½ turn until drum is in proper range. Tune and match pitches at each tension rod. Match the other drums to the first tuned drums checking each drum frequently. Tension rods should be greased with white lithium grease when changing heads. Use a large marching drum key to save wear and tear on fingers.

Care and Maintenance

Covers – All battery instruments should be covered for rehearsals and storage. This will protect the finish from scratches and other damage. Mallet instruments should also be covered for transport and storage and to protect against sun damage. Covers can be home made by boosters or purchased through the percussion companies. Moving blankets work well for this as well. Plastic tarps are needed for rainy days and should be readily available for sudden weather changes.

Frames should be tightened regularly and kept in good repair.

Hardware – Maintain small hardware such as felts, washers and keep extra replacements in a repair box.

Cases – battery percussion should be stored in cases or on secure carpeted shelves.

A percussion storage room is ideal for keeping the instruments organized and safe. Keeping it neat and orderly is a good student leader's job. Shelving can be purchased or built and use carpet on the shelves, if cases are not used.

Percussion Technique

Percussionists are challenged with the most technically demanding music in the marching band.

A foundation of solid technique is critical for successful marching band percussion performance. This is the main area where a percussion specialist is needed and a chapter in this book will only scratch the surface. The band director needs to have an understanding of the principles of marching percussion to oversee the program and if necessary, teach the percussion section.

Concert vs. marching—technique is basically the same. Quality is quality indoors, outdoors, marching snare or concert snare. What is written for the percussion section, the dynamic range and the instruments themselves are very different in the two genres. However, the intense training that the percussionists receive in the fall will carry over throughout the year in the total band program.

There are many approaches to marching percussion by specialists in the field but they are fundamentally very similar. It is important that the overall approach be based on relaxation and not tension—relaxed arms, wrists and fingers.

The first place to start, and this does not take a percussion specialist, is with posture, visual uniformity and discipline. The marching percussion section is very much a physical activity and it is important to make a strong visual impression. A frequent statement in regards to this is:

"You can't sound good until you look good!"

Starting with the first percussion rehearsal, perfect posture should be required. Sticks should be moved in a uniform manner from a rest position (sticks in) to a ready position (sticks out) with precision. The first note should not be played until this is perfected, and then it should be required before every start. Once this routine is established, students usually take great pride in this discipline. They want to look good and strong and make a great impression.

Two rehearsal concepts that are important are "tracking" and the use of Dr. Beat. Once the music and technical exercises begin to solidify in standing rehearsal, tracking should be used on a regular basis. Tracking is simple marching in block form while playing exercises and show music segments. The Dr. Beat or other electronic amplified metronome should be used **all of the time** at the **beginning** of the season to insure perfect timing and precision. **Caution** should be taken to be very careful of hearing damage, a serious potential problem for percussionists. The volume should be kept to the lowest possible setting that can still be heard, and quality ear plugs should be worn in rehearsal at all times. It is important to "wean" the section off of the Dr. or the first performances will be a disaster.

Sectional rehearsals should always be held in an organized setting, preferably outside (for volume and hearing considerations). A suggested rehearsal set-up:

Battery Section

Cymbals

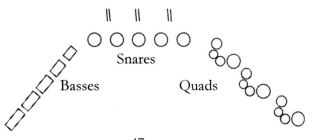

Snares

Basses   Quads

An in-depth analysis of technique is not possible here, but it is important for the non-percussionist band director to understand a few basic terms.

Traditional vs. matched grip – The first decision in snare technique is to use traditional or matched grip. Why use traditional grip? Two reasons – because it "looks cool" and is "traditional." Since using the traditional grip is much more difficult, it is imperative that the battery is taught by a percussion specialist and that the snare players are mature players. Otherwise, **use matched grip**. Matched grip is uniform in all percussion playing with only minor variations—quads, bass drums, timpani, and concert percussion. Therefore this is the place to start in the young and developing section or with a non-percussionist as an instructor. Refer to any good percussion text for correct grip position.

Legato stroke is the basic stroke or motion of the percussion technique. It is one quick down/up motion initiated from the wrist in a smooth non-stop motion. The players should focus on the up stroke (or rebound) and not the down stroke.

Dynamics are based more on stick height than on actual volume in order to attain uniformity in the section. The following stick heights are generally used for dynamics:

p	=	1"	f	=	9"
mp	=	3"	$f\!f$	=	12"
mf	=	6"	$f\!f\!f$	=	15+" with full (visual) arm

Front Ensemble

Sample front ensemble set-up (keep Marimba 1—section leader in center):

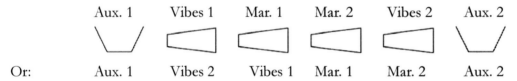

Aux. 1	Vibes 1	Mar. 1	Mar. 2	Vibes 2	Aux. 2

Or: Aux. 1   Vibes 2   Vibes 1   Mar. 1   Mar. 2   Aux. 2

Mallet technique – Two-mallet technique (one in each hand) should be mastered before attempting four-mallet technique. Refer to any good percussion text for correct grip position. The four-mallet technique needs the attention of a percussion specialist to execute correctly. For outside field performance, the mallets should be played with 10% more stroke when needed.

Piston stroke or legato stroke is the same as explained above.

Shift – Use the return (up) stroke to travel to the next note when changing notes.

Dynamics - The following stick heights are generally used for dynamics:

pp	=	1 ½ "	mf	=	6"
p	=	3"	f	=	9"
mp	=	4 ½ "	$f\!f$	=	12"
			$f\!f\!f$	=	15+"

Basic Technique Exercises - Daily Warm-up

The basic techniques for battery and front ensemble should be played *daily* in percussion sectional settings to work on specific techniques. There are many resources for technique exercises: see websites and search engine under "Percussion Technique." If the percussion section must warm-up with the winds, the *Daily Warm-up* will match and cover most skills.

Snare Drum

Daily Warm-up

Wayne Markworth

Mallet Instruments # Daily Warm-up

Wayne Markworth

Percussion Arranging

*Arrangements for the battery and front ensemble will have a
big impact of the total marching band's success.*

The quality of the percussion arrangements can make or break the overall success of the band's musical production. Too often the percussion arrangements create a negative effect by either overpowering the winds or being out of characteristic style for the music selected.

The band director needs to be aware of the characteristics of good percussion writing to make wise decisions regarding the percussion arrangements. It is the director's role to make sure that the total musical production is uniform in style, well balanced and creates a strong combined musical effect.

Great care needs to be taken in either choosing a percussion writer or in analyzing the music to be purchased. It is possible to use a published arrangement and have the percussion parts custom written to match the level of the percussionists.

Characteristics of quality percussion arrangements or compositions:

- Most important—research and listen to the **original** source of the music. Do not use DCI percussion as source material. Drum corps are wonderful and exciting but a totally different activity than marching band with great emphasis placed on percussion "pyrotechnics" often at the expense of a truly balanced musical production.

- The percussion arrangement should enhance and slightly augment the original source material to make it come to life on the football field and needs to be **idiomatically** appropriate to the style. If it is a concert band piece, it should be an enhancement of the concert percussion score. If it is a rock or jazz piece, it should be a re-creation and augmentation of the drum set part (there **must** be an obvious ride cymbal part!).

- The main role of the percussion section is to support and enhance the wind writing, second to create a rhythmic pulse when appropriate and last to highlight the percussion in a featured role. (This is where it differs greatly from DCI.) A good model for this musical balance is in the contemporary wind ensemble literature.

- The percussion writer should work closely with the wind arranger in initial show planning with the goal of creating a final musically balanced arrangement. Generally the wind arrangements are written first. The front ensemble mallet parts should be written as a sketch by the wind arranger because it is an element of the total music score. It can be a one or two line mallet sketch or even simple comments like "vibes sustain chords" or "marimba arpeggios here." The wind score with mallet sketches should be a complete musical package. It is no longer musically appropriate (if it ever was) for the front ensemble writer to introduce new musical material that is not a part of the original music intent of the wind arranger. Otherwise there are too many conflicting musical lines and too much clutter rather than a unified musical arrangement.

- Consider the front ensemble as a fourth section—woodwinds, brass, battery and front ensemble. Use interplay and combinations to create interesting orchestrations.

- **Do not overuse** the front ensemble – they should **not** be playing non-stop throughout the show anymore than the woodwinds, brass or battery should.

- Write fewer musical lines for the mallets. Look at the wind score—there is usually a melody, a rhythmic and/or harmonic accompaniment, a bass line, and possibly a counter melody. Counting harmony parts, there can easily be 8–12 separate wind parts. In that case, simple mallet parts—one for marimbas and possibly one for vibes is best. The color of those two instruments should not always be utilized together. Make sure the total musical intent is very clear and that usually means fewer lines.

- Mallets should double the woodwinds only sparingly. Accompany the woodwinds the same way a piano would accompany a woodwind solo.

- Write the auxiliary percussion parts as a composer for concert band or orchestra would—sparingly. It is more effective if these colors are not overdone. Make sure the instrument is musically appropriate and can actually be heard outdoors. Timpani in a Tower of Power soul tune does not belong! A drum set can be appropriate if the music calls for it, there is an excellent player and it is not overdone throughout the show.

- Use full battery ensemble sparingly, even with a large band. To support the winds, it is best to use one sub-section of the battery (e.g. just the bass drums). As the music builds a second sub-section can be added in. Save the full battery for full impacts, fills and solis.

- Battery parts should be rhythmically fitting for the musical intent. Don't mix triplets and sixteenths and quintuplets just to "get credit." They must make musical sense relative to the wind parts.

- Include dynamics (lots of them) in the initial writing and not as an afterthought later. Use crescendos and decrescendos to create musical phrasing the same way the winds do. Rarely should the percussion section play the same dynamics for more than 8 measures.

- Create interest in solo/soli sections with dynamics. *Music without dynamics is boring.* Too often drum features are simply loud the whole time and not effective, even when played fairly well.

- Create interest in solo/soli sections by *developing* rhythmic motives. Fast notes get *boring* unless there is a logical development into them.

- Make sure the level of difficulty of the percussion music is achievable by mid-season. Music should be challenging and educational but within the grasp of most players. The percussion still lays down a solid rhythmic foundation for the entire ensemble and this needs to be happening by the first performances. It is better to write on the easy side and "beef them up" later in the season rather than writing too hard with the intent of "watering down" afterward. The tendency for most instructors and writers is to predict the ability level to be higher than it usually turns out to be. ("Hope springs eternal…")

- Be flexible and willing to re-write once the music gets on the field. Balance is never the same on the field as it is on a computer music writing program.

- Listen to the wind score with and without the battery and front ensemble parts added in. Make sure it sounds better and is an improvement when added. If not, leave it out.

Percussion Staging and Marching

The percussion section makes a huge visual impression—good or bad.

Because of the physical size of the percussion instruments, the battery is always "in view" of the audience and needs to march well and be staged well. Don't forget that the front ensemble is very visual too. They need to look good, professional and involved with the music.

Most percussion specialists include marching as part of their duties in rehearsing the section. It is truly integral to the entire percussion performance.

Staging

The location of the battery on the field has as much or more to do with total band balance than the volume played. The most important rule is to stage the battery **behind the winds** and **close to the center of the field** as much as possible. The battery behind the brass section will create the most unity of sound and precision.

For the majority of the drill, keep the sub-sections together in horizontal lines and the entire battery close. It is not easy to hear, play well and project the sound forward when the section is moved into vertical lines or too spread out.

One word of caution regarding staging battery features is in order. Although the section needs to be staged front and focused for the feature, be cautious of placing them in front of the wind section for the end of the previous musical statement. The battery will overpower the winds. A good solution is to have the battery in the middle of the winds, say at the front hash mark. As the battery feature begins, they can move forward to a staged location. This will also create musical and visual interest as the introduction crescendos while they move forward.

Most percussion sections use a verbal count-off by the center snare or others to bring in the section together following longer rests. This is generally done using the syllable "duht" for each count. Care should be taken that the audience or judges do not hear this. Judges will generally forgive this early in the season but by mid-season, if it is audible, it becomes part or the musical texture and will be evaluated as being inappropriate musically.

Timing is an important consideration in regards to the location of the battery. **"Listen back"** to the percussion is the general rule of thumb for the winds and the front ensemble. When the battery is off-center, adjustments in timing will need to be made based on the arrival of the sound in the audience area. In general the front ensemble should **not** watch the conductor but listen to the sound of the battery.

Many bands have the drum major focus on the center snare drummer's feet while the lead snare focuses on the drum major's pulse.

Marching

Marching skills for percussionists are covered in Chapter 5: The Marching Program. It should be emphasized that the marching can hardly be separated from the playing in the percussion section. Attention should constantly be given to the visual aspects of the percussion section. As soon as music is solidified standing in place, the battery should start tracking and use it on a regular basis. "Visuals" (stick, arm or body moves) can add interest but should not be distracting or musically inappropriate. Watch outstanding drumlines for visual ideas.

What do front ensemble musicians do in parades? They can march (make sure they march during marching basics) and play cymbals, small percussion or carry water bottles for the others. They generally want to be included, unlike DCI groups, and enjoy being involved.

Electronic Instruments

The musical production can be enhanced with the judicious use of electronic instruments.

Electronic music instruments can be used as part of the front ensemble to add colors and variety to the sound palette. They should not be used to double or replace instruments except in a small band setting. Effective instruments to use are the electric bass, guitar, synthesizer, drum pads and MalletKat. Using a synth and/or bass is a great tool, especially for the small band.

A quality sound system is essential to the use of electronics in any kind of music ensemble. Care needs to be taken to balance the volume with the entire ensemble. It is best to err on the side of being too soft rather than too loud.

Resources

There is a great amount of material available to help with the marching percussion section.

Educational downloads from Websites:

Innovative Percussion, Inc. at www.innovativepercussion.com

Vic Firth, Incorporated at www.vicfirth.com

Dynasty USA at www.dynastyband.com

Pearl at www.pearldrum.com

Yamaha at www.yamaha.com, go to Yamaha USA > Products > Marching Percussion

DVD - *The Outdoor Gig The Scott Johnson Approach to Marching Percussion featuring the Blue Devils Drum Line.* DVD available at www.bluedevils.org produced by Dynasty USA

Summary

The percussion section can make or break the band.

The importance of having a dedicated percussion instructor with the percussion section at all rehearsals and performances cannot be overemphasized. The percussion area is very complex and out of the realm of most band directors' preparation. Further, the wind and percussion sections need to be separated during much of the rehearsal time due to the different skills being taught. The percussion students deserve a complete music education in their area as much as the wind players.

The percussion section can be a source of pride and spirit in the school further increasing the support, image and recruitment for the total band program. Band directors should not hesitate to support the school by playing at pep rallies and spirit functions (with the battery, a pep band or the entire band) as long as it does not infringe upon needed rehearsal time. The highest musical standards can still be maintained at these functions and further the performance experiences of the students.

Chapter Four

The
Color Guard

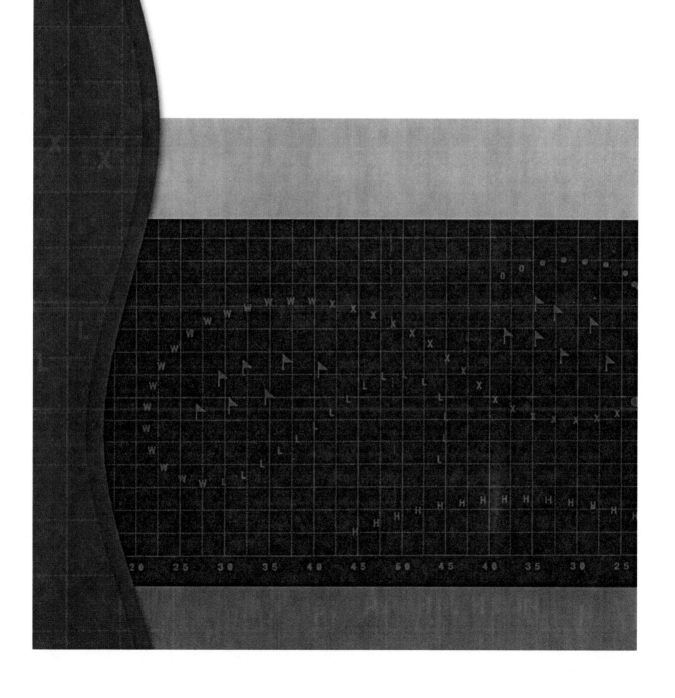

The Color Guard

Chapter 3 covered the marching band percussion section and emphasized the need for a dedicated percussion specialist to work with the section at all rehearsals and performances. This is typically the case since most band directors are not percussion specialists. That being said the topic of the color guard is even further removed from the knowledge base and comfort zone of almost all band directors. While most, if not all, colleges have a Percussion Techniques class as a requirement, it is doubtful that any colleges have Color Guard 101 as a requirement for future band directors. Yet the color guard is an important segment of the total band program that can involve many non-musician students (as well as musicians) and give them the opportunity to participate in a meaningful activity.

A color guard specialist is absolutely essential to teach the guard on a daily basis.

A color guard instructor can be someone with teaching experience in a DCI or WGI group or another high school band. If an experienced instructor cannot be found, someone with experience as a color guard member, with interest in learning the teaching aspect, can do an adequate job. Without a dedicated instructor, there should be no color guard until that time when an instructor can be secured. It is more than a band director can handle with all of the other duties required.

There is a substantial expense in properly maintaining a color guard for equipment, costumes and staff, but it is well worth the cost in terms of value to the students and the marching band.

This chapter will be a brief overview of the marching band color guard section. It will cover what the band director needs to know to supervise the program.

Role and Function

The color guard adds "color" and visual enhancement to the marching band program.

The color guard provides a visual interpretation of the music, style and theme of the show. A well-written and performed guard can enhance the music and make it come alive. For example, it can give the illusion that the band is louder or more beautiful than it really is. The guard adds to the overall visual (and musical) effect of the performance. By contrast, a poorly performing guard can detract from an otherwise strong visual and musical performance. It is therefore important to fully support the color guard program. The opportunity to involve more students in a worthwhile activity is a further reason for the school and boosters to support the program.

Recruiting

Wanted: Color guard members—no experience necessary.

The entire student body is the market for the high school color guard since, unlike playing an instrument, years of practice are not required. The only training ground for the color guard, other than being in a guard, is dance lessons. Therefore, the students who have had dance training should be a target group. Most marching bands have some members who play band instruments who are interested in the color guard. If it is a small band, this can be a problem. It is hard to deny a student access to the guard when literally everyone else in the school is being recruited. If wind instrument players are needed, some gentle "arm twisting" may be needed, but students should not be denied the opportunity to try out.

Since color guard is a very physical activity and coordination is required, auditions should be held to select the members. Even if the guard is small and a developing program, it is important that only members who are coordinated make the audition. Plus it will become more prestigious and eventually grow in numbers, if it is an accomplishment to "make it." Occasionally a school administration is opposed to tryouts for guard, in which case a comparison must be made to the athletic teams in the school and their tryouts.

See Chapter 11: Marching Band Recruiting for more information and coordinating the guard recruiting with the rest of the marching band. Some specific color guard recruiting ideas are:

- The guard is always recruiting for the future, so make sure the performances are always first class, and that it is an enjoyable experience for the members.

- "Word of mouth" from the current members is always the best recruiting tool.

- Make sure the costumes are attractive in the sense that others would see the group and want to be a member. No one wants to be in a group that looks shabby or dumpy.

- Make posters one month before the auditions and distribute them everywhere—high school, dance studios, middle schools, etc. Make sure they look professional and attractive, which is relatively easy to do on the computer. Use the band's website, newsletters and the community's newspaper to further inform people.

- Send a brief informational recruiting letter home to every student in the eighth grade and freshmen class, with school administration permission.

- Perform in school and community activities whenever possible. Create an assembly, if possible, three weeks before auditions – winter guard works well for this.

- Run a three day clinic & tryout. This gives the staff time to watch how quickly skills are learned and to see if students are dedicated in attendance and attitude. Teach some basics, a simple 16 count routine and a little dance. Keep it short and simple.

> ### The Marching Tigers
> ### Color Guard
> ### Clinics & Tryouts
>
> No Experience Necessary
> Dance & Flag Skills will be taught
>
> April 26, 27 & 28 - 6 – 8 pm

Costumes

Color guard costumes should be visually appealing and match the theme of the show.

Most competitive bands utilize a costume for their show that is new each year and in the style of the show concept. These can be purchased from the uniform companies and can include designs or can be sewn by skilled boosters. The consignment services mentioned in Chapter 13 are a good resource for a developing program. The winter guard and percussion groups also use yearly costumes. If budgets are not developed to accommodate this, costumes could be utilized for two or three years. See the Uniform section in Chapter 13: The Band Boosters for more information on designing and purchasing costumes. Make sure the costumes are fitted well before ordering and re-fitted when they arrive. Alterations should be made as needed to assure a good fit for each member. Order a couple of extra costumes for emergencies and any additional late joining members. Many companies handle color guard costumes and equipment. Two reputable companies are listed below:

Fred J. Miller, Inc.—Costumes and all color guard equipment: www.fjminc.com

The Guardroom, a web based company—Costume & equipment consignment company:

www.theguardroom.com

Equipment

In a novice or developing guard, start with just flags. When the numbers reach 12 to 16 and the members are proficient, add a weapons section starting with rifles. This would be dependent on having a guard instructor who is knowledgeable on weapon techniques.

Flags – Flags are available in aluminum and fiberglass and in various lengths with 5', 5 ½' and 6' the most frequently used.

Flag Designs – There are many ready to use designs in the catalogs and websites. Custom designs by staff or companies can be used as well. Flags are frequently made by band boosters to save money, using fabric purchased from the same companies.

Rifles – Rifles can be purchased in various weights and sizes. The companies can recommend which are best for novice groups. They are generally painted white to be most visible on the field. A small group of rifles can be used to portray the music for part of the show, but they are generally not used throughout.

Sabres – For the more advanced color guard, sabres can add another visual dimension to the visual program. It is recommended that the guard become very proficient in flags and rifles before adding a sabre section for part of the show.

Guard Mom

It is highly recommended to have a color guard parent who is interested in being the designated booster/guard coordinator usually called the "guard mom." This person can have a committee to help if the group is large. They can take care of makeup, hair, accessories, uniforms (fitting, storing, cleaning, transporting, etc.)—anything logistical that can help the guard staff.

Be cautious about giving the guard mom too much authority or decision-making because they have been known to become overbearing and controlling.

Technique and Terms

The band director needs to know the basic terms of color guard.

In order to properly supervise the total marching band, the band director needs to know the basic terms and fundamentals of flag technique. In the absence of Color Guard 101 in college, it would be a good idea for the young director to at least learn how to hold and spin a flag. The color guard staff should teach a solid foundation of technique on a daily basis, the same as the other sections of the band. Careful attention should also be given to body conditioning and movement.

There are excellent resources for developing a technique program. Highly recommended is the Cavaliers color guard DVD mentioned in the resource section following. Also excellent for a novice guard in particular, is sending the guard or at least the leaders to a summer camp. There are many quality camps around the country such as those sponsored by Fred J. Miller, Inc. and Bands of America.

Attention – flag is vertical on right side of the body with right hand on bottom of flagpole in front of right hip and left hand on flagpole (under chin), forearm is parallel to the ground

Hip Shoulder Angle – left hand on flag in front of left shoulder, right hand on flag in front of right hip

Ready position – flag in the up location, left hand at belly button, right hand at forehead, ready to spin (drop spin)

Front Present – the position with the flag extended at a 45° angle from the waist, left hand at belly button, right arm fully extended

Flat – flag is horizontal at waist with arms bent and elbows popped, could be a right flat or left flat depending which side the flag is on

Drop spin – the basic spin technique

Choreography and Staging

The location of the color guard in the drill can enhance the visual effect of the show.

The choreography and equipment work needs to be written at an appropriate level for the talent of the guard. An important element of the color guard is body movement or dance, both with equipment and without. The music should dictate what type of visual enhancement and interpretation is best. A talented color guard writer or designer should be hired to create the equipment work and choreography. This person does not need to be on staff but can do the writing and come in to teach it early in the season.

The color guard should be staged by the drill writer, using input from the guard staff and band director on the Data Module sheets. (see Chapter 7: Show Planning) A variety of staging options should be utilized: backdrop behind the instrumentalists, integration in the forms and features in front. Careful planning on the change of equipment (i.e. from one flag to another) needs to be incorporated in the drill and conveyed to the drill writer on the Data Module sheets. Generally the entire guard should not leave the field to change equipment at the same time.

Winter Guard

The winter guard program can be an important part of the guard program.

The development of the winter guard activity has created opportunities for those students who wish to participate in the guard activity throughout the winter and early spring. It is a great opportunity to raise the performance level. With a fall and a winter guard, neither one should be thought of as the main activity but rather a total guard program. Each activity reinforces the other. It is recommended that the winter guard be an optional program since some guard members will have other winter and spring activities. Other members of the band program and new recruits can also participate and have the opportunity to experience guard through the winter guard.

One special aspect of the winter guard is that the guard members are the sole "stars" of the show. That is one characteristic that has made winter guard so appealing to many programs. Further, it is a good recruiting tool for the fall guard.

Resources

There are great resources available for the guard members, staff and band director.

There are many excellent resources to use to increase knowledge, skills and motivation for the color guard—DVD's, summer camps and clinics for the students and/or leaders, live performances of great color guards in marching band, winter guard and drum corps.

One highly recommended instructional DVD is "The Cavaliers – Current Approaches to Color Guard" available at www.cavaliers.org at and as well as many educational and performance videos and DVDs on the Winter Guard International website www.wgi.org/store.

Summary

The color guard is an essential part of the marching band.

Band AND Color Guard

Do not use the phrase "Band and Color Guard" as that implies that the guard is separate from the band. The band has three sections – color guard, winds and percussion. Even though the sections rehearse separately much of the time, the unity of the band family is important.

It is essential that the color guard, if it is to exist as part of the marching band, has a dedicated color guard specialist to be at every rehearsal and performance. This cannot be emphasized too much to the school administration and band boosters. The guard is a great opportunity to involve more students in this worthwhile activity.

The camaraderie that develops in most active color guards is special. It is one of the most important experiences of most members' school years.

Chapter Five

The
Marching Program

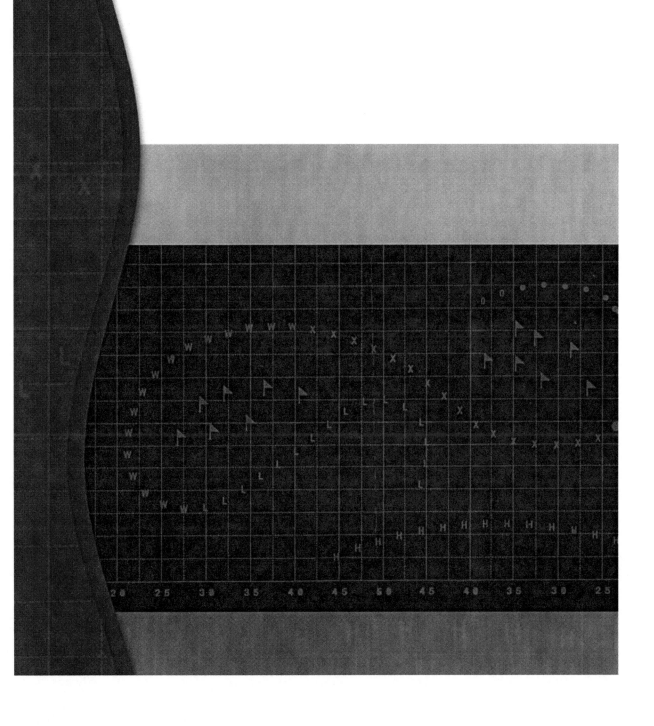

Marching Program Overview

Since "marching" is the first name of the marching band, it is important that marching techniques are taught with the same detail, organization and commitment as the music.

Whether the marching band is competitive or non-competitive, it is important that the band marches well and with a style and technique that allows the players to play well. It is an important element of the performance whether that performance is a parade, football game or competition. Audience members easily recognize a quality visual performance regardless of their knowledge of music. It has been said, "Anyone's grandpa and grandma can tell if a line is straight or not!" It is important that the marching band remain within the realms of music education, but if the members march poorly and look bad because of a lack of attention to the visual aspects, the band's performance will not be viewed favorably. Further, a band cannot perform musically to its potential, if good posture and marching technique is not being utilized.

There needs to be a solid fundamental program of marching techniques just as there is in the music area. This should include an organized and *progressive* method of teaching and reinforcing skills as well as a daily marching warm-up and development of ensemble uniformity. The same fundamental approach for musical development (scales, long tones, flexibility, etc.) should be applied to the development of visual skills (posture, foot technique, 8 to 5, etc.).

Since many young music educators have a strong background in the study of all aspects of music, but little background in the pedagogy of marching skills, time and energy needs to be invested in learning as much as possible to do a good job of teaching this major element of the marching band program.

Vocabulary for Marching Band

A guide to the foreign language of marching band

Since marching band uses a vocabulary that is foreign to most rookie members, it is necessary for each member to have a printed copy of the "Vocabulary for Marching Band." This will also help staff members who may have various backgrounds in marching bands and drum corps to all know and use the same terminology. The Word document is available online: www.dyanmicband.com, and may be modified to fit the terms familiar to the director.

ABOUT FACE – (also right & left) military turn in place, not often used today

ABOUT TURN – (also right & left) turn body facing 180º (or 90º)

ALIGNMENT - dress by rank and cover by file

ANTICIPATION - beginning a movement early

ARC - a curved formation which is part of a circle

AT EASE – relaxed position in place, no talking

ATTENTION - the basic standing position

BACK or BACKFIELD – the side of the field opposite the press box

BY THE NUMBERS - to rehearse a maneuver by counting or calling steps aloud

CHOREOGRAPHY – any physical movement other than drill

CLEAN – to make precise (*adj.* precise)

COLUMN - a line of individuals, one directly behind the other

COMPANY FRONT - standing or moving in a lateral line, in a large form

COVER - the straightness of a line of individuals front to back (*v.* to align)

CURVILINEAR DESIGN - any design utilizing arc or curved segments

DIAGONAL – two or more members in line at an angle to the yardlines

DISTANCE - the space between members from front to back

DRESS or GUIDE – check the straightness of a lateral line, standing or moving

DRIFTING – gradually shifting out of position

FALL IN - take up position in formation designated

FLANK - abrupt change of direction 90º to the right or left, by each individual or rank

FILE - a line of individuals, one directly behind the other

FLOATING TURN – an advanced technique to change direction while in motion

FOLLOW THE LEADER - a group of people that are led in a predetermined path

FRONT – towards the press box side of the field

GATE - the movement of a form with one end fixed as a pivot

GRID SYSTEM – the mathematical subdivision of the football field into steps

HALT - individual or group stopping all movement

HESITATION - beginning a movement late

HIP SHIFT – an advanced technique to change from forward to backwards march

HIT - a major impact point in the show

HOLD or FREEZE - stand in place, no motion

HORNS or HORNLINE - all wind instruments

HORNS UP (DOWN) - maneuver to bring instruments to playing position (or down)

HORNS TO THE BOX - horns are raised at an angle towards the press box

INTERVAL - the space between members side to side

JAZZ RUN – a technique to cover large distances with large step size

LEFT (or RIGHT) GUIDE - band member at extreme left (or right) of rank

MARK TIME – marching (foot motion) in place

OBLIQUE - a movement or facing not 90, 180, 270 or 360 degrees to original line of march

PARADE REST – a relaxed position of attention, no talking

PHASING – lack of group precision or timing, musically or visually

POSTURE - carriage or bearing

PRECISION – uniformity of movement

PREPARATORY COMMAND - tells you what to do before you start

PUSH - a major impact point which directs sound and moves toward the audience

RANK – group of three or more members side to side, usually within a block formation

READABILITY - the clarity of the design presented on the field

ROTATION - taking a form and moving it about on any point or axis

SEQUENCE – the same movement or segment repeated at different times, visual or music

SLIDE – instruments and shoulders face 90° to the right or left of foot direction, usually to front

SMOOTH – a gradual movement executed in one or two counts

SNAP – a quick movement usually executed in a half a count

SPACING – the physical distance between members in any direction

SQUAD – grouping of three or more members into a unit

STACKED FORMS – grouping of similar forms layered front to back

STAGE – to present an individual or group (verb), the area of presentation (noun)

TIMING – precision

TOUCH AND GO – a technique to change directions, usually 180°

TRACKING - basic marching in block form while playing exercises and show music segments

WHEEL - the rotation movement of a form while maintaining the form

8 to 5, 16 to 5, etc. – number of equal sized steps per 5 yards

Marching Fundamentals

A guide is needed for all members to detail the instructions for marching fundamentals and maneuvers.

The details of learning marching fundamentals can be overwhelming to new members. Rookies need to have the information printed out so they can practice or review at home with correct instructions. Instructors should be careful not to teach too many skills at each session. This guide and the Vocabulary for Marching Band should help the members and staff in developing uniformity of marching technique and instructions. This could be a section in the Band Handbook given to each member. The staff and Drum Majors use verbal commands for initiating marching fundamentals. Everyone should give verbal commands in rhythm using the same cadence. All CAPITAL letters are the accented or emphasized syllable.

There are several excellent instructional videos available for marching technique that are excellent to show rookie members. ("A picture is worth a thousand words" so a DVD must be worth a million words.)

The term "toe" is used throughout these instructions but actually means the ball of the foot. Using "toe" is simpler to use when giving instructions. It also conveys more of a raised position.

Fall-In

This is used as a command for students to take their position as instructed. They are to be in place but relaxed. The right foot is in place. No talking is allowed.

For example: "Fall-in in block band." ("Fall-in at Parade Rest" can be specified)

Posture

Good posture is the most basic element of good marching and playing. Uniformity must be maintained when moving and a halt.

- Chin up slightly
- Stand tall (as if someone were lifting you from the top of your head)
- Legs straight (but do not lock knees)
- Heels – Back of shoulders - Back of head in alignment (as against a wall or pole)
- Stomach in
- Rib cage expanded/Chest out
- Shoulders relaxed, pulled back and down
- Shoulder exercise – shoulders up towards ears, pull shoulders back, then down
- Eyes look straight ahead or direction of focus
- Posture exercise - raise up on balls of feet slowly four counts and down four counts – maintaining balance and posture

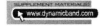

Parade Rest

The purpose of Parade Rest is for the band to be in a uniform position ready to move to attention (or relax/at ease).

Verbal Command:

Band – paRADE Rest (Move)

1   2   3   4   1

- Good posture
- Feet 22 ½" apart (one 8 to 5 step size)
- Toes angled out slightly (some bands keep toes straight ahead)
- Instruments should be held uniformly in each section

  (there are many options for each section—must be uniform)
- Instrument should be ready to move easily and smoothly to Attention
- No talking
- No moving
- Focused attitude

Attention

The purpose of Attention is for the band to be in a uniform position ready to begin marching or bring instruments up to playing position. *Any group of students* can be taught to stand at Perfect Attention and look great! (Explain the importance. Take pride in it. Make a game of it. "Let's practice standing at perfect attention for 30 seconds." Then keep adding on. Rehearse Attention anytime the band does not do it well just like anything else.)

Verbal Command:

Band – ten HUT (Move)

1   2   3   4   1

- Good posture
- Left leg closes to right leg (right foot stays in place)
- Toes angled out 45% (some bands keep toes together)
- Instrument held in both hands (hands in playing position on instrument)
- Uniform instrument height in each section (match mouthpiece height within section)
- Arms relaxed – Elbows out slightly
- No talking
- No moving
- Focused attitude

Horns Up

Instruments must be brought up to playing position with a quick precise movement. This is part of the visual performance and often the first impression. At times, a slow *Horns Up* is effective as well (e.g. in a ballad) taking three counts and in place on count four.

Verbal Command:

Band -   Horns UP   (Move)

1   2   3   4   1

- Horns move quickly (snap) to playing position
- Each section needs to be uniform in instrument carriage
  (Flutes and brass must be parallel to the ground)
- Arms at 90% in an inverted V
- Slow Horns Up can be coordinated to fit the music (usually 3 counts)

Horns Down

Instruments must return to the attention position with a quick precise movement. At times, a slow *Horns Down* is effective as well (e.g. in a ballad).

Verbal Command:

Band -   Horns DOWN (Move)

1   2   3   4   1

- Horns move quickly (snap) to position of attention
- Slow Horns Down can be coordinated to fit the music (usually 2-4 counts)

Dress Right/Left/Center

Dress Right, Left and Center are movements to check and adjust alignment in a block or linear formation.

Verbal Command:

Dress [Right] Dress   (Move)

1   2   3   4

- Horns move quickly (snap) to Horns Up position (usually Tubas keep the instruments at Attention Position)
- Head snaps to the direction called
- Maintain good posture
- Quickly adjust alignment
- Band member on end of line (dress point) keeps head forward and checks location of feet
- Dress Center aligns to designated center of line, members to right do a Dress Left and members to the left do a Dress Right

Ready Front

Ready Front returns band members to the attention position.

Verbal Command:

Ready		**FRONT**	(Move)
1	2	3	4

- Head and instrument returns quickly to Attention position

Mark Time

Mark Time is marching in place with no forward motion.

Verbal Command:

Mark	**Time**	**MARK**	(Hold)	(Move)
1	2	3	4	and

- On the "and" of count 4 the left heel is raised so the bottom of shoe is even with the top of the right shoe (just below ankle). The left toe stays down.
- If Attention is toes apart 45o, then toes move together (parallel) on counts 1 and 2.
- On count 1 the left heel is lowered to the ground and the right heel is raised to the top of the left shoe (just below the ankle).
- The motion continues with the left heel down on counts 1 and 3 and the right foot down on 2 and 4. Heels are up on the "and's."
- The balls of both feet remain planted on the ground.
- The knees will move forward in a natural motion.
- The movement should be continuous and smooth.
  (some older band styles call for a snap & freeze motion)

Halt

Halt stops the movement of either *Mark Time* or *Forward March*.

Verbal Command:

READy		**HALT**	(Left foot stops)		(Right foot stops)
1	2	3	4	and	1

- On count 4 the left foot stops in place. (subdivide count 4)
- If Attention is toes apart 45o, then left toe is placed out 45o on count 4 and right out 45o on the next count.
- On the second count 1 the right foot stops in place and all motion ceases.
- A position of Attention is assumed.

Right/Left/About Turn

Right, Left or About Turn is a simple maneuver to get the members to face 90° to the right or left or 180° to the rear. Some bands use a military right, left, and about face in addition to or instead of the *Turn* maneuver. *Turns* are recommended since they are easier to do than the military facings. Further, they are rarely used in a show so little time needs to be devoted to them.

Verbal Command:

RIGHT	**turn**	**ready**	**MOVE**	(Hold)	(Step)	(Step)
1	2	3	4	1	2	3

- On count 1 left foot does one mark time
- On count 2 right toe rotates 90o to the right, pivoting on heel
- On count 3 left toe rotates 90o to the right, pivoting on heel

Verbal Command:

LEFT	**turn**	**ready**	**MOVE**	(Step)	(Step)
1	2	3	4	1	2

- On count 1 left toe rotates 90o to the left, pivoting on heel
- On count 2 right toe rotates 90o to the left, pivoting on heel

Verbal Command:

aBOUT	**turn**	**ready**	**MOVE**	(Hold)	(Step)	(Step)	(Step)	(Step)
1	2	3	4	1	2	3	4	5

- On count 1 left foot does one mark time
- On count 2 right toe rotates 90o to the right, pivoting on heel
- On count 3 left toe rotates 90o to the right, pivoting on heel

Forward March

Forward March is the basic technique to move forward with a smooth glide step. (There are other techniques used for Show Band and old Big Ten style with exaggerated leg lift. These are difficult for high school musicians to do while playing.) This is typically done from a *Mark Time* but can be done from a *Halt*, but is somewhat awkward.

Verbal Command:

FORward	MARCH	(Lock)	(Move)	(Step)
1	2	3	4	and 1

- Out of a Mark Time the right foot should lock in place on count 4
- On the 'and' of count 4 the body should begin its motion by moving forward leading from the center of the body (but not leaning forward.) The right foot and leg initiate the body motion by pushing forward. See Figure 1.
- Also on the 'and' of count 4 the left foot should move forward with the toe raised up and the heel down low enough to just clear the ground.
- On count 1 the left heel should be down and the toe pointed up at a 45o angle. See Figure 2.
- Also on count 1 the right heel is up and the right toe is down.
- If Attention is toes apart 45o, then toes move together (parallel) on counts 1 and 2.
- The body should be motionless from the waist up.
- Good posture should be maintained. Do not lean forward.

Forward March continues with the left heel down on counts 1 and 3 and the right heel down on counts 2 and 4. See Figures 3 & 4.

Figure 1: "And" of 4

Figure 3: "And" of 1

Figure 2: Count 1

Figure 4: Count 2

Mark Time 4 and freeze on 1 Balance Exercise

This is a basic exercise to unify the step-off technique, balance and step size.

Mark time 4 counts and Forward March 1 freezing all motion on count 1

- Left heel is down and toe is up

- Right toe is down and heel is up

- Body weight should be centered and balanced on both feet

- Good posture is maintained

- Hold this position motionless

- On command, smoothly shift weight forward so left foot is flat with all of the weight over the left foot. Right toe is down and heel is up.

- Check alignment, step size and posture.

- On command, smoothly shift weight backward so right foot is flat with all of the weight over the right foot. Left toe is up and heel is down.

- Check alignment, step size and posture.

- Also do exercise Mark Time 4, Forward 1 and Freeze on 2 (then to 3, then to 4)

Backward March

Backward March is the basic technique to move backwards. Most bands do this style on the balls of the feet and keep the heels off the ground. This demands a little more balance but reduces the chance of bouncing and stumbling.

Verbal Command:

BACK	**MARCH**	**READy**	**Move**	(up on toe)	(Step)
1	2	3	4	and	1

- Out of a Mark Time or Forward March the right foot should go up on the ball of the foot on count 4

- On the 'and' of count 4 the body should begin its motion by moving backward leading from the center of the body (but not leaning.) The right foot and leg initiate the body motion by pushing backward.

- Also on the 'and' of count 4 the left foot should move backward with the heel raised up and the toe down.

- On count 1 the left toe should be down.

- Toes (balls of the feet) should be on the beat and heels stay up.

- Legs should remain straight.

- The body should be motionless from the waist up.

- Good posture should be maintained. Do not lean forward or backward.

Slides

Slides are done in the context of the drill or in a Box to the Right (or Left) Exercise or Slide Exercise. The purpose of the maneuver is to keep the body orientation/shoulders flat to the front and instrument direction (if horns up) to the front. This is typically done while marching towards an end zone and facing front. It is not done with a verbal command but instructions and then:

Verbal Command:

ONE	**TWO**	**READy**	**MOVE**
1	2	3	4

- At a halt, feet are facing the end zone and upper body and instrument are facing front   (90o to the right or left). Shoulders should be squared flat to the front.
- Hips should be at a 45o angle.
- Forward or backward march while maintaining this body orientation.

Crab Step **(Percussion)**

The *Crab Step* is done by the percussion section instead of the *Slide* for ease of playing the drums. Generally the percussion section automatically substitutes this move for the *Slide* in the drill or exercises. On occasion the entire band might utilize the *Crab Step* for effect, however adequate time would need to be devoted to its mastery. It also is not done with a verbal command but instructions and then:

Verbal Command:

ONE	**TWO**	**READy**	**MOVE**
1	2	3	4

- Moving to the right - on count 1 the left leg crosses over the right and takes a ¾ size step.
- On count 2 the right leg takes a 1¼ size step to the right.
- Moving to the left - on count 1 the right leg crosses over the left and takes a ¾ size step.
- On count 2 the left leg takes a 1¼ size step to the left.
- Maintain good posture and avoid bouncing.

Plus One Step/Minus One Step

Plus One Step and *Minus One Step* are fundamentals used in rehearsals to improve change of direction and transitions from one page of drill to the next. The Plus One is executed at the end of a drill move by adding one count or step in the next direction. For example, in an eight count drill move, marchers would take step nine in the direction and step size of the following move, hold for three counts and return the feet together (to location on count 8):

(Move) -							Step	(Hold) - - - - - - - - -			Close
1	2	3	4	5	6	7	8	1	2	3	4	5

Minus One starts a drill move by presetting the right foot from the last count of the previous direction and step size. This is executed on count 5 of the count-off (verbal or Dr. Beat©):

(Count-off)				Step back	(Hold) - - - - - - - - -			Move
1	2	3	4	5	6	7	8	1

High Mark Time

High Mark Time is mark time with an exaggerated leg lift. This is used by show and big ten bands and occasionally in competition shows to create an energetic look for a few counts, usually four to eight. It is also an excellent balance exercise, especially when done very slowly. Big Ten and show bands sometimes do this as a chair step—lower leg not pulled in against knee.

Verbal Command: (Explain this is High Mark Time)

Mark	Time	MARK	(Hold)	(Move)
1	2	3	4	and

- On the "and" of count 4 the left foot is raised so the middle curve of the foot is against the right knee and the toe is pointed down at a 45o angle.
- On count 1 the foot is down.
- On the "and" of count 2 the right foot is raised to the left knee (as above)
- On count 2 the foot is down.
- As a balance exercise Hold the "and's" and counts and then very slowly in rhythm (eighth note = 60 bpm)

Touch and Go

Touch and Go is the technique used for reversing direction when not changing the body orientation (forward march to backwards march). It is not done with a verbal command but instructions.

- The last count of the forward or backward motion is a "stab step" –both heels off the ground.
- Count 1 of new direction is a re-placement of the left foot in spot.
- When going from backward march to forward, the re-placement is on the heel.
- The left leg and abdominal muscles initiate the move on the "and" of 1.
- On count 2 the right foot continues in the new direction.
- Maintain upper body posture.

Hip Shift

The *Hip Shift* is the technique used in a Slide to change from a Forward March to a Backward March while maintaining the same direction of motion. (i.e. Forward March towards an end zone in a Slide, continuing in the same direction and changing (using a Hip Shift) to Backwards March. It is not done with a verbal command but instructions.

- While moving in a Slide, on count 8 the right foot is a "stab step" (toe down, heel up) straight to the front sideline.
- During counts 8 thru 1 the hips should rotate to the right while the left foot changes from forward to backward (heels off the ground). This should be a smooth motion.
- The shoulders and instrument maintain flat to the front position.
- By count 2 the body is now in a Backward March/Slide and continues.
- Once the Hip Shift from Forward to Backward is comfortable, the Hip Shift from Backward to Forward should be learned using the same procedure.

Jazz Run

Jazz Run is an advanced technique utilized to cover large distances (usually 4 to 5) and create a great deal of motion. It is not done with a verbal command but instructions. It is usually preceded by a Forward March and not a Halt.

- On count 8, right toe goes out at a 45o angle and knees bend to lower the body center of gravity.
- On count 1, left toe goes to a 45o angle.
- Foot should contact ground in this order: toe–ball–heel with very little weight placed on heel.
- Maintain good posture and avoid leaning forward.
- On the 'and' of the last count of Jazz Run, the body should begin to return to normal tall marching position.

Tracking

Tracking is a very important exercise for playing while marching.

Marching and playing at the same time is one of the most difficult tasks to master for the rookie, particularly for the wind instrument players. An exercise that greatly helps the transition from standing and playing to playing in motion is the tracking exercise. It is simply marching and playing easy scales, exercises and eventually show segments in a block formation in a straight marching situation like on a track (hence the name). Tracking can be done anywhere there is a level surface and some distance, including the practice field. This exercise is helpful in both small and large section contexts and full band. In small sections, instructors have the opportunity to hear and help the individuals. (Rookies should not march next to each other.) Tracking should begin in band camp.

At the beginning, use the following sequence:

1. Mark time 8 and then play a unison Bb concert long-tone for 16 counts, release and halt on count 17. MM = 120
2. Same as above but Forward March while playing. Rookies will need to force themselves to play, even though it is difficult to hold a steady tone. (It will get easier!)
3. Students should concentrate on no motion from the waist up.
4. Battery (or Dr. Beat) should play quarter notes to help maintain the pulse.
5. Mark time 8 and then play the Bb concert scale up and down marking time. Last note off on count 5 and halt.
6. When this is somewhat comfortable, play the scale in half, quarter and eighth notes.
7. Rookies should be urged to at least play all the way through the half notes.

It will take more than one session for the rookies to get comfortable tracking with scales. It needs to be done daily for several weeks, gradually adding other scales and exercises like #3 on the *Daily Warm-up*. Eventually 8–16 measure phrases from the show material should be added. A sequence should be used of continuous marching while alternating playing and not playing. This is also a good endurance builder. The segments in the show that are difficult should be tracked regularly throughout the season. The *Daily Warm-up* should be occasionally played in a block formation, and the rhythmic exercises should be tracked.

Physical Training

Marching band needs to be approached as an athletic activity because it is!

Stretching and Conditioning

Marching band is obviously a very physical activity, and careful stretching and conditioning need to be part of the routine. Many schools are offering physical education credit for participation and justly so. This is especially true where marching band is an after school, co-curricular program. It is highly suggested that the band director talk to the school's athletic trainer about a stretching and conditioning program for the band. Show him/her what the demands are by inviting them to attend a rehearsal. This will also be good for building Athletic and Band Department relations.

There are some good resources available for band stretching. One recommended video is *Fitness for Band* available from Marching Show Concepts at www.msconcepts.com.

As a daily routine, the band should start the rehearsal in Block Band, and the Drum Majors should immediately start the stretching routine. Attendance can be taken and the director and staff can supervise and take care of the last minute pre-rehearsal details.

Because of the special physical demands of the Percussion and Color Guard sections, they should do some extended stretching and conditioning that is relevant to their needs. Percussion should pay particular attention to back and ab muscle development, and the Color Guard should work on dance/body movement stretching and conditioning.

Since marching band is physically demanding, it is important that a conditioning program be established and utilized especially in the summer to get the members in shape. Once the school year begins and the students are more in shape, less time needs to be devoted to physical conditioning but it should not be totally abandoned. Aerobic breathing should be incorporated with conditioning, which will have a direct correlation to wind instrument playing in particular.

Marching Aerobics

Many bands run for conditioning but there are problems associated with running that must be considered. Running, especially on hard surfaces, can be damaging to the knees and some students already have knee problems. Some students can only walk, and there is always the track star that wants to go faster. A more **relevant form of conditioning**, that also greatly improves the basic marching technique, is Marching Aerobics. This is defined later in the chapter. Marching Aerobics should be done immediately following stretching and any other conditioning.

Nutrition

Teenagers today, by and "large," are not particularly keen on observing good nutrition. It is important that good nutrition is emphasized throughout the season. For example, when a break for a meal occurs, give a simple reminder to eat healthy and avoid junk food so you can be in top form for the next rehearsal. (Drive safely too!) An Attitude Session (Chapter 9) could be devoted to the importance of good nutrition and performance. A health teacher or trainer might be happy to help with this presentation.

Daily Marching Basics Routine

A daily routine is needed to establish good technique and uniformity in the band.

Just as a Daily Warm-up is needed musically, the Daily Marching Basics Routine is needed to establish good habits and uniformity. Although it takes some time, the improvement of performance in the drill will make the time spent worthwhile. These can be done in a block band formation or in company fronts. **Attention to detail** and setting **high standards of excellence** are the keys to developing **excellent marching technique**.

1. **Daily Marching Aerobics**
   a. Company fronts on yard lines or in end zone (2 step spacing). Use Dr. Beat®.
   b. MT 8 and then FM 8 to 5 full length of the field at MM = 120, Halt
   c. Relax, Turn around, Attention
   d. MT 8 and then FM 8 to 5 length of field at 130, Halt
   e. Repeat at 140, 150, 160 & 170 (6 lengths of field total)
   f. During season build up to higher tempos (130 to 180, 140 to 190, etc.)
   g. Alternate Horns Up & Down
   h. Also do some sets 6 to 5 at the slower tempos

2. **Parade Rest, Attention, Dress R & L**
   a. These are simple skills that establish the foundation for all other techniques. They can be mastered by anyone regardless of experience.
   b. Do not continue until they are at the highest level possible.

3. **Balance/High Mark Time** (optional)
   a. Balance - Hold each count and 'and'
   b. Slow Tempo (8th = 60)

4. **Mark Time & Freeze on 1**
   a. See page 74 for details
   b. Also freeze on 2, 3, and 4

5. **8's & 8's** - MT 8/FM 8/MT 8/FM 8 etc. to Halt
   a. This is the basic foundation for great marching. Insist on good posture and foot technique.
   b. Last four counts give verbal "READy–HALT"
   c. Also do MT 8/FM 6 going 6 to 5
   d. Also do Backwards March 8 to 5
   e. Also do Halt 8/FM 8 (in the show this is more common than MT)

6. **8–7–6–5–4**, 10 yards each - 8 to 5, 7 to 5, 6 to 5, 5 to 5, 4 to 5
   a. Horns Down
   b. Horns Up
   c. Start the season with only 8–7–6 and then add on as skills develop

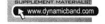

7. **Slide Exercise 1**
   a. Preparatory Exercise with horns up
   b. At a halt, turn upper body and instrument slowly (1–2–3–4) to right 90° and hold (hips should be at a 45° angle), pause, stretch a little bit farther but don't force, return to 90°, return front slowly (1–2–3–4)
   c. Repeat to the left
   d. Slide Exercise 1. Do above to the right & hold, then FM 8 to 32 counts and Halt.
   e. Repeat exercise to the left

8. **Slide Exercise 2 (in motion)** - Face end zone – Horns up – MT 8/FM 8 (horns move slowly front & right 5 6 7 lock on 8), /FM 8 (horns return 5 6 7 lock on 8)/Halt
   a. Repeat exercise to the left

9. **Box to the Right** – MT 8/FM 8/R Slide 8/BackM 8/L Slide 8/Halt
   a. Horns remain the same direction
   b. Horns Down
   c. Horns Up
   d. Also do Box to the Left and both in sequence

10. **Touch and Go** - MT 8/FM 8/Touch and Go/BackM 8/Touch and Go/FM8/Halt
    a. Horns Down
    b. Horns Up
    c. Horns Front

11. **Hip Shift** - Face End Zone & Horns Front - MT 8/FM 8 (Hip shift on 8)/ Backwards March 8/Touch and Go on 8/FM 8 (Hip shift on 8)/ Backwards March 8/Halt

Optional Exercises

Use these for advanced techniques if used in the show.
1. **Floating Turns**
   a. Back to Front
      i. Back step on 1
      ii. Turn on 2 to right (Foot & Shoulders 60°)
      iii. Continue on 3: Right Foot crosses over (Foot & Shoulders 120°)
      iv. Regular step on 4 (180°), FM on 5–6–7–8, Halt
   b. Front to Back
      i. Forward on 1
      ii. Turn on 2 to right (Foot & Shoulders 60°)
      iii. Continue on 3. (Foot & Shoulders 120°)
      iv. Regular step on 4 Right Foot crosses behind (180°), Back march on 5–6–7–8, Halt
2. **Jazz Run**
   a. See 6. Above
   b. See page 77 for details

Daily Marching Basics Routine
SUMMARY

1. **Daily Marching Aerobics**

2. **Parade Rest, Attention, Dress R & L**

3. **Balance/High Mark Time (optional)**

4. **Mark Time & Freeze on 1**

5. **8's & 8's**
   a. Forward 8 to 5
   b. Forward 6 to 5
   c. Backwards 8 to 5

6. **8-7-6-(5- 4)** - 10 yards each - 8 to 5, 7 to 5, 6 to 5, (5 to 5, 4 to 5)
   a. Horns Down
   b. Horns Up

7. **Slide Exercise 1**
   a. Preparatory Exercise with horns up
   b. Slide Exercise 1 – Do above to the right & hold, then FM 8 to 32 counts and Halt.
   c. Repeat exercise to the left

8. **Slide Exercise 2 (in motion)**
   a. Exercise to the right
   b. Repeat exercise to the left

9. **Box to the Right**
   a. Horns Down
   b. Horns Up
   c. Box to the Left
   d. Both in sequence

10. **Touch and Go**
    a. Horns Down
    b. Horns Up
    c. Horns Front

11. **Hip Shift**
    a. Front to Back
    b. Back to Front

Optional Exercises
Use these for advanced techniques if used in the show.

1. **Floating Turns**
   a. Back to Front
   b. Front to Back

2. **Jazz Run**

Central High School Marching Tigers
MARCHING PROGRAM

Check-off System*

Level One:
>Attention/Parade Rest/Ready Position
>Right/Left Dress
>Horns Up/Down
>Turns - Right/Left/About
>Mark Time
>Forward March 8 to 5 (8 & 8 Exercise)
>Forward March 16 to 5 (16 & 8 Exercise)

Level Two:
>Slides (Horns Front)
>Box Eight Exercise
>Backwards March 8 to 5 (8 & 8 Exercise)
>Backwards March 16 to 5 (16 & 8 Exercise)
>Forward March 6 to 5

Level Three:
>Touch & Go
>Hip Shift
>High Mark Time
>Other Techniques called for in the Drill
>Drill "Excerpts" from the Drill

Other Exercises:
>Circle Rotate
>Accordion (Expand & Contract spacing)
>Stop Sign
>8-7-6-5-4
>Jazz Run
>Diamond
>Asterisk

* See Chapter 6, page 100 for Check-off System information.

Chapter Six

Rehearsal Techniques

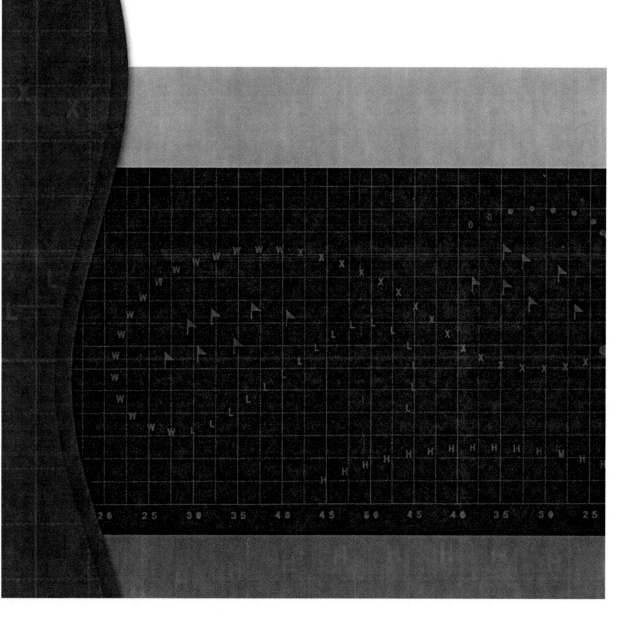

Rehearsal Philosophy

The director must start with an overall approach of how rehearsals will be run before the season begins.

With a rehearsal philosophy clearly spelled out, day-to-day and person-to-person consistency will result in effective rehearsals. It is important that all band staff members adhere to a uniform approach to rehearsal philosophy and procedures. No two people use the same techniques, but an overall uniformity in approach is vital for success. The students can then expect consistency on a daily basis, regardless of which staff member is running the rehearsal.

(A Sample Rehearsal Philosophy)

The Central High School Marching Tigers Rehearsal Philosophy

Rehearsals will be conducted with a positive attitude in a pleasant atmosphere. Students will be focused, energetic and relaxed in order to achieve the outstanding results desired. The director and staff will be organized and efficient through careful planning and goal setting. These qualities will make the experience enjoyable and productive for students and staff alike.

Rehearsal Goals

Goals must be clearly established and reviewed to keep the band "on course".

The Rehearsal Goals will be the tools to achieve the Band Goals. Various levels of goals must be established by the director prior to the start of the season. These should be long term (seasonal), middle term (weekly) and short term (rehearsal) in nature. This will keep the staff and students focused on what is to be achieved during the various time intervals. It is easy to get over-involved with problems in rehearsal and not stay on schedule without this kind of roadmap to maintain focus. For example, many directors plan to complete the show, at least in a rough form, by the first performance. Spending too much time cleaning the opener can prevent the band from reaching that goal. A clear set of goals, precisely communicated, will keep staff and students on target. The Rehearsal Goals will help implement the overall Band Goals as discussed in Chapter One.

1. **Long Range Goals** – Seasonal Goals should be established by the director, with input from the staff, on several topics—rehearsal efficiency, attitude, behavior, level of achievement, etc. These statements and ideas can be general in nature but should lead to specific actions and activities in the middle and short term goals.

    A director might decide, for example, that the band needs to achieve a higher level of performance in rehearsal (and therefore in shows) than the previous year. While this seems an obvious goal, it must be stated in specific terms in areas such as marching, music, color guard, percussion, winds, etc.

Sample Long Range/Seasonal Goals

Rehearsal Efficiency – The band will rehearse more efficiently utilizing good rehearsal etiquette, careful planning by the staff and attention to time-on task. The members will rehearse with relaxed focus and perform with energy and excitement, keeping in mind the concept of "rehearsal equals performance."

Music – A higher level of music performance will be achieved by dedicating more attention and time to this aspect in the wind and percussions sections. Warm-ups and basic technique development will be used daily and will be not omitted as the season progresses.

Marching – The high level of marching realized in the past will be maintained through daily basic technique drills and marching and drill emphasis in full ensemble rehearsals.

Color Guard – The color guard standard of performance will be raised to match that of the winds and percussion. More attention will be placed on staffing and design. The color guard will establish quality fundamentals using daily technique and skill development.

Timeline Goals – At the Parent Show at the end of Band Camp, the band will march and play the Opener plus stand and play the school songs and Star Spangled Banner. By the beginning of school, the band will march and play the second show song. By the first show, the band will perform the entire show.

2. **Middle Range Goals** – Weekly goals will be written at the conclusion of the previous week while the accomplishments and problems are fresh in the director's mind. They will be broken down by sections while being more specific in terms of music and drill. Caption heads can do their own section's goals in writing and submit to the director.

Sample Middle Range/Weekly Goal

Day	Woodwinds	Brass	Percussion	Color Guard
Monday	Opener Ltr. E Closer Drill 65-74-------- Full Ensemble–Closer	Opener Ltr. E ------------------------------ 1st Half---------------------	Opener Intro & Ltr. A Closer Feature ------------------------------	Opener Feature Closer Feature ------------------------------
Tuesday	Closer Ltr. B Ballad Ltr. D Full Ensemble----------	Opener Ltr. E Closer Drill 75-86---------- Closer 2nd Half------------	Opener Ltr. E ------------------------------ ------------------------------	Closer 65-74 Closer Feature ------------------------------

3. **Short Term Goals** – Daily Goals can simply be written on the Daily Rehearsal Plan sheet with time allocations. It is important to follow the time schedule or the other goals will not be achieved. There is never enough time and staff members need to learn to stop each segment on time. These should include specific music rehearsal segments and drill pages. Goals will be achieved in sectional and full ensemble rehearsals.

Sample Short Term/Daily Goals

Time	Woodwinds	Brass	Percussion	Color Guard
3:15	Inside **Daily Warm-up**	Inside **Daily Warm-up**	Outside Warm-up	Outside Stretch
3:45	Opener Ltr. E-------	-----------------------	Closer Drill 65-74	Opener Feature

Rehearsal Methods

The director should implement successful rehearsal methods to assure efficiency, enjoyment and long lasting results.

With a rehearsal philosophy clearly defined and goals established, the director and staff need to implement effective rehearsal methods and procedures for efficiency, enjoyment and long lasting results.

Atmosphere of Rehearsals

The atmosphere of the daily rehearsal will, to a great extent, determine the ensemble's ability to perform to the best of its ability. This is based on the Rehearsal Philosophy and Goals created by the director, stated previously. The members should rehearse with *relaxed focus* and perform with *energy and excitement*, maintaining the concept that "rehearsal equals performance." A relaxed focus denotes that the members pay careful attention but are not rigid and tense both physically and mentally. A tense, uptight mood creates mistakes and nervous performances in rehearsals as well as shows. "Relaxed" should not translate into "talking" on the part of the students. The staff (in particular the person leading the rehearsal) controls the atmosphere and the success of the practice. Yelling and screaming at students creates a negative mood with short term results, but little progress and long term damage.

Concepts for Members

Band members need to be taught and periodically reminded of a few concepts of rehearsal.
- "You are your own best teacher."
    - Awareness – the more you become aware, the more you can improve
    - There are mathematically too many things for the staff to fix
    - Ownership – the band and the performance belong to you
    - "Fix something in every letter or drill move"
    - Keep a mental checklist of what to work on in the future
- Mistakes—How to deal with them
    - Without mistakes there is no learning!
    - Again, *awareness* is what is important
    - Be appreciative of a correction—that is how you improve.
    - Don't be afraid to ask questions if you are uncertain of what to do or how to do something.

The director and staff members should keep the following rehearsal concepts in mind:
- **Focus on one thing to fix at a time** (next repetition fix the next problem)
- Don't make mistakes the focus (no anger or blame)
- **Talk less—Play more!**

Individual Attention

The success of the marching band performance depends on the ability of *every member* to perform to the highest possible level of achievement. Although most rehearsals are full ensemble or sectionals, attention needs to be paid to the learning and performance of the individual. Some ideas that will help:

- Devote a significant amount of time to small group rehearsals in the initial stages.
- Rehearse and warm-up the wind instruments in a large circle or arc so the individuals can be heard and corrected. Staff members, if available, should float in front of the players to assist.
- From the first rehearsals, make the individuals *responsible* for their own preparation. (see Check-off information on page 100.)
- Identify individuals by name, in a pleasant manner, for corrections. (Otherwise they do not know you are talking to them.)
- Use peer teaching with student leaders and individuals on basic music and marching skills.

Efficient Use of Time - The Law of Diminishing Returns

The Law of Diminishing Returns states that as the rehearsal continues:
- *Improvement* will occur
- Improvement will *level-off*
- *Regression* will occur

The key to a successful rehearsal is being aware and stopping as soon as *level-off* begins to occur. Then move to something different—new section, song, etc. or take a break. Further improvement can and will occur at the next rehearsal segment.

Fighting the *Law of Diminishing Returns* or trying to overcome it **never** works. It only creates frustration and regression on the part of staff and members (although at first it is hard to see).

Efficient Use of Time - Breaks

- An efficiency expert in any field (business, physical fitness, musician) will state that periodic breaks are essential for efficiency and success.
- Take a 5-10 minute break every 60 minutes (maximum) to
  - Relax - Refresh - Recharge - Refocus
    - Muscles (get off your feet)
    - Brain
    - Spirit
    - "Chops"
  - Improves focus, energy, improvement, retention, positive attitude
  - Minimizes injuries

Summary Thoughts

- The staff controls the atmosphere and efficiency of the rehearsal.
- Telling the students to do something is *not* teaching! The instructor must, through a series of events, make the action occur.
  - "Don't miss that step-off" is not teaching.
  - "Let's practice the step-off by playing four measures and then taking one step only and freezing." This approach will work and is an example of isolating the problem.
- Understand the concepts of productivity.
  - Students will be most productive mentally and physically in the **middle** of practice.
  - The first **part** of practice should be music and visual warm-up and basic technique.
  - The middle **part** of practice should be the intense portion that requires the most concentration and focus.
  - The last **part** should be review and continuity using longer segments closing with a "run thru" of the show.
- Talk less—Play more
  - After an initial introduction to a topic, talk less—play or march more.
  - Say *one* sentence (occasionally two), then play with that idea as focus.
  - Students remember the last phrase you say (teenage attention span!).
  - Then state the next idea or concept and play.

"I hear and I forget.
I see and I remember.
I do and I understand."

—Confucius

Rehearsal Etiquette

"Rehearsal etiquette" is a phrase that invokes respect between staff and students.

Band directors usually refer to the terms "discipline" and "behavior" when addressing this topic. Using the phrase "rehearsal etiquette" when speaking to the band members immediately makes the frame of reference one of respect. For example, "we need to work with a little better rehearsal etiquette when we stand at parade rest and listen to instructions." This conveys to the students an expectation of good manners, efficiency and respect, which will achieve the common goals.

Therefore, the director needs to demonstrate good etiquette in his/her attitude when speaking to the band. The director should be business-like and teach as one would a private lesson. Young musicians will not display good etiquette nor work hard if they are being yelled at constantly.

1. **Foundation -** Time must be taken at the beginning of each season, *before* the first rehearsal begins, to clearly define what is meant be the phrase "rehearsal etiquette" and what is expected of the students both in and out of rehearsals. Start with a foundation for good rehearsals and behavior. See "Attitude Session 10" in Chapter 9: Attitude.

2. **Expectations -** It is expected that all members (and staff) will follow the motto "Be Your Best" *at all times*. Here are a few comments to give the students on how the phrase "Rehearsal Etiquette" relates to the marching band:

    *   Be silent when someone is addressing you or the group.

    *   Make eye contact with the speaker—you will hear more when you do!

    *   In full rehearsal, when the instructor says your section's name, everyone should raise their hands. In that way, the instructor knows the group being addressed is listening.

    *   Participate if asked a question. For example, "How many of you arrived at your set early that time?" Raise your hand. The instructor is trying to assess the situation and needs an honest response.

    *   Speak only at the appropriate times. Talking keeps you and others from hearing and learning. It is also rude behavior to the instructor (poor etiquette).

    *   Listen carefully to directions for the next move. Repeating instructions and moves wastes everyone's time.

    *   Move quickly and efficiently to the position for the next segment.

    *   Think independently. Do what you are supposed to do, when you are supposed to do it.

    *   Don't wait for everyone else to do something.

3. **Behavior/Discipline -** The goal is for the band members to be *self*-disciplined and *self*-motivated. Discipline and motivation need to come from within the members and not imposed by the staff. If the band members feel *ownership* of the band and show, they will work harder and be more cooperative. They must be involved in understanding **what** is being done and **why** (long, middle and short term goals). If the staff feels it is "dragging the band by a rope" in order to motivate them, it will be frustrating for both the members and the staff.

Rehearsal Procedures

Specific procedures need to be uniform from day to day and person to person.

Specific procedures or routines are needed for rehearsal efficiency. These procedures relate to verbal commands, counts, instructions, movement, etc. Students need to have consistency from the instructors if they are expected to be consistent in their actions. Routines need to be consistent regardless of which staff member is running the rehearsal and whether it is a small group or full ensemble. Some terms used below are explained in Chapter 5: The Marching Program.

Rehearsal Routine

Band members learn the complex skills of marching and playing (or spinning) together in a layered fashion using the *spiral technique*. Skills are learned separately and *gradually* combined. The following sequence should be used when rehearsing drill and music on the field after the music and drill have been learned separately. The front ensemble should always play in the following routine.

- **Play** a segment in place marking time.
- March the segment **without playing** (singing). The battery should play if they are confident.
- Reset and **march and play** the segment.
- Repeat the focus above that needs the most work.
- Gradually the combined music and marching become automatic.
- Once the playing and marching is solid, the routine should only be used when needed.

A consistent method of starting marching or playing is needed to avoid confusion. There should *always* be an eight count "count-off" by either the conductor or Dr. Beat® (more on Dr. Beat® follows). The members should *routinely* start after the count-off. Using a random number of counts with the Dr. Beat® is a waste of rehearsal time and creates confusion. The Drum Major should conduct large beat patterns on 1, 3, 5, 6, 7 and 8 as a count-off.

Levels

Levels are used to identify the overall tone or intensity of the rehearsal situation. These range from casual and relaxed to performance simulation. Some bands refer to these as modes of rehearsal. It is important that the students understand which level or mode is being used.

Rehearsal Level One - (Instructional Mode)

Used for basics, fundamentals, learning drill, choreography & music, explanations, new material. Use Parade Rest, Attention, etc. but say "Relax" before conveying information. Students stand in a relaxed manner but are still focused. The pace should be *slow enough* that there is not too much confusion, and *fast enough* to keep it interesting and not waste time (a difficult balancing act). The atmosphere should be kept relaxed and pleasant.

Rehearsal Level Two - (Rehearsal Mode)

Basics are relatively solid and new material has been taught and understood. This is the *cleaning and continuity* phase. One staff member is in charge of the rehearsal with the microphone (Mic).

Procedure:

1. Fall in at "(Parade) Rest Position" Clearly define:
   a. starting and **stopping** point
   b. **to play or not** and what the goal is
   c. **music or visual focus** of rehearsal needs to be clear

2. "Set" command from Mic (or Drum Major)—band comes to attention with instruments up or down as called for. (If everyone is not ready, "Band Ten-Hut" or "Horns Up" without impatience in voice—see if there is a problem or confusion)
3. Don't start until attention is set and 3—5 seconds of silence has elapsed to establish "focus."
4. Eight count count-off from conductor or Dr. Beat
5. End the move with a "Plus one step" (see Chapter 5) and hold position and silence. (The staff needs to hold the 3-5 second silence as well to maintain the quiet mood)
6. Check form & spacing with "eyes only" on command—do not move.
7. "Adjust" command from Mic (or Drum Major)—make adjustments in spacing and alignment
8. Optional—"Check set"—paint marks or step it off. Fall in at attention.
9. "Rest Position" from Mic (or Drum Major)
   a. **First** – Microphone comments (one person only at a time)
      i. Give *clear and brief* corrections
      ii. Compliment (better, good, almost) or "we need to repeat that"
   b. **Second** – Field staff makes quick comments (on "field staff" cue), *clear and brief* (if they need time or have full ensemble comments—communicate to mic person)
   c. **Third** - Mic instructions
      i. "Reset back to___" or
      ii. "We are going to continue and stop at ___"
10. Repeat - "Reset" - move quickly - don't need to run or be silent, sometimes ask squad leaders to make helpful comments, field staff and mic staff can make more individual or small group comments
11. Members should fall in at "Rest Position." "Set" from Mic is the cue for leaders and staff to be silent and members to be at attention and ready to move (back to #2 above).
12. When the rehearsal and marching skills have reached a good level of consistency, each step-off should begin with a "Minus one" to solidify chart–to–chart direction changes.

Numbers 1 thru 9 should all be done in silence.

Try to keep all of the members **involved**. If there is a small group problem, find something else to do with the others or let them sit and relax (or fix the problem in a smaller group setting.) Sometimes the student leaders worry that every problem is not getting fixed. The staff needs to assure them that they are aware of the problem and will take care of it in the future.

The field staff has a better grasp of when the members need a quick water or longer break or when the students mentally need to move on, and review it next rehearsal. **The field staff must maintain good rehearsal etiquette & attitude on the field.**

The band director and staff **must know drill page numbers and the music** and how they relate. See sample score with drill page numbers available online at www.dynamicband.com, for a method to keep organized.

Rehearsal Level Three - (Performance Mode)

This is the "Run Thru" level when everyone's attitude and performance should be just like a show, whether it is a small segment or the entire show. It is a state of mind. (Although "Rehearsal equals performance" conflicts with this concept a little bit!)

The staff should avoid interrupting the performers as in a show. It is a good opportunity to make lists of what needs to be accomplished at the next sectional or full ensemble rehearsal.

Staff Rehearsal Meeting
Staff Rehearsal Techniques
Meeting Outline

(The following is a sample outline to use in a preseason meeting with the marching band staff to establish a uniform approach to rehearsal. It is meant to encourage discussion and communicate the rehearsal philosophy of the band director. Printed copies of the band's philosophy, goals, methods, procedures and etiquette should be distributed. Questions at the end are to reach a consensus on consequences. Staff meetings should be held every two weeks during the season to discuss progress, show concepts and changes.)

It is important that the staff has a uniform approach to rehearsal philosophy and procedures. While no two people have exactly the same approach, being on the same page matters. The students can then expect consistency regardless of which staff member is running the rehearsal.

1. **Positive Attitude** - The atmosphere/attitude must be positive, and any quality band staff in the country would concur. Maintaining that attitude throughout a season of rehearsals is difficult. A few phrases (and the opposites) that are more specific are:

   - Encouraging   (not critical/demeaning)
   - Goal-oriented/organized   (not random)
   - Patient   (not impatient)
   - Serious   (not frivolous)
   - Constructive   (not critical/destructive)
   - "We" oriented   (not "I/me")
   - Expecting/encouraging excellence   (not demanding it)
   - Pleasant or business tone of voice   (not angry)

2. **Some overall rehearsal concepts**
   - Relaxed focus—Students are relaxed (not tense) and focused (not inattentive).
   - There is nothing easy or difficult, only familiar or not.
   - Approach problem solving in rehearsal as one would in a *private lesson* setting in regards to attitude and voice control. Look for the right words and actions to improve the performance.
   - Be aware of the "Law of Diminishing Returns"
   - Be Organized. "Organization is the key to success"

3. **Behavior/Discipline** - The goal is for the band members to be *self*-disciplined and *self*-motivated. Discipline and motivation need to come from within the members and not imposed by the staff. If the band members feel *ownership* of the band and show, they will work harder and be more cooperative. They must be involved in understanding **what** is being done and **why** (long, middle and short term goals). If the staff feels it is "dragging the band by a rope" in order to motivate them, it will be frustrating for both the members and the staff. We need to discuss and reach a consensus on the following:

   - What do we do about mistakes, mental lapses, lack of effort, etc.?
   - (Mistakes are part of the learning/improving curve. You can't improve without them.)
   - Punishment/Consequences? (push-ups?) Self-imposed?
   - Do we demand they "self-impose" them???
   - Punishment/Consequences for everyone if one person makes a mistake? (team effort vs. resentment/rebellion)

Consequences - Over the years, we have tried every approach with varying degrees of success. I feel that when we went from a punitive approach (especially "take a lap") to an educational/cooperative approach ("we need to fix... or improve...let's do it again" or "the problem is...") we made greater progress, and the attitude of the band as a whole improved. When there are rehearsal problems, we need to take time and pause, have everyone gather together and give a quick talk/reprimand. A punitive approach creates short term results and long term resentment and burn out (and therefore more punitive efforts).

(Discussion: Possible consequences when necessary: push-ups, take a lap, stand at attention, individuals removed from rehearsal or show, others?)

Be very careful about assuming that a member has a "bad attitude" or "is not trying". (I have made some huge mistakes in this area.) It often *appears* as such. A member who simply cannot do something very well, will often behave poorly or appear to have a bad attitude rather than simply saying "I just can't do this right now." Take a problem solving approach and involve the student one-to-one.

4. Recommended approach to discipline problems:
  • Individual behavior problem
    - Speak to individual outside of the rehearsal (avoid confrontation)
    - Identify the problem factually
    - Seek a solution <u>with</u> the student
    - Give a warning & establish future consequences
      • A removal of privileges (such as marching for a day)
      • Removal from a performance if more serious
    - Follow through if there a continued problems (make no idle threats)
    - If CHS Rules & Regulations have been broken, the Director must be notified and will follow stated school policies.
  • Group behavior problems (i.e. excessive talking, lack of effort)
    - Speak to group in a close setting about the problem and why it is interfering with a productive rehearsal.
    - If behavior continues, use a group consequence such as standing at attention or parade rest and "rehearsing silence."
    - Maintain a business-like tone of voice (not an angry one).

5. Review Rehearsal Methods, Etiquette and Procedures and distribute copies.

"That government is best which governs the least, because its people discipline themselves." – Thomas Jefferson

Dr. Beat® and Electronic Aids

The marching band has at its disposal a myriad of electronic aids to assist in instruction.

Band directors need to take advantage of the many electronic devices to make teaching marching band easier and more efficient. Gone are the days of using nothing but a hand held battery operated megaphone. Of course, with any electronic gadgets, there are problems that do regularly occur and must be remedied.

Sound System – A quality sound system is necessary for the instructor to be heard clearly by the band members. A quality system is well worth the investment and can be utilized in the total band program throughout the year. Speakers should be in the front, up on stands and not too close to the field or some students will be deafened and some will not hear. If it is a large band, it is better to have more speakers to cover a wider distance without having to turn up the volume excessively. The same° system can also be used for amplified instruments and solos. Care must be taken to not over-amplify solos, while the goal should be to make it acoustically audible. It is better to be too soft than too loud. The sound system can also be used to play music CD's for stretching and fundamentals, judges' taped comments and recordings of the band in rehearsal and performance. It is best to have a cabinet on wheels that contains the entire system and accessories. The sound system should include a mixer, amplifier, two speakers as well as any needed extra peripherals. A power source outlet or generator is necessary.

Portable Sound System - There are portable sound systems that can be utilized (Long Ranger®, MegaVox®, etc.) that are easy to transport and set up. These are great for vocal instructions and metronomic pulse but are not usually adequate for fidelity in music amplification. A combination of a quality sound system (for music, instructions and amplified instruments) and a portable sound system (for voice and Dr. Beat®) is probably the best scenario. The director's instructions should come from the front of the field and the Dr. Beat® should come from behind the band. Some band directors still use the hand held power megaphones, particularly at shows, to insure that all communications are heard clearly.

Dr. Beat® – Dr. Beat® is the most well known of the digital metronomes but there are other good brands. They have programmable tempo and rhythm changes, subdivisions, tuners and different sounds. They can be amplified through a sound system for the whole section or band to rehearse with a metronome. This is very important in establishing a strong pulse, steady rhythm and maintaining tempos. It should be used frequently with the marching band and especially with the percussion section.

Two Cautions:

1. Severe hearing damage can occur if the volume is too high. Students standing within close proximity should wear quality ear protection.

2. Be careful of over-reliance on Dr. Beat®. Don't wait until the last rehearsal before a show to rehearse without it. Gradually "wean" the band or section off of it or early performances will be disastrous. Use it less frequently as the season progresses.

Two-way Radios – Two-way radios are excellent for staff on the tower to communicate with staff on the field. Time can be saved and communication can be far quicker and clearer.

Tuners – Depending on the band director's philosophy, tuners can be utilized to aid intonation. Some use them daily; some at shows only, while others never use them, preferring to do all tuning by ear. If electronic tuners are part of the concert band program's resources, then they should be utilized with the marching band as well. (see Chapter 2 section on Intonation)

Wireless Microphones – Wireless microphones (mics) are used by many bands to amplify solo wind instruments and vocals. This allows them to be staged anywhere rather than near the front sideline where a wired mic would be. There is the good possibility of interference (which is hard to eliminate) and other electronic failures. It is recommended to use wired mics whenever possible if staging is not an issue.

Computer Drill Programs – Most drill writers today use computer programs that can animate both the drill and individual members. This can be educational and very interesting for the students to watch. They can even log in and watch on their home computers.

Computer Music Programs – Programs like Finale® and Sibelius® can play back original compositions with perfect precision and intonation. This is a great aid for student musicians. Further, practice CD's can be burned with variable tempos to gradually develop technique and accuracy for individuals. Other programs like SmartMusic® can be used to practice tempos, loops and analyze performance.

Videos, DVD's and Projectors – An essential teaching tool for the marching band is showing the performances and occasional rehearsals, preferably on a big screen. Students will not really understand their role as part of the whole picture until they can see the whole picture. Further, it is very motivational for the members to watch their shows and see the improvement as the season progresses. The sound can be run through a sound system for maximum effect and enjoyment.

Sound Person – As electronics become more utilized and more complex, a full-time sound person is necessary. Many bands have student managers, who do not march, to fill this role. It is also helpful if an electronically educated staff member or band parent can supervise, especially at shows.

KISS – As the electronics become more complex, it is hard for the director to stay current with it. Workshops, convention sessions and books are available. It is best however to retain the "keep it simple" philosophy in purchasing and utilizing equipment. Only buy and use what is manageable by the people available or the situation can quickly become nightmarish.

Rehearsal Tower – Although not an electronic aid, it needs to be mentioned here that it is essential to have a rehearsal tower that is at least 16 feet above the field level. This is the only way to accurately assess and rehearse music and visual precision and balance. It is crucial that the tower is secure and safe. It is a good idea to have a knowledgeable person from the school maintenance department check it for safety.

(Don't forget the batteries!)

> # Be Prepared
> ## Know the Score & Drill
> *Good Communication is Essential for Successful Rehearsals*

Rehearsal Set-ups

Indoor and outdoor set-ups can affect the ensemble rehearsal or performance.

Rehearsal set-ups or seating arrangements can help or hinder the ability of musicians to hear and perform well. They can be utilized with or without percussion. Some concepts that help music performance are listed at the bottom of the page. Look at the charts on the following pages for reference. Use assigned seating (standing) for uniformity and quick assembly.

Outdoor Warm-up Circle – This is used, as the name implies, for outdoor warm-up and rehearsal. Many band directors prefer an arc or two rows of arcs. They work in similar fashion and can be interchanged or alternated depending on the site and amount of space. If percussion is included, the arc form is better with the battery added behind the winds. The circle works well for student focus since they are facing the conductor in the center and are equidistant. Extra staff members can float around the circle to listen to individuals. The members need the individual help in matching tone quality, balance, blend, posture and instrument position. It is easy for them to "hide" in a traditional, standing concert band set-up. Switch instrument locations from time to time including mixed instrumentation. The students will also develop independence, which will then carry over to the drill formations on the field.

Outdoor Concert Formation – This arrangement is for performing outdoors in a "concert" setting but can be used for rehearsal as well. Instrument direction must be uniform and towards the audience.

Block Band – The block band form is the standard set-up for starting outdoor rehearsals and taking attendance (sometimes referred to as Attendance Block.) It is also used as a parade block. Instruments are usually grouped in ranks (rows) with brass in one block and woodwinds in another. Traditionally trombones are put across the front but it is not necessary. Percussion is placed in the middle of the block so the pulse is centered with tubas nearby. Color Guard is in front for visual interest as well as for them to hear the music. A block band name chart should be used in order for everyone to learn names as quickly as possible.

Indoor Rehearsal Set-up – Indoor seating arrangements are much like the indoor concert band. There are many options just as in concert band. If the area permits, an aisle in the middle is helpful for the director to move closer to sections.

Concepts for musical uniformity
- Location of instruments assists matching sonority, blend & balance and rhythmic precision.
- Keep the woodwinds together and the brass together to facilitate rehearsing these segments.
- Keep low voices together and middle voices together.
- Place battery in back of the winds and front ensemble in front of winds. Place the front ensemble behind the conductor if space is limited, while keeping the conductor closer to winds.
- In any form that is **going to be used for performance**, the directional brasses should all be facing the same direction. In all forms, the sound will seem balanced to the conductor; however in performance, trombones playing in one direction and trumpets in another will be a balance problem for the audience. A curved row, with some pointing one way and others another, will cause balance problems as well. This is true for concert bands also. The directional brasses need to face the same direction.
- In multi-part sections, the first part should be placed where the seconds and thirds can hear them—in the middle of an arc or behind them in stacked forms.
- Directors should experiment with what works best for the instrumentation and adjust as needed.

97

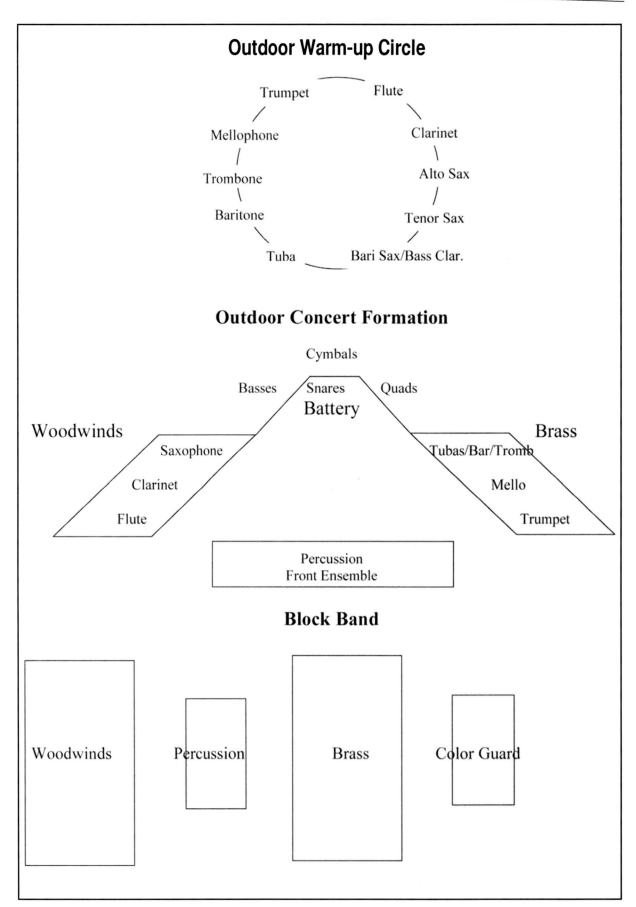

Outdoor Warm-up Circle

Trumpet   Flute

Mellophone   Clarinet

Trombone   Alto Sax

Baritone   Tenor Sax

Tuba   Bari Sax/Bass Clar.

Outdoor Concert Formation

Cymbals

Basses   Snares   Quads

Battery

Woodwinds   Brass

Saxophone   Tubas/Bar/Tromb

Clarinet   Mello

Flute   Trumpet

Percussion
Front Ensemble

Block Band

Woodwinds   Percussion   Brass   Color Guard

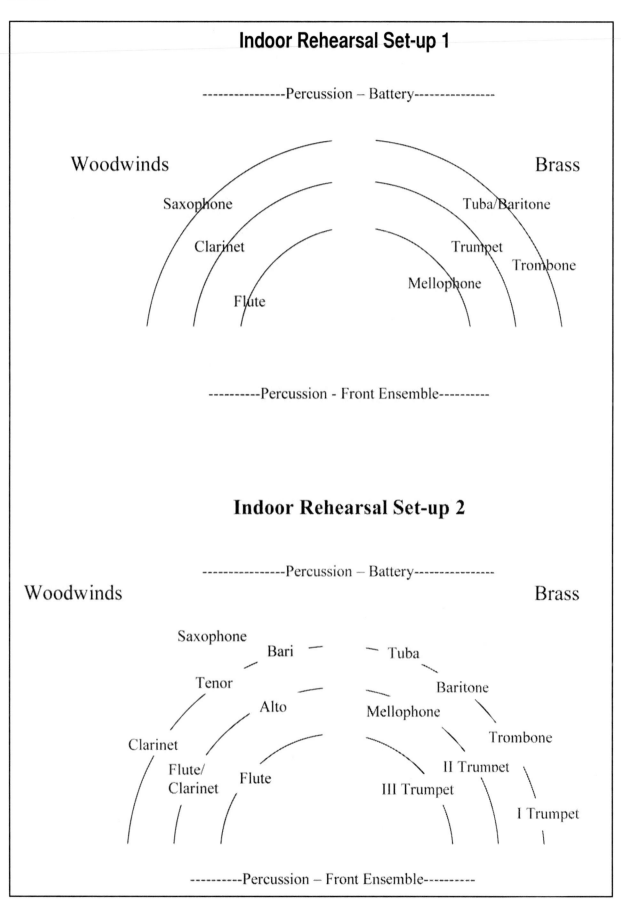

Indoor Rehearsal Set-up 1

---------------Percussion – Battery----------------

Woodwinds   Brass

Saxophone   Tuba/Baritone

Clarinet   Trumpet

                                                              Trombone

Mellophone

Flute

----------Percussion - Front Ensemble----------

Indoor Rehearsal Set-up 2

----------------Percussion – Battery----------------

Woodwinds   Brass

Saxophone
                    Bari   Tuba

Tenor
                                                    Baritone
                    Alto
                                        Mellophone
                                                              Trombone
Clarinet
                                                          II Trumpet
Flute/   Flute
Clarinet   III Trumpet
                                                              I Trumpet

----------Percussion – Front Ensemble----------

Check-off System

A system of checking individual members for skill and memory achievement will make staff and students aware of progress.

The check-off system is used for both music and marching skill development. Staff and student leaders can be involved in the testing (checking) process. The various levels are used to create achievable goals for all students. For example, Level One Music is playing music while reading the printed page. Too often directors skip this important step and assume students are on target. However, students often memorize music with incorrect rhythms or articulations and this is very difficult to "unlearn." Results are posted in the Band Room Area using poster board grids readily available at educational supply stores. Names can be listed down the vertical column and music pieces to be learned and visual skills can be listed along the top horizontally. Students can easily see on what they need to work, while the staff can gauge progress and what needs to be emphasized in rehearsals. Deadlines should be announced and posted well in advance and adhered to with appropriate consequences.

"You have to know your music for memory by Monday." It is a fact that if there are no consequences, there will be little progress. It is much more effective to say, "… and we will do a quick check-off on Monday afternoon" and then follow through. Remember that *telling* the students to do something is *not* teaching! Students become responsible when they are held accountable.

Music

Level One:

       Play music **while** reading the printed music—accurate notes, rhythms,
           articulations, slurs, **slow/steady** tempo
       Music check-offs can be broken up in segments (i.e. #1–4 of Warm-up)
       Summer/Band Camp goal

Level Two:

       Play music **from memory**—accurate notes, rhythms,
           articulations, slurs, **moderate** tempo
       September goal (before first major performance)

Level Three:

       Play music **for memory**—accurate notes, rhythms, articulations, slurs, plus
           dynamics & excellent style at **full** tempo
       End of October goal

Marching

Marching Program and check-off levels are outlined in Chapter 5: The Marching Program.

Chapter Seven

Show Planning

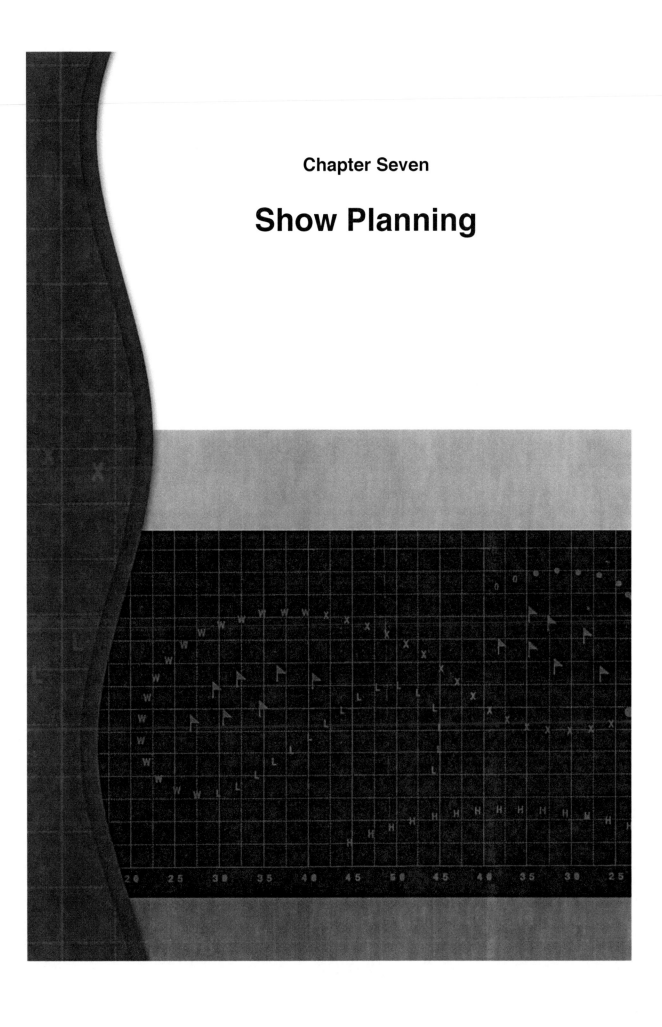

Guidelines

The band staff must plan and be highly organized to insure a successful season.

The band director and staff must do careful planning well in advance, whether it is a Friday Night Football Band performing three shows for the season or a complex custom designed show for a competition band. The timeline for planning will depend on the style and type of the band and whether the show will be purchased or custom designed. A band that utilizes published arrangements need not plan quite so far in advance, since there is little delay in getting the music. All bands regardless of style and type however, should follow the same guidelines presented here in planning and producing quality shows that are musically educational for the students.

For bands using custom arrangements and visual drill, the process is almost a full year production. It starts with review and evaluation of the current season while it is in progress, noting what is working well and what is not.

In planning the show, the band director and staff need to be excited about the new package and season or the students will not be motivated. The following important topics in show planning are discussed on the subsequent pages.

1. **Published vs. custom arrangements** – Choosing to use published or custom arrangements for the marching band is one of the first considerations.

2. **Music and theme selection** – The most important element of show planning is picking the music and possible theme.

3. **Timeline** – A schedule of show planning from brainstorming sessions to getting the show on the field will keep everyone on target.

4. **Data Module Sheet** – Once the music is selected, the details and form of the arrangement need to be organized with contributions from all key staff members. This is sent to the designers—winds, percussion, drill and choreography.

5. **Effective music repertoire in a nutshell** – The effectiveness of the music is the main concern in selecting music for the marching band show. If the music is not effective, the show is not effective. Some considerations are presented here.

6. **Visual considerations** – Before the music selections are finalized, attention needs to be given to the visual program.

7. **Small band considerations** – There are some special considerations that need to be given to smaller bands when selecting music and planning the show.

Published vs. Custom Designed Arrangements

The first decision to make is the source of music arrangements.

There are successful marching bands that use published and custom written arrangements. Depending on the situation, one of these options will be preferable. The choice will considerably change the show planning process in selecting the music to perform. It will also affect the achievement level of the marching band either positively or negatively.

Published Music Arrangements

There are some excellent publishing companies and arrangers available.

- **Pros**
    - Arrangements and recordings are readily available for perusal.
    - Large selection and variety of music is obtainable.
    - Music is graded and accessible to all bands.
    - It is a simple process to select and order music.
    - There are no special copyright permissions to obtain to perform published arrangements.

- **Cons**
    - Published arrangements are written to be accessible to a great number of bands and therefore not "special" or unique. Limited range, keys and tempos are utilized.
    - Safe scoring is utilized for most arrangements, with frequent doubling, giving them a generic sound. The sound and texture of published arrangements is similar from song to song and band to band.
    - The best arrangements each season are popular, and many other bands may perform the same music at a performance.
    - Syncopated rhythms are often "watered down" losing the flavor of the song and an opportunity to teach those skills. (In pop and rock music that is known by the students, it is easier to play a syncopation than a simplified version.)
    - The difficulty level and instrumentation may not match the particular needs of the band in all sections. Solo parts may not match the strong soloists in the band.

- **Summary**
    - As a starting point for a novice or developing band, published arrangements are a good way to begin.
    - Careful research should be done to find the best quality arrangements.
    - Seek different arrangers or publishers for the various songs in a show to create more variety of sound.

Custom Music Arrangements

Custom arrangements allow for more flexibility and creativity.

- **Pros**
    - The choice of music is almost limitless. (See copyright restrictions)
    - Special arrangements are written for the strengths and weaknesses of a particular ensemble, including solos and solis.
    - Form of the arrangement can be created by the staff to match the needs of the show.
    - The music selected is unique to that band and will probably not be performed by another.

- **Cons**
  - Custom arrangements must receive permission from the copyright holder, usually a publishing company or the composer, using the "Permission to Arrange" form. There is usually a fee involved to receive permission.
  - There is a financial obligation for the above permission and for the arranger's fees.
  - More planning is involved to get the product desired.

- **Summary**
  - To get a more unique arrangement that accomplishes the goals of the show, a custom arrangement is preferable.
  - Details of the band's instrumentation needs to be sent to the arranger.
  - How many in each section (i.e. four 1st trumpets, six 2nd trumpets)
  - Strengths and weaknesses (i.e. 1st trumpets to written G^5, two strong soloists, 2nd trumpets to D^5, simpler rhythms)
  - Overall level of the band (i.e. Brass grade 3, Woodwinds grade 4)

Quality Music Arrangements

Regardless of the source, quality arrangements must meet the following standards:

- Variety of orchestration techniques
- Dynamics and shaping clearly marked for every phrase
- Articulations for every note clearly marked or indicated
- Interesting melodies, countermelodies, harmonies and rhythms
- Music should have direction, builds, impacts, tension and release
- Key centers utilized for resonance of the wind instruments, particularly at impacts
- Music selected should be challenging but achievable by the middle of the season

A word of *caution* is in order. The biggest mistake made by groups is choosing music that is *too difficult*. Directors want to challenge the students, which is a good goal, but when the level is beyond their reach, there is little music learning taking place. The level of difficulty needs to be such that the majority of the students can achieve it by mid-season. Then the other musical elements can be attained such as style and expression. It is better to make small strides each season and gradually reach the goals of the band program.

Another Resource

There is another resource to consider when choosing music. There are several companies that provide music arrangements and drills to match the size and level of the band. Original music written for the marching band is another option available as well as color guard choreography, flags, costumes and theme T-shirts. The designers utilized are well-respected professionals in the marching band activity. Shows are packaged and themed with a great selection available. One such quality company is Marching Show Concepts. Visit www.msconcepts.com for more information.

This is a highly recommended entry level option for the young band director with a novice or developing band who is not comfortable writing drill, has limited staff or does not have the resources to hire an experienced professional. It eliminates the need for some of the show planning discussed in this chapter. It is almost "one-stop shopping" for marching band.

Music and Theme Selection

The music selection is the most important decision of the season.

Choosing the music for the marching band can launch the band on a successful season or doom the band to many months of problems, frustration or boredom. It must be carefully considered, not rushed and involve the members of the marching band staff.

Trends and fads in marching band come and go much like the fashion industry. It is currently in style to have a theme or at least a title to the marching band show that creates interest and unifies the show. Several years ago it was in fashion for bands to do a variety show. These typically had a classical opener, a jazz or Latin number, a pop ballad and a classical closer, often a reprise of the opener. There was variety and interest but little continuity. These shows may come back in vogue since most things go in cycles.

Which should come first, the theme or the songs?

Great shows have been created both ways. Sometimes a fascinating theme or concept is chosen and then music is found to fit the theme. Other times great music is selected and a theme is found to tie the music together or unify the selections. *The music selected must be effective* regardless of which is chosen first. Weak music with a clever theme or concept will be a weak show.

Several examples will illustrate the value of the different approaches. A band staff selected *Bizarro* by Michael Daugherty because they thought it would be an effective and interesting piece on the field. A theme of "Outside the Box" was then created as a visual concept to work together with the music. The concept was not directly related to the music (other than it is a bit "outside" or bizarre) but worked well as an effective production.

Another show was created based on the concept of a poem titled "The Man Who Wasn't There." Music was then researched and selected to highlight the dark and mysterious mood of the poem. Music eventually chosen was *Psycho* by Bernard Hermann, *Color and Light* by Stephen Sondheim, *Let Me Fall* by Benoit Jutras and *Candelabra Tango* by Michael Daugherty.

In a third example, a combination of the two approaches produced a successful show. The band staff got the idea of doing a contemporary version of *Take Five* by Paul Desmond. In brainstorming for other songs, they started looking at "number" tunes such as *Four Brothers*. The theme developed with a title of "Countdown – 5 4 3 2 1" using original music and short excerpts from the tunes above and *Fanfare for the Common Man* (a three note motif from *Symphony No. 3* by Aaron Copland), *Just the Two of Us* and *One is the Loneliest Number*. As many visual and musical ideas were used as possible to highlight the theme.

Brainstorming

The first step begins with a staff meeting that includes the director and key staff members. If local, the arrangers, choreographer and drill designer should attend. A brainstorm is a sudden and exciting idea. The show selected must be exciting to the staff or the season will not be exciting for the students.

All staff members should feel free to bring any ideas for music or themes to the table. A white board or large paper on easel will help to focus ideas. Recordings should be listened to and a free discussion of all ideas should ensue. Unless everyone immediately agrees on an idea as *The* show to do next year, it is best to let everyone think about it for a week or two and do more research and listening. A second meeting can produce the show or narrow it down to a few ideas and finalize it at a third meeting. The marching band works on a show and lives with it for many months, so this is not a decision to be made too quickly.

Some key concepts to keep in mind in choosing the music:

- The music is the most important element of the show. Nothing will make up for poor music choices.
- The effectiveness of the music is a primary concern for both audience and adjudicator. It is generally the most important category in competition and applies equally well to a half-time show. See "Effective Music Repertoire in a Nutshell" on page 108.
- If published arrangements are being used, listen to all available on sample recordings and websites. Make sure older arrangements are still available if selected.
- Consider the "Quality Music Arrangement" checklist mentioned on page 105.
- Be cautious in searching for a song that "no one has done before" as a primary consideration. There often is a very good reason some music has never been performed on a marching field!
- Most esoteric and avant garde music is only loved by the composer's mother and not even all of them. Be extremely cautious about picking this type of music. A good rule of thumb is to ask yourself "Would you want to come to band every day for months and play that music?" Do not forget that you need the support of the parents, administration and community for your program. This type of music education is best left to the concert stage (and in small doses).
- Design a show that "the popcorn eaters" at the show will "get" and enjoy (and then the judges will get it too!) If you need a libretto to understand it, choose something else.
- Most problems in music selection occur because the music is too difficult for the ability of the band. It is always a tricky balancing act to pick music that is challenging but achievable by the middle of the season. Make sure the band is familiar with the style of music. For example, a band program with little jazz experience should not be performing a jazz show.
- The second biggest problem is picking band music that is too easy. This is sometimes done intentionally for the purpose of being clean and not exposed for adjudication errors. This is not justifiable for band directors who should be music educators first.
- The third area of concern is picking music with tempos that are either too slow or too fast for the marching ability of the group. Always use a metronome when selecting music because tempos can be deceiving on a first listening (or march around the room to the music).
- Avoid overdone songs and themes. Everyone has heard _____ (fill in the blank) too many times.
- Caution should be exercised when selecting popular music even for half-time shows. It often lacks musical content or is monotonous and will get old to the players, staff and audience by fall.
- **Essential music elements**
  - Melodic content
  - Harmonic content
  - Rhythmic content
  - Tension and release
  - Form and development
  - Variety of styles, moods and expressions, tempi, scoring/voicing textures (orchestration)

Effective Music Repertoire in a Nutshell

An understanding of what makes music effective from the viewpoint of the adjudicator (and audience) will help in the selection of music and show concepts.

Direction

The music must have direction or forward motion. This is achieved through:

    a.   Melodic line

    b.   Harmonic progression

    c.   Rhythmic progression

    d.   Tension and release

    e.   Form and development

Variety

To achieve a high level of effect, the music program must demonstrate variety of style, moods, dynamics, scoring/voicing textures, and tempi.

Melodic Content

The use of quality melodic lines is still a priority regardless of the style of music selected —classical, jazz, pop and contemporary. This area is not about quantity (lots of notes & difficulty) but about quality.

Problem Areas in Music Repertoire

Direction

"Goes Nowhere, Does Nothing" (GNDN) The lack of direction in musical design is the main problem in programs that do not achieve a strong musical effect. The question that must be asked throughout the program is "Where is this going?" If the answer is not a positive one or a question mark, there is a problem. Great harmonic progressions, melodic lines and the other factors create an interesting program for the listener.

Variety

A lack of variety creates a boring show.

Melodic Content

The current trend heard sometimes in contemporary marching programs is a lack of high quality melodic content. This is a serious concern. When the question "Where is the melody?" is asked by the audience and judges, little music effect is being created.

Creating a Show

From great music to a great show

Once some great songs have been selected, the staff needs to mold them into a cohesive and entertaining show. Use the "Show Planning Guide" on page 111 to list several options for each part of the show – opener, second song, etc. Then mix and match and listen to possible combinations. Make sure there is variety, continuity, direction and a satisfying conclusion.

Answer the following questions as the show begins to take shape:

- ❖ Will the show or theme match the identity or traditions of the band? Can you "see" the band performing this show?
- ❖ Will the show be innovative – "bring something new to the table"?
- ❖ Will the show highlight the strengths of the band (and minimize the weaknesses)?
- ❖ Does the show have an interesting beginning and a satisfying ending?
- ❖ Are the "pieces of the puzzle" put together in the right order?
- ❖ Is the music program strong enough to stand on its own without the visual?
- ❖ Will the show maintain interest for the members and staff for an entire season?

Ingredients for a successful show

The current recipe for a successful marching band show calls for certain ingredients. Make sure to stay current because these change over the years. Current ingredients that are "the unwritten compulsories" for the competitive activity are:

- ❖ The "essential music elements" (see page 107)
- ❖ Woodwind technical moment(s)
- ❖ Brass a capella (no battery) sustained sonority moment
- ❖ Percussion feature as part of a full ensemble music production (and not an isolated feature)
- ❖ Color guard full ensemble moment(s)
- ❖ Featured solos and sections if musically appropriate

The "original" music option

Quite a few bands are successfully using music originally created for them to get a unique show. They can obtain the exact style, form and pacing that they want and be thematically coordinated. The band can also avoid the expense and difficulty of obtaining Permission to Arrange clearance.

Caution: Make sure a *quality* composer is commissioned to do the writing, and that the music is carefully critiqued and edited when necessary. There are too many original compositions heard on the field that are lacking in melodic content, harmonic development and musical direction.

"Marching band is the art of the obvious."

Show Segments

The various segments of the show each have a function.

The function of each song in the show should be considered when "piecing the show together." Although there are many variations and exceptions to these standard practices, the following ideas will lay a groundwork for a well-functioning show.

Opener

The opener sets the mood of the show. It usually has an introduction that is dramatic, suspenseful or intriguing and developmental in nature and often leads to an impact within the first minute of the show ("Hello, here we are!"). It is typically up-tempo following the introduction and has a strong ending although not the biggest moment of the show.

Production number

The second song is traditionally called the "production number." It is usually a change in style, tempo and orchestration and often features sections or soloists.

Ballad

The third number is often a ballad to showcase the sonority and expressive qualities of the band. In a three song format, a lyrical segment can be utilized within another song. The ballad should not be too long because it is hard to maintain interest visually as well as musically.

Closer

The closer should bring the show to a satisfying conclusion. It is generally up-tempo and has the biggest impact of the show. This does not need to occur at the very end, and is often about one minute prior to it. "Down endings" can be very emotional but are very difficult to accomplish successfully.

Data Module Sheet

Once the music is selected, all musical and visual ideas are assembled.

A Data Module Sheet is now written to assemble all of the ideas in one place. Many band staffs call this "developing the storybook." This is the place to get all of the musical and visual ideas formulated and organized. One of the most important functions of a good drill is to have the sections staged in the right place at the right time. The Data Module Sheet is an excellent vehicle to communicate those needs to the drill writer. It should be referred to as the show gets put on the field and also later in the season to make sure all (or most) of the ideas become realities. (See page 112.) A blank Data Module Sheet can be found on-line, www.dynamicband.com.

With the songs and theme selected, research all ideas regarding the theme, music and composers. Find what can be used to add to the interest of the show and include those comments in the data sheet.

See the following sample Data Module Sheet for *The Raven* as submitted by the composer. The next step (on this sample) is for the color guard and visual staff to add their comments and drill requests for the drill writer. They would also follow along a score and an MP3 recording.

Band:

Theme/Title:

Show Planning Guide
Music

Titles	Composer	Arranger	Publisher	Style	Tempo & Key	Length
Opener:						
#2:						
#3:						
Closer:						

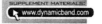

Title: The Raven - Part One

Measure	Counts	Time	Melody	Background	Ideas
					The Raven Part One is not in a clear key center to create a mysterious mood. (See Raven Keys and Scales) The music follows the general outline presented.
1	24	:00	W.W.	Sustain bass BD - 5's	Starts soft and thinly scored. 5 bass drum for tapping repeats several times. W.W. arpeggio background Brass gradually add in.
7	20	:20	Trpt. Solo Mello Solo Trpt.Soli		"The Raven" theme (3 notes) Echo in Mello
12	16	:31			Accel. To Ltr. A Melodic fragments from section to section
A 16	16	:40	Full Ens.		HIT Perc. 5 Raps - Everyone look at door on field Text "only this and nothing more."
B 20	16	:47		Synth bass Tromb. To Trpt.	MOVEMENT ONE - *Tempo = 144* Intro to Theme
24	32	:53	W.W.	Mello echo Trb. & Trp. Cont.	W.W. melody
C 32	48	1:07	Full Ens.		Full Ensemble Impact
44	8	1:27			Vocal: "Darkness there, and nothing more." Optional rhythm for this in the synth. part
D 46	32	1:30	Upper voices Echo midd.	Lower voices	The Raven melody
54	8	1:43			Diminuendo lst 8 cts. of melody
E 56	32	1:47	Trpts. then W.W.	L.B. Bass and Synth.	Fade away and slow down to end Fragments from Intro from section to section Low Brass play "Lenore, Lenore, Lenore" Others chant

Timeline

A schedule from brainstorming sessions to getting the show on the field will keep everyone on target.

A suggested show planning timeline follows. Every situation is a little different, and the schedule will depend on winter band activities, availability of staff and whether published or custom designs are utilized. It is better to be prepared too early than too late.

Design Completion Dates

Date	1. Opener	2. Production	3. Ballad	4. Closer
April 1	Winds			
April 15	Percussion	Winds		
May 1	(Numbers to drill writer)			
		Percussion	Winds	
May 15			Percussion	Winds
June 1	(Music to students)			
	Drill			Percussion
June 15	Choreography	Drill		
July 1		Choreography	Drill	
July 15			Choreography	Drill
August 1				Choreography
Band Camp	Learn			
August		Learn	Learn	
2 weeks before first show				Learn

Notes:

There is a "domino effect" if one of the designers gets behind—everything else will be late.

Color guard is always at a big disadvantage because they are the last link in the chain. They should learn in segments rather than in sequence—in place (halt) segments first. Learn "traveling music" parts later.

It is usually very time consuming to teach drill once school rehearsals begin. Finish in the summer!

There is another "school of thought" and that is to go slowly and include all the details, and it is okay if the show is not done until the end of the season. The drawbacks to that approach are the lack of time to revise once the show is completely done, and the closer is usually not as solid as the opener.

The Visual Component

The visual program interprets and enhances the music to make it a complete package.

With a solid musical foundation established, the show must also work well as a visual production. The visual caption is often out of the band director's area of expertise and therefore, the color guard and visual specialist must be consulted to be sure the show lends itself well to a visual production.

The visual elements—drill, color guard, marching and body movement—should interpret and enhance the music. The most effective shows have a blended and coordinated musical and visual program. Other visual considerations concern possible use of props, color guard costumes and flag designs.

The color guard is an important element of the successful marching band, and the input of their staff is very important at this point in the planning process. The color guard caption head, with the band director's concurrence, should communicate to the drill writer requests for staging, equipment choices and changes using the Data Module Sheet. He/she should also inform the drill writer of numbers, strengths and weaknesses including how well the members move. Make sure the music is appropriate for the talent level of the color guard. If the music "calls for" dance, the color guard must be able to effectively communicate this style.

A word of caution to the band director—color guard staff members are famous for being very creative. However, they sometimes are not very practical, so careful attention needs to be paid to budget, costumes, flag designs and choreography to make sure everything aligns with the overall show theme and the band director's vision of the show. The band director should not be a micro-manager but does need to be the overall boss of the total band program.

Ballads are inherently difficult visually because the tempo is slow and there is less motion. Bands often march very slow tempos to the eighth note pulse to achieve more visual interest. Care must be taken to maintain a smooth technique that is not distracting to the music played.

Although ideally every music phrase should be interesting, in reality, this is impossible. Therefore, there are moments, such as music transitions, where the visual program needs to maintain the interest of the show. The visual can also smooth out the connections that may be abrupt or fragmented in the music.

Marching tempos need to be considered carefully as they relate to the music. Sometimes a difficult music passage needs to be played at a halt in order to achieve a strong performance. In such cases a body pose or slight movement can visually enhance the effect of the moment. The music performance must always be the top priority.

Visual and Musical General Effect

There needs to be an *effect or applause point* every 20–30 seconds in the show. It can be a "stand up and shout" moment or it can be a beautiful phrase that "takes your breath away," but it must be something —musical or visual—that makes the audience react. Every few minutes there needs to be a very big "Wow" moment that is memorable.

Small Band Considerations

An important part of the show planning process is keeping in mind the size of the band.

It may seem obvious, but band directors sometimes forget the practicality of matching the show selected with the band performing it. An honest evaluation of the band's projected size, as well as level of ability, needs to be in the forefront of everyone's mind. Every year there are very effective small band shows, but they were always planned with the size of the group in mind. Too often a small band tries to perform a show that would be well suited to a large band or DCI group with unsuccessful results.

Some thoughts to keep in mind when planning for the small band:

❖ Most important – choose appropriate music for the size of the ensemble. A large symphonic work such as *Great Gate of Kiev* or *Star Wars* is not going to be successful with a small band.

❖ Reduce the practical field size by the use of props or tarps. With a small band, there is no need to go beyond the 30 yard lines or behind the back hash. Props or backdrops can focus the attention of the viewer and portray the theme in a convincing manner. Make sure the props are as professional looking as possible.

❖ Keep the wind instruments close together when playing section features so they can perform with confidence and a unified sound.

❖ Use bright colors in the flags and costumes, if appropriate to the show theme, to make a bigger visual presence.

❖ Integrate the color guard in the forms frequently rather than using them as a separate entity or backdrop.

❖ Make sure the marching technique and execution is excellent. Although there is greater exposure (no room to hide), in many ways it is easier to clean a small band visually than a large one. Take advantage of this opportunity.

❖ Avoid ballads or use them in short segments as part of another production. It is difficult for the small band to sustain the quality of sound, balance and blend.

❖ Be extra cautious in getting accurate numbers to the drill writer. One missing wind player can make a big difference in the drill and sound of the band.

❖ If there are not enough numbers to have a balanced battery and front ensemble it would be better to place them all in the front ensemble. The percussion can then function as a concert band percussion section. An option is to have the battery march only a portion of the show, perhaps the opener and/or closer, to get variety and also develop marching skills for the future.

❖ Use a synthesizer with a good sound system, if a good player is available, to fill out the sound. Simple sustained sounds and solos are effective and better than doubling melodies in the winds.

❖ Be creative!

Chapter Eight

Drill Design

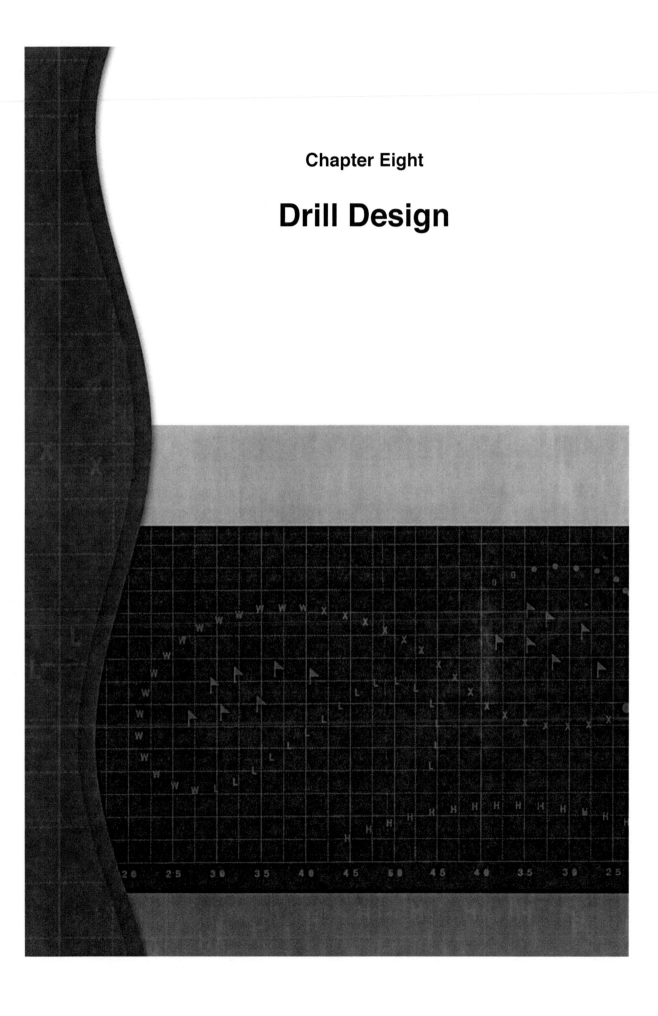

Drill Design

A well-written drill adds visual impact and interest and boosts the music effect.

The three main areas of concern to the band director are music selection, drill design and performance quality. Following the selection of a strong music program, an excellent drill must be obtained to complete the package. A good drill design will strengthen the visual program, giving credit to the marching ability of the members and for the artistry of the drill itself. A high-quality drill design will also enhance the musical production allowing the music and its performance to achieve its maximum potential. Conversely, without a good drill design, the music and visual performance will suffer because of poor staging, unnecessary difficulty in cleaning the visual program, too hard to perform the music and lack of interest in the drill.

Drill Design Options

There are several options in attaining a quality drill for the marching band program, whether the band is competitive or not.

Hire a drill writer – Highly competitive bands generally hire an expert drill designer to custom design a drill for the band. At that level, it is important that all elements of the band and the show are first-rate. In competition, typically the music captions account for 50 to 60% of the score with the remainder going to the visual captions. So the visual captions, being 40 to 50% of the total, are a very important part of the total show. The drill design, as mentioned above, will positively or negatively affect the music performance as well. The positive side of using a custom designed drill is getting exactly what the director and staff wants for the show. This is communicated through the Data Module Sheets mentioned in Chapter 7.

There are some negative aspects of getting a custom designed drill. The first is the expense. Most experienced professional drill designers write as their full time job and each drill is very time-consuming, justifying the expense. A younger, budding drill writer will be less expensive but the quality of the product may not be as strong.

The second possible negative is getting the drill on time. Drill writers, including some of the finest in the business, are notorious for having difficulty meeting deadlines. They are artists! This can cause difficulties for band members being prepared in time for performances, utilizing precious rehearsal time and for the band director's stress level.

Here are some recommendations to minimize this potential problem:

- Plan ahead and start early (December or January is not too early to plan the show.)
- Have a contract or verbal agreement with the drill designer
- Let the drill designer set the timeline for delivery of segments of the drill
- Follow up verbal agreements with written documentation ("Here is what we agreed to...")

- The director and staff must meet their deadlines
  - Data Module Sheet delivered on time
  - Music scores delivered on time
  - Number of musicians in each section and guard delivered on time
  - Color guard requests delivered on time
- Communicate with the drill writer for progress reports (without being pushy)
- Be patient! Even with the best intentions and plans, drills can be late. If they are, make sure the band is performing to the highest level of achievement on what they have. Don't complain until that point is reached and you are truly waiting for the next drill page with "nothing to do." If it is a major problem, next season choose another drill designer.

Do it yourself – If there is not a need for a "state of the art" drill, it can be written "in house" and many of the potential problems can be avoided. Plus, as the season progresses, changes can easily be made, if needed (and they frequently are).

Some band directors are outstanding drill designers. For novice and developing drill writers who have a strong interest in this area, this can be a good situation for the band. It is highly recommended to use a quality computer program like Pyware 3D Java and study the text *Techniques of Marching Band Show Designing* by Dan Ryder. Both are available from Dan Ryder Field Drills at <www.danryderfielddrills. com>. It is also recommended to become a "student" of the art of drill writing by studying live and recorded performances, attending workshops and clinics and seeking input from experienced drill writers, judges and band directors. An essential feature is the print out of the individual coordinates for each member of the band. The Pyware program can also animate the drill on screen with MIDI files of the music.

All band directors, whether writing drill or not, should become familiar with the above software program and text to learn the intricacies of drill design. This will help the director to better understand, analyze and teach whatever drill is used.

Experience in drill writing is the best teacher and always improves with time.

Purchase a package show - The third option in obtaining a drill is purchasing a ready-to-use or pre-designed drill and music package. There are several companies involved in providing this service. One reputable company with many choices of shows, including published and original music, is Marching Show Concepts <www.msconcepts.com>.

This method is **highly recommended** for the young band director in his/her first few years in a new position. Unless there has been a tradition of using a particular drill writer, this will bring about the most satisfactory results in a new situation. These companies have experienced, high quality drill designers on staff to write the drills.

A standard drill for each music program is written for several band sizes and then is custom adapted to the band director's input on number of members. There is regional protection so that bands attending particular contests will not see another band performing the same show.

A band director, especially in a new situation, has enough to occupy his/her time and worry about, without the stress of drill concerns. A quality product is delivered *on time* including the music. There are other options available such as guard costumes, choreography, T-shirt and flag designs.

Drill Considerations

The band director's drill preferences need to be communicated to the drill designer. The writer may have a different perspective, but the director is the client and needs to dictate preferences.

❖ The first purpose of the drill is to stage the music – the instrument groups must be in the right place at the right time.

❖ The second purpose of the drill is to create motion that matches the music.

❖ Finally, the drill should be visually interesting in and of itself. It needs to have several special moments that create applause simply because of the drill.

❖ The needs of a high school marching band are very different from that of a drum corps. Make sure the designer understands the differences, especially regarding difficulty, woodwinds and placement on the field for volume.

❖ In featured segments, woodwinds and small groups need to be staged close to the front. Winds should not be too spread out, especially sections that play similar music lines. The battery should be centered and behind the winds as much as possible.

❖ The drill should be relatively easy to execute and play or spin. A drill that is too hard just to "get credit" is not worth the effort. Sometimes simple details make cleaning the drill difficult. For example, spacing that changes frequently (i.e. 3 step to 2.5 step to 3.25 step) is difficult to maintain. It is much better to maintain the same spacing for many pages and change the form shape or length. Perfect circles are difficult to clean, especially if they are floating, but easy to design on a computer. An advanced level of band can handle something of that nature but not an average or novice group.

❖ The drill must allow the musicians to perform the music well. A spectacular drill that does not allow for good music performance is not spectacular at all. The band must sound good as the top priority.

❖ Very slow and very fast tempos are difficult. Make sure the level of the band's marching skills matches that of the drill.

❖ A lot of members doing small steps (baby steps) for any length of time is difficult and does not create any motion or interest. 8 to 5 and 6 to 5 are the most comfortable step sizes and look the best.

❖ Keep in mind that if there are many requests for staging in the Data Module Sheet, it is sometimes not mathematically possible to achieve everything. Staging for a featured group often takes many previous pages to prepare. Make sure the designer knows what are the *most important* moments.

Teaching the Drill

The process of teaching the drill must be organized and efficient.

It is time consuming at best to initially teach a new drill. It is therefore very important that the band director and staff are well organized and plan ahead. There are many successful approaches and methods that work and several options will be presented here.

Start with a session explaining drill charts, terms and learning methods in a seated classroom environment (Drill 101). The band room works fine for this. Do not *assume* the students understand drill charts, even the veterans.

Drill Philosophy

There are two main philosophies regarding how to move from set to set. Both are based on the premise that each member must know their drill coordinates, step size, counts and direction for each page.

1. **Guide the form** – using peripheral vision, maintain form spacing and shape while moving to the correct location.

    a. Pros – spacing, form maintenance and posture are generally better; visual awareness is strong

    b. Cons – forms sometimes drift from actual location; members tend to "follow the crowd" rather than really knowing their sets

2. **March dot to dot** – move from exact location of one set to the next without concern for other members (spacing, form shape, etc.)

    c. Pros – form location is generally better; members must really know sets

    d. Cons – one cannot look down with peripheral vision to see the last 2 or 3 steps into the set, so it is hard to actually march dot to dot; posture can therefore suffer; much time is spent with members "stepping off" their drill sets; individual 8 to 5 must be flawless or this process is a waste of time; spacing and form shape may not be good until mid-season

Directors are quite adamant about the merits of each system. The young director will have to choose the system to use based on the pros and cons of each. It can be said that most high school bands use the "guide the form" method, while emphasizing knowing the drill sets.

Drill 101

1. Students should have a drill/music 3-ring notebook, 2 pencils and a Hi-Lighter with them at all rehearsals.

2. Some groups give each student a copy of the complete drill so they can see what the forms look like. Keep in mind that there are many learning styles—visual, auditory, and kinesthetic. Most people are a combination, so the more approaches one takes—the better the learning and retention. Seeing the forms on paper can help students visualize how they look on the field. Some bands give a copy of the drill only to student squad leaders.

3. Coordinate Books – every student should have a small notebook with their individual drill information. 3 x 5 index card notebooks work very well and some bands have a printer make and bind these notebooks. Each page should contain: drill page number, music measure, coordinates, counts to arrive at this page and any additional special information. Drill Mapbooks are similar to this, but only have blank grid paper. Students then mark 4 to 6 sets on a page and connect them with lines. This, in graphical form, shows direction and distance covered and transfers well to the field. Either type of notebook should be on a lanyard or long shoestring and worn around the neck or waist at *every* rehearsal.

4. The director or staff member should teach drill terms and how to read a drill chart and mark the drill books. See Drill 101 football field grid with drill terms (page 126). Each member should get a copy of this. Remind students that when they are on the field, they should hold the drill charts flat and aligned with the field. That means if they are facing front, the drill paper should be upside down. This avoids a lot of confusion.

5. Drill Quiz – give the students a blank field grid with the assignment to mark with dots 10 drill coordinates. Then have the squad leaders grade them to make sure everyone understands. (See supplementary material online, www.dyanmicband.com.)

6. Pass out drill and/or coordinate information for beginning of actual drill. Have students enter their individual information in Coordinate Book or Drill Mapbooks for about 10 pages. Staff and student leaders should assist, answer any questions and make sure the younger members understand the process. Highlight individual position on drill charts.

7. Mark the drill page number in the music. The relationship of the music measure or phrase to drill page will automatically be learned every time the music is rehearsed. Directors need to mark their music scores so they know how drill pages and music align. (See score page online, www.dyanmicband.com.)

8. The Drill 101 class will save a lot of time and avoid confusion once the actual drill learning begins on the field.

Learning the drill on the field

1. Marking the field –
   a. Yard lines/hash marks - The field must be painted with accurate yard lines & high school hashes (mark college hashes if the bands performs on fields so marked).
   Four-step grid – Mark a dot or diamond every four steps for the entire field; students can quickly check their sets relative to this grid.
   b. Concrete, asphalt or grass field – The band practice lot can be any of these surfaces Concrete or asphalt is good because it is always level, never muddy and the lines and markers remain visible, but it can be very hot in warm weather and more demanding on the legs and knees. (Directors usually do not have a choice!)
   c. The 22.5" step size is a myth! It is accurate for marching yard line to yard line, but front to back is actually 22.86". This may not seem like a large difference, but the 22.5" step size will be off by 10" marching from one hash to another. Paint the grid accordingly. The article "Moving Dot to Dot" in the Spring 2007 *Fanfare* publication presents an excellent solution to this problem, (www.msconcepts.com).

2. Marking individual sets or dots on the field – Several methods can work. (Some bands do not mark any individual sets but "step off" whenever necessary.)

   a. Hard surfaces - Paint drill sets with small dots and/or page numbers, sticky dots, chalk, tape or soap.

   b. Grass surfaces – Paint (non-damaging paint is available), small marking flags or colored poker chips can be used. A different color is used for each of 4 or 5 sets learned. Then chip or flag #1 is picked up and becomes #6 and so forth.

   c. All sets can be marked but this gets confusing when there are too many marks. Some bands mark only the difficult or curved sets. Also on a hard surface, the previous year's drill may still show through. (Use cheap paint.)

   d. The drill is learned faster if the sets are marked. The group marches the number of counts and halts. The members then are told to check the form and adjust. Then check the marker and adjust. (See Chapter 6: Rehearsal Techniques)

3. Procedure

   a. Carry drill notebooks and/or coordinate books (no instruments).

   b. Find location and go to position on page 1.

   c. Look at drill or coordinate sheet and **look** at location on the field for page 2.

   d. **Walk** in tempo, correct number of counts to page 2 set, looking at the set.

   e. Stand at attention facing correct direction. The director corrects drill sets and form from tower and field staff does the same on field. When it is accurate, members or leaders mark the set (if that is the system). Members should stand at attention then and become *visually aware* of how the form and spacing looks and feels.

   f. Walk quickly back to page 1 and fall in at attention.

   g. **March** from page 1 to page 2 *not* looking down and halt.

   h. On command, check form with eyes only (don't look down) and adjust.

   i. On command, check set marker and adjust (or "step off" position).

   j. Once form is set, stand at attention and look to become *visually aware* of how the form looks.

   k. Reset and repeat process (g–j) as many times as needed for the members to feel comfortable (maybe 4–8 times)

   l. Learn page 3 using the same process (b–k) reviewing only 3–4 times

   m. Go back to page 1 and run 1 to 2, halt and check. Then pages 2 to 3, halt and check. Repeat if needed.

   n. Run page 1 to 3 non-stop until it is comfortable.

   o. When a new page is learned, go back to page 1 and review in sequence, first with halts in between and then non-stop. This sequential learning **increases retention**.

   p. Continue this sequence until an ending point is reached that constitutes a rehearsal segment, a halt or the end of a section of music. This segment might be 4 to 10 pages long.

q. Start the process anew with this rehearsal "starting point" as the point of return and learn that segment. The starting points might be every 3–5 rehearsal letters of music in logical divisions. It *saves* time because students can quickly get to these drill pages, as opposed to expecting students to quickly start on any page of the drill. (i.e. It only takes a few extra seconds to start at page 8 (a starting point) than page 10 which is the targeted rehearsal page. The other approach can will take much more time to find a random page.)

r. Music can be added, when it is memorized, working in segments always beginning at "starting points."

Summary

- Learn page 1

- Learn page 2 (repeat as needed)

- March 1–2 (repeat as needed)

- Learn page 3

- March 2–3 (repeat as needed)

- March 1–3 (repeat as needed)

- Continue add-on process until a new rehearsal starting point is reached.

Cleaning the Drill

Cleaning the drill is a season long process.

See Chapter 6: Rehearsal Techniques—Procedures—Level Two for general ideas. A few key concepts to review:

- Music or Visual focus of rehearsal needs to be clearly defined.

- Use the spiral learning method for music and visual for each rehearsal segment

  - *Play* only – stand at halt or mark time

  - *March* only – don't play – focus on the visual

  - *March* and *Play*

  - Then move to the next rehearsal segment

  - Each focus will gradually improve and become automatic as the other is added.

- Work in rehearsal segments (often referred to as "chunks"). Use consistent "starting pages" throughout the season to save time.

- Don't overuse Dr. Beat©! The band performs without an amplified metronome, so they must frequently rehearse without it. Suggested percentage of rehearsal use of Dr. Beat©:

  - Band Camp 100%

  - Two weeks before first show 75%

  - Last rehearsal before *any* show 25%

  - Remainder of season 50%

  - Last week of season 0%

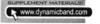

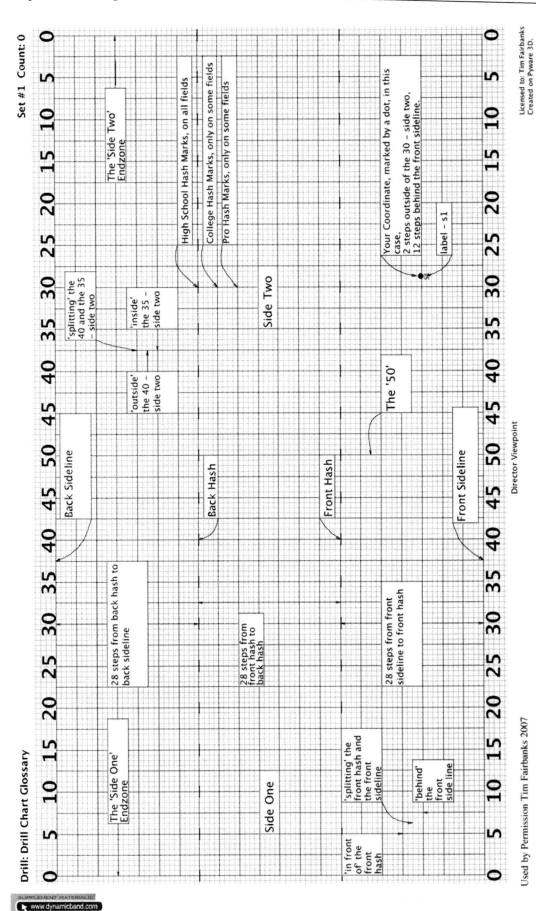

Set #1 Count: 0

Drill: Drill Chart Glossary

The "Side Two" Endzone

High School Hash Marks, on all fields

College Hash Marks, only on some fields

Pro Hash Marks, only on some fields

'splitting' the 40 and the 35 – side two

'inside' the 35 – side two

'outside' the 40 – side two

Side Two

Back Sideline

Back Hash

Front Hash

The '50'

Front Sideline

28 steps from back hash to back sideline

28 steps from front hash to back hash

28 steps from front sideline to front hash

Your Coordinate, marked by a dot, in this case, 2 steps outside of the 30 – side two, 12 steps behind the front sideline.

label – s1

The 'Side One' Endzone

Side One

'splitting' the front hash and the front sideline

'behind' the front side line

'in front of the front hash

Director Viewpoint

Chapter Nine

Attitude

Attitude

"It's all in your attitude" is a saying that is very important to the successful marching band.

A positive attitude on the part of the director, staff and students will create an enjoyable experience *more than great achievements* in marching and music. Everyone has the choice every day to embrace a positive or negative attitude. It is always amazing to hear students talk, following the same event, class or activity and one is glowingly positive and the other can be luke-warm or negative. "It's all in your attitude."

How can the director and staff *affect* the attitude of the students? The attitude of the director and staff will rub off on the band members whether it is desired or not. Teenagers are easily influenced by their teachers, and this must be utilized to create positive benefits for the individual members.

Much of this was addressed in Chapter 6: Rehearsal Techniques under Staff Rehearsal Philosophy, Methods and Atmosphere. It is important to briefly review since nothing will affect the band members more than the atmosphere of rehearsals, performances and how they **perceive** they are being treated.

- **Attitude—Philosophy**
  - Positive
    - Reinforce good performance
    - Approach problems as a need for improvement
  - Remove negativity (anger, sarcasm, emotion, blame)
  - Businesslike
    - "Just the facts"
    - Staff to Students same as Staff to Staff
    - Non-emotional

- **Method—Approach**
  - To students
    - "You are your own best teacher."
    - Self-awareness is a goal for students
    - Ownership
    - Ask members to keep a mental checklist of what to work on
  - Mistakes—How to deal with them
    - Without mistakes there is no learning!
    - Don't make mistakes the focus (no anger or blame)
    - AWARENESS is what is important
    - Negative reinforcement
      - Fear creates mistakes & a lack of confidence (especially in shows)
    - Negative reinforcement/Fear is successful but only in the short term.
  - Private Lesson Approach = Ensemble Approach
    - As a teacher, what can I do to help the student solve the problem.
  - Elicit student input
    - "Does everyone understand?"
    - "What would help you…?"
    - "Are there any questions?"

What if you are just not in a good mood someday due to any number of reasons? Everyone has a bad day every now and then, so what do you do? **Fake it!** (What? And be insincere?) **Yes!** As a teacher, you are an actor on stage. (All great teachers are great actors!) You need to motivate, inspire and model the behavior and attitude that you want your students to exhibit. You even need to be overly dramatic sometimes. After pretending to be positive and enthusiastic, pretty soon it starts to become sincere.

The second half of developing a positive attitude in the band is *communicating* to the band members. It cannot be assumed that the students understand attitude, nor can it be communicated in a few brief comments in rehearsal. Time must be dedicated outside of the normal rehearsal setting to address attitude and other important life-skill issues. An approach to this communication—The Attitude Session— follows on the next few pages.

The topic of attitude cannot adequately be addressed in a few pages but is a lifelong pursuit of great educators. There are many resources to periodically study including many books in libraries and bookstores, DVD's and lectures, clinics and workshops.

Resources

(See supplementary material online, www.dynamicband.com.)

Books – Refer to Music Educator's Resource List in Chapter 18: Appendix material online.

There are many speakers and clinicians in this field. Here are two highly recommended music clinicians in the areas of attitude and leadership.

Dr. Tim Lautzenheiser – www.attitudeconcepts.com

Fran Kick – www.kickitin.com

Try a Google search for "positive attitude" – over 2 million hits!

Band members in Attitude Session.

What Is an Attitude Session?

Attitude Sessions are an opportunity to address the important non-performance topics that are often neglected.

An Attitude Session is a meeting or class setting where non-performance topics can be discussed. These life skill subjects range from positive attitude to dealing with performance nervousness, as well as band expectations and traditions. It is an opportunity for the band members to focus on these issues without the distractions of a large rehearsal setting. Too often these topics only get addressed after a problem or crisis arises in the band. These issues are very important to the band members individually and the development of teamwork and band unity.

Here are ten topics that can be used for sessions early in the year to establish good student attitude, focus and teamwork. All Attitude Sessions can be found in supplementary material online, www.dynamicband.com.

Ten Topics for Attitude Sessions

1. **WHAT IS THIS THING CALLED "BAND"?** The first day of band can be intimidating to the new member. The band director can alleviate those fears and kick off the new season with his/her plans for the year.

2. **BAND EXPECTATIONS** Every good band has expectations or rules and regulations. In order to have efficient rehearsals and be fair to all members, it is important that everyone knows the expectations and understands the reasons for them.

3. **REHEARSAL SKILLS** There are student rehearsal skills and procedures that allow band members to achieve their potential and make the rehearsals efficient and enjoyable.

4. **POSITIVE ATTITUDE** Developing a positive attitude is an essential life skill for all people. It takes practice and understanding.

5. **PHILOSOPHY OF COMPETITION** Understanding the band program's philosophy of competition is important for all members. Competition as a fact of life that needs to be addressed so it is a learning tool and not a negative force.

6. **WINNING ATITUDE** In life there are winners and losers. It is significant to develop a winning attitude and to understand that this is different from winning awards.

7. **PERSONAL RELATIONS** Getting along with people is an essential skill but especially important when band members spend hundreds of hours working and socializing together over a period of many months.

8. **LEADERSHIP SKILLS** A strong student leadership program is vital for the success of the marching band program. It will benefit all members to understand these skills.

9. **STAGE FRIGHT** Performance nervousness is a concern to many band members as well as professionals. There are techniques that help performers reach their potential.

10. **OPEN MIC** Having an Attitude Session devoted to the band members expressing themselves and the importance of band in their lives can be a powerful event.

Relaxation & Breathing Techniques

An **optional** element of the Attitude Sessions is to develop skills in focused relaxation and deep breathing. These are techniques that help directly in musical and visual performance but are important life skills as well. As students move from high school to college to adult life, tension and stress becomes more and more of a serious health and performance concern. When the students are relaxed, the topics of the Attitude Sessions can be addressed. Soft, soothing music can help with relaxation techniques. Instructors interested in this aspect of stress reduction are encouraged to read one of the many fine books on the subject.

1. Find a large area that is free of distractions. Partially lower the lighting.

2. Students are encouraged to lie on the floor on their backs and close their eyes. (optional)

3. They are to center themselves with an imaginary line running from the center of the top of their head down through the center of their bodies.

4. **Deep Breathing** – Begin by focusing on breathing in for a slow count of four through the nose and exhaling through the mouth for a count of four. The instructor can count and snap fingers to establish a pulse. Students should keep all the breathing muscles relaxed and fill their lungs with air so their stomach rises as they inhale. They should expand the counts to five in—five out, then six in—six out, etc. Allow students to settle in on their own to whatever feels comfortable and relaxed. Students should *focus* on the feeling of the air inhaling and exhaling.

5. **Muscle Relaxation** is achieved by focusing on the muscle groups and *allowing* them to relax starting with the toes, then moving to the feet, the legs, torso, arms, shoulders, neck, temples, forehead, cheeks, mouth, eyes and jaw.

6. The mind should think about the muscle groups and periodically go back to attention on the relaxed breathing. Be passive and don't try too hard. These are skills that take practice.

7. The topic for the Attitude Session can be discussed at this time.

8. When the session is finished, students should roll to their side (if lying down) and remain quiet for a minute. Then they should sit up and remain quiet for a minute and then stand up slowly.

9. Students generally find these sessions very relaxing and centering.

Performers should remember the **deep breathing** techniques and use three four-count inhales/exhales just prior to a performance or taking a written test in class. This is very helpful in calming the nerves and focusing the attention on the performance.

 **Attitude Session 1**

What Is This Thing Called "Band"?

The first day of band can be intimidating to the new member.

Everyone is filled with all kinds of emotions as they first begin an activity like marching band —excitement, anticipation, hesitation and probably fear. Most rookies think that they are the only ones to feel fear. They don't know what to expect and are not sure they will be able to rise to the level needed for the band's rehearsals and performances. I would be surprised if every veteran in the band did not feel some or all of these emotions when they were rookies. So it is to be expected! When the rookie looks around at the veterans or watches a video of last season's show, they need to realize that everyone they see was a rookie once. They all started from ground zero with the same feelings.

What Can You Expect?

Hard Work
You will probably work harder in marching band than you ever have in your life, but you will love it! The more you put into something, the more you get out of it.

Exciting Performances
Few people get to perform in front of thousands of enthusiastic fans. It is truly exciting to perform in a marching band of this caliber.

Friends
Most members make some of their best friends in band. Ten–twenty–thirty years from now, you will probably have many of the same friendships that started in band.

Memories
You will have memories that will last a lifetime! When band alumni come to visit, they still talk about their band experiences

Sense of Belonging
You are an important part of a great organization. The band is a family that you belong to. You have a place to go and people you can count on.

Life Skills
In addition to the musical and visual skills that you learn, you will learn about attitude, organization, responsibility, teamwork, leadership and many other important life skills.

Tradition
You will be part of the tradition of this band that has been established over the years. You are now a part of this great tradition!

Band Motto

Be Your Best

Be Your Best is a goal that everyone can achieve. This is not the same as "Be The Best" which is something that few can achieve. It is all that is expected of you, but it is expected all of the time—every minute, every practice, every day and every performance. Further, it is expected that you will Be Your Best outside of organized band activities, as well as in rehearsals and performances.

You can measure your success and do not have to wait until someone else, like the director, senior or band judge tells you. You know!

Band Expectations

Show Respect

Respect yourself. Respect others. Respect the band facilities, equipment, and uniforms.

Be Prepared

Band members are responsible for doing their best, working on their individual skills, and practicing. All equipment must be brought to rehearsals as requested.

Be on Time

Students should arrive at the building 15 minutes *before* the rehearsal is scheduled to begin in order to be ready to start on time. If you count on someone else to get a ride to practice, tell him or her the time you have to *be there*, not the time rehearsal begins. With this concept, you will be prepared physically and mentally to begin the rehearsal and not flying in at the last minute or worse–late. You also will have a cushion of safety if there is extra traffic or you are running a couple of minutes behind.

Band Expectations

Every organizition has expectations of conduct or behavior.

It is called many terms—behavior expectations, conduct, discipline, rules and regulations—and is essential for a successful band program. For the most part, band members want to be good and reach their potential. They understand that this is not possible without good conduct on their part.

- Without discipline
  - The group does not achieve its potential.
  - Students are not focused and do not hear information.
  - Too much time is wasted.
  - It is not enjoyable/fun (contrary to what some may think).
- With discipline
  - The band operates in a **spirit of cooperation**.
  - Students are focused and hear information.
  - Rehearsals are efficient.
  - Members take pride in being a part of the band and in striving for excellence.

We prefer to call the topic "behavior expectations" because this is how we, as a staff, *expect* the members to act. Some organizations have many rules for every detail and possible situation. We think it can be summed up in a few simple phrases—the Band Motto and three Band Expectations. Of course all high school rules and regulations *always* apply. The Band Expectations are the foundation on which our band operates, so it is important to review them.

Be Your Best

Strive to be your best and make the best decisions possible in all you do. The best award we receive is the compliment that the band members were mature, well mannered young ladies and gentlemen. We hear that compliment frequently and want to maintain that tradition.

Show Respect

If you are "being your best" you will at all times show respect to other members, to the staff, to the parents and other adults who are here to help you and of course yourself. Respect the band facilities, equipment, and uniforms and the traditions of the band program.

Be Prepared

Band members are responsible for doing their best, working on their individual skills, and practicing. All equipment must be brought to rehearsals as requested.

Be On Time

In order to be prepared physically and mentally to begin the rehearsal, arrive 15 minutes before rehearsal time.

Questions or Problems – talk to your leaders and then the staff to resolve them. Don't hesitate.

Attitude Session 3

Rehearsal Skills

Members need to understand their role in achieving great rehearsals.

The following is the band's rehearsal philosophy:

Rehearsals will be conducted with a positive attitude in a pleasant atmosphere. Students will be focused, energetic and relaxed in order to achieve the outstanding results desired. The director and staff will be organized and efficient through careful planning and goal setting. These qualities will make the experience enjoyable and productive for students and staff alike.

Why is it important to have a rehearsal philosophy? A philosophy is an overall way of thinking about a subject. It helps to keep everyone's attitudes on the same page. In order to have efficient, productive rehearsals, we need to have an approach that will be successful and this will happen if everyone maintains the ideals set forth.

What kind of cooperation is needed? Band is a team endeavor and only is successful if the teachers and the students work together in a cooperative effort. The staff has the knowledge and background to direct the team and the students have the skills, energy and enthusiasm to bring the performance to life. Any weak links in the team will cause the team to not reach its full potential. Each member is important in this effort.

How can the students be active participants in this process? "You are your own best teacher" is a quotation that is very applicable to the marching band activity. There are literally thousands of visual counts and musical notes in a marching band show, and it is impossible for the staff members to correct everything. You are an active participant on this team and not a passive observer. Don't wait to be told to fix a problem—fix it yourself. You can then take pride in truly being an important team member.

What is the band member's role in this process? You should strive at all rehearsals to "Be Your Best" of course, but what does this mean? Here are a few ideas:

❖ Be prepared—within the available time, come to each rehearsal improved.

❖ Be aware of your performance and everything around you—visually and musically.

❖ Try to make an error only once.

❖ Try to improve one thing in every segment visually or musically. Don't wait for someone else to tell you.

What about mistakes? Without mistakes there is no improvement. It is the natural way we all get better in all endeavors. The important thing is that you are aware so you can make improvements.

How should I feel if I am corrected for an error? Thankful! You appreciate a private lesson teacher for making a suggestion that makes you a better player. So it is in band. We are always trying to solve problems and make the performance better. Go ahead and say "Thanks!"

Rehearsal Etiquette

Many directors talk about rehearsal discipline and behavior, but we like to use the phrase "rehearsal etiquette." This phrase immediately brings to mind the meanings of the word "etiquette" that everyone has strongly imprinted on their brains. The meaning is "correct or polite behavior in social or professional settings."

All of you as band members should keep in mind in rehearsal, indoors or outdoors, good rehearsal etiquette. Here are a few thoughts about how the phrase relates to marching band rehearsals:

- Be silent when someone is addressing you or the group.

- Make eye contact with the speaker—you will hear more when you do!

- In full rehearsal, when the instructor says your section's name, everyone should raise their hands. In that way, the instructor knows the group being addressed is listening.

- Participate if asked a question. For example, "How many of you arrived at your set early that time?" Raise your hand. The instructor is trying to assess the situation and needs an honest response.

- Speak only at the appropriate times. Talking keeps you from hearing and learning, as well as those around you. It is also rude behavior to the instructor (poor etiquette).

- Listen to directions for the next move carefully. A student not knowing what to do wastes everyone's time and the instructions must be repeated.

- Move quickly and efficiently to the position for the next segment.

- Think independently. Do what you are supposed to do, when you are supposed to do it. Don't wait for everyone else to do something.

"Do what you are supposed to do, when you are supposed to do it" is what you need to do every rehearsal. It is a waste of time and energy to question and complain about what you are asked to do, whether you do that mentally or verbally. If you cheerfully follow directions you will be happier and enjoy the rehearsal.

Good rehearsal etiquette (or discipline or behavior) does not create a negative, unpleasant atmosphere. It creates a relaxed, pleasant environment that is productive and efficient.

Everyone wants to get better, have the band improve every day and have an enjoyable experience. Good rehearsal etiquette, a positive attitude and following the motto – "Be Your Best" is how we get there.

This is your band! Make it great by being an active participant.

Positive Attitude

"It's All in Your Attitude"

Everyone has heard phrases like "It's All in Your Attitude" and seen many attitude posters and signs. We all know that someone with a positive attitude is much more pleasant to be around than someone who is grouchy. But how does this apply to marching band and how can you, as an individual, work on maintaining (or getting) a positive attitude?

It certainly is not as simple as it sounds. Those of you who are student leaders can have a big impact on the overall band's attitude by presenting yourself in a positive manner. Everyone can make a contribution to the overall band feeling because a positive attitude is infectious (and so is a negative one).

Let's begin by looking at a few words that define "positive" and think about what each one means to you:

Optimistic	Constructive
Helpful	Encouraging
Affirmative	Upbeat

Let's have a discussion about what these words mean to you. Someone raise their hand and tell us what "optimistic" means to you. (Discuss meanings of each of the other words.)

What can we do outwardly to promote a positive attitude?

* ❖ Be friendly—not just to your friends but everyone, especially the younger members.

* ❖ Adopt the motto "What Can I Do to Help?" and try to help others before they ask.

* ❖ Try to look happy and put a smile on your face when you greet someone.

* ❖ Be patient with each other.

* ❖ Avoid criticizing others in public. It never does any good.

* ❖ Try to speak in a pleasant tone of voice.

* ❖ Be "We" oriented and not "I/Me"

Can someone be too positive? Sure. We all know people who are just too much, but it is usually insincerity that bothers people. Be honestly upbeat and this is not a problem.

We live in a negative world; all one has to do is read the paper or watch the nightly news. The negative people and troublemakers always seem to get the attention in school (and maybe in band?). That is why they act inappropriately! We can, at least in a small way and in our band, do our best to create a positive environment where everyone cooperates towards a common goal. We can also make sure we give our attention to what is right and positive.

Certainly none of this is new information or a revelation to any of us. However, the more we think about being positive and how we can translate those thoughts into action, the more we can positively affect the band and the world we live in.

"This band has a great attitude!"

Philosophy of Competition

Attitude Session 5

"Why Do We Compete?"

As we are approaching the first competition of the season, it is important for you to understand our philosophy of competition. Although there are pros and cons to competing, we feel the positive values far outweigh the negatives. We choose to compete in marching band because we feel it is the best motivator for you to excel as individuals and as a group. Our band's motto is "Be Your Best." We strive to achieve this every day and not just in show performances. However, we all tend to prepare better when we know there is a performance approaching, and a competition focuses this even more than a football halftime show or other performance. It is the same with academics—we all tend to study and learn more if there is a test than no test.

I think there is competitiveness in human nature that can be either good or bad. When friends get together and shoot baskets, it is not long before they are playing a game. When people go bowling or play a card game, they soon start keeping score because that is part of "playing the game." Band competitions should be treated as a game with no more or less emphasis put on it. When used as an enjoyable activity and means to achieving other goals, it can be very rewarding.

We treat competitions as a test or exam and use the score as a measurement of our success and improvement from show to show. Of course, there are always variations in scoring since it is a human activity. We will tell you if we think the score was accurate or perhaps too high or low for the particular point in the season. Just like in school, our goal is to get 100 points. In band there is no perfect score, but our approach is to strive for excellence and perfection. If your goals are to be just pretty good, it is too easily achieved. Since scores start low and improve as the season progresses, we use the score as a benchmark compared to previous contests or seasons. We set goals such as "we hope to break a score of 80" by a certain time in the season. If we reach that score, and we think it is accurate, we have achieved a goal or plateau for the week.

When we rehearse, perform and compete, we only have control of ourselves—how well we practice, how well the show works and is written, and how close we come to achieving our potential. We do not have any control over what other bands show up at the contest and how well they are achieving their goals. Other than doing our best, we have no control over how the judges evaluate us. Our goal is to compete in great stadiums and where great bands are competing whenever possible. We want you to be challenged in rehearsing and want you to see the great bands of our activity.

We try to define the terms winning and losing in other than placement terms but in life skills terms. We have all seen first place groups that acted like losers and last place groups that were really winners in their behavior and attitude. We expect you to react the same regardless of what place the band receives—congratulate others and be humble if complimented. Human nature being what it is, we all prefer to place higher rather than lower and that is okay. The marching band competition scene should be viewed as part of the educational process of our band program. It opens up many opportunities for learning that cannot be duplicated elsewhere.

You have the joy of competing in exciting performances.
Enjoy every minute of it!

Attitude Session 6

Winning Attitude
Winners in Life

The topic of a winning attitude is another way of approaching the subject of positive attitude. It is an important characteristic for everyone and relates to our previous focus on a philosophy of competition. There are three types of people in life—spectators, losers and winners. We are not talking about winning games or contests but about life and people skills.

Spectators are the people who don't like to get involved and prefer to watch others for fear of being rejected or defeated but also for fear of winning. If there is no commitment then there is no failure. It is safer that way. These types of people are usually not involved in marching band since it takes a huge commitment of time and energy to be a member. However, within the group, some people from time to time tend to slide into this mode of "let everyone else do the hard work and I'll just watch." There is no failure but there is no enjoyment or reward either.

Losers in life wear a sour face, put others down, have a negative attitude and don't listen well. Unlike the spectator, they sometimes do participate in activities but they strive to bring others down with them. They give little or no effort and are okay with failure. It is also safer that way. "I don't really care" is a safer response than saying "I just couldn't do it." They also have little enjoyment or reward other than the attention they sometimes get.

Winners are happy, satisfied people. They set realistic goals for themselves that are achievable but challenging. When this goal is met, they savor the moment and then set a new goal and pursue it. They are supportive and appreciative of others. Winners are aware of their strengths and limitations and strive to improve. They are life-long learners and strive to expand their knowledge in a wide range of interests. They are content and cheerful people.

Everyone chooses what type of person to be each day. You can choose to be a spectator, loser or winner. The spectators and losers don't risk much, but they don't gain anything either. Choose to be a winner and a happy person. It is your Winning Attitude that is the key to your happiness and success.

It is amazing that two people can sit next to each other in class or band and experience the same things and have totally different reactions. What is the difference? Of course, the difference is attitude, usually starting as soon as they walk in the door. If you think this will be an interesting activity and you can learn some new things, it will be. Don't be overly influenced by what others say and do.

Most people know the difference between right and wrong when they have to make a decision. Winners choose the right and losers choose the wrong. It makes all the difference in the world.

> *"True winning is no more than one's own personal pursuit of individual excellence."*
>
> – Tim Lautzenheiser

You are a winner whenever you strive to
Be Your Best!

Attitude Session 7

Personal Relations

We can create a family atmosphere in the band.

Unless one is a hermit living in the woods, we must interact with other people on a daily basis. What happens in these interactions can make us happy, sad, frustrated or any number of other emotions. Our band is a family, we would like to say happy family, but it is not always so. Just like a family there are occasional squabbles and bickering but hopefully those are few and far between and quickly resolved.

What do we mean by personal relations? "Personal relations" means acting together, working together, cooperating, networking and intermingling. For this to work in a band organization, you need to move outside of your small circle of friends and relate to everyone, especially those in your immediate section.

What can you actually do? With everyone "working together" we can make the concept of a band family become a reality with everyone working towards a common goal. The upperclassmen need to take the lead here. Remember how you felt when you first joined the band? It can be an intimidating and lonesome experience. Here are some things to keep in mind as all of you make an effort to include everyone in your "network:"

- Speak to people
- Smile at people
- Learn everyone's name and use it
- Be friendly
- Be honest and sincere
- Be thoughtful
- Be generous of your time
- Be aware of other people and their feelings
- Be patient
- Be humble
- Have a sense of humor

Go out of your way to do these things, not just when it is convenient. It seems like a lot of work at first, but you will be rewarded knowing that you made a positive difference in other people and in the band.

Does this mean that everyone has to be your close friend? No, but it does mean that you need to be friendly to everyone and work together. If everyone can act together, work together and cooperate then the band can achieve a family atmosphere. Ever band member can have a sense of belonging and enjoy being a part of a great group.

"People are about as happy as they make up their minds to be."

- Abraham Lincoln

 **Leadership Skills**

Strong student leadership is necessary for a successful band.

Much has been written about leadership and we try to give our student leaders as much information as possible in their meetings. It is important for all of you, as band members, to understand how the leadership system works and to know your role.

Young band members often ask, "How can I become a leader or drum major?" The answer is that the auditions began the minute you walked in the door. The most important quality of a leader is being a strong and dedicated member. Although there is an application and audition process, we observe you from your first day until the decision is made. You don't need to do anything outstanding or be a superstar, you just need to be a good member—do what you're supposed to do, when you're supposed to do it. You can't decide at the last minute to become a strong member in order to be a leader.

What does it really mean to be a great member? The great member has the qualities we have been talking about—positive/winning attitude, self-disciplined, friendly, helpful, and always strives to Be Your Best, Show Respect, Be Prepared and Be on Time.

Then what are the qualities of a leader? They are actually the same traits but to a stronger degree with a few more added. The following traits establish a strong foundation for leadership:

- Confidence—to lead others

- Enthusiasm & Energy—to go above and beyond the call of duty

- Persistence—to finish the job you start

- Patience—there is no standard time for how long learning takes

- Friendliness—to everyone

- Honesty—to tell the truth

- Self-motivated—don't wait to be asked to do something

- Dedication—to the band program and all the members

- Self-disciplined—you naturally do what you are supposed to do

- Humility—to have all these strong traits and remain humble

It would be very difficult to exhibit these qualities every minute of every day, but we strive for these high ideals and do our best.

What can I actually do as a member to demonstrate leadership qualities? Strive for excellence in all you do. Do what you are asked to do and be appreciative of corrections and help. Never drop below your highest level of achievement.

The majority of the time finds a leader not leading, but simply being a strong member marching and playing. The leader is the person "first in line" and everyone else follows his/her example.

Great leaders lead by example.

 **Attitude Session 9**

Stage Fright

Stage fright and nervousness can be a good thing!

As we approach the first big performance of the season, it is a good time to discuss how to deal with nervousness. Almost everyone gets nervous when they perform in front of an audience. Some very famous professionals in all fields get literally sick before a performance, but they have learned how to deal with it. Generally with more and more experience, the nervousness diminishes and sometimes disappears.

Understand that most fear usually occurs before the performance and pretty much disappears as the show progresses. Here are some things you can do to help alleviate this problem, first in rehearsal:

- **Be prepared**—the better you know your music and marching, the more confident you will be and the less nervous. Practice until it is easy.

- **Treat all rehearsals, especially "run thru's", as performances.** If you are in performance mode every day, shows will be routine and normal.

What you can do immediately before you step onto the field for a performance:

- Do your breathing exercises.

- Visualization—picture yourself performing the best you have done in rehearsals and what it feels like.

- Look at the audience, stadium and press box as you approach the field and become familiar with it. Then it is not a surprise when you get ready to start the show.

- Imagine the audience responding positively to the band's performance.

- Make eye contact with the members around you. Remember that you are part of the marching band and that it is a team effort.

- Transform the nervousness into energy and excitement and enjoy the exhilaration.

What you can do during the performance:

- Use good breathing skills during the show whenever you can.

- Focus on one thing at a time. Don't worry about the whole show—just what you do next.

- If you make a mistake (and almost everyone does), recover and get right back into the flow of the show. Don't dwell on what happened, but concentrate on what is coming next. The recovery is more important than the mistake. Even if you fall down (and many members have), it really does not affect the outcome of the contest.

Remember nervousness does not show a fraction as much as it feels.

**Let the nervousness become energy and excitement and
enjoy the exhilaration!**

Enjoy the show!

Attitude Session
10

Open Mic Session

This is an opportunity for the members to stand up and speak.

(Director's note: This is something that the older members look forward to all year. It is sometimes hard to get the students to start speaking, but once it gets going, it is hard to stop. The director will have to put a time limit on the session. Encourage polite applause after each speech and try to discourage discussion after each talk. This is more like a testimonial.)

One of our traditions each year is for you to get the opportunity to be an active part of the Attitude Sessions. We try to do this at the end of Band Camp (or other culmination of preparation sometime before the first big show). No one needs to feel an obligation to speak but don't be shy either. We are all friends and part of the band family. We especially like to hear from the seniors as a chance to tell us what you think about the band experience and what it has meant to you.

There are only a few guidelines we would like you to follow:

- ❖ Your comments must be positive and related to band.
- ❖ Try to keep it at about 25 words or less. (It is not a big speech.)
- ❖ Please do not mention names of people.
- ❖ Please no discussion after each talk.
- ❖ Stand up and speak.

Here are some topics you might want to talk about:

- ❖ What did you feel like your first few days of band as a rookie?
- ❖ How have you changed over the years because of band?
- ❖ What does being in band mean to you?
- ❖ What is it like to be in an exciting show event in this band—especially the last show of the season?

The mic is all yours!

Chapter Ten

Student Leadership

Leadership Philosophy

A strong student leadership program can be a great asset to the marching band.

Many band directors are apprehensive of allowing very much leadership on the part of the students. They feel it is letting go of authority and that students cannot possibly teach as well as a trained music educator. This is true! However, with proper training and coaching, the student leaders can fill in the gaps in the overwhelming job of achieving the potential of the marching band. There simply is way too much to do for most band directors; they need all the help they can get! There are times when the director can become a supervisor watching many student leaders work, and thus have more impact on the student's learning process. The director is not losing control of the learning environment but actually getting more out of it.

As an example, the music check-off system (Chapters 5 & 6) is designed to motivate and insure that music is actually memorized accurately by the individual members. Except in the small band situation, most band directors simply do not have enough time to check Level One and Two before the music is added to the drill on the field. The admonition "make sure your music is memorized by Monday" will have little effect in most situations, unless there is some follow-up to make sure it happens on an individual basis. By allowing the student leaders, to check-off the memorization for Level One, the director and other staff members will have the time to check-off Level Two. The leaders can also check-off music such as the school songs and National Anthem. The leaders, being more experienced, can assist the younger members in how to memorize in a small group or one-on-one setting.

An equally important aspect of the student leadership program is developing a sense of ownership of the band program. The marching band belongs to the members, not the director (a reminder to avoid the phrase "my band"). The more they participate and are involved and informed, the more they will "buy into" the program and work hard to make it great.

There are many non-rehearsal things that the leaders can do to augment and support the work of the director. For example, on occasion students leave a rehearsal upset, disgruntled or frustrated. The student leader is first of all more aware of this than the director and can usually smooth things over. (i.e. "When I was a freshman I had so much trouble memorizing the music too. Can I help you with that tomorrow?") Further, they should be trained to refer serious problems to the director.

A key to the success of these concepts, in addition to training, is allocating only small time allotments for leaders to work with students (10-20 minutes). Even a good leader, given forty-five minutes to work with a group of students, is going to lose effectiveness and not maintain a good learning environment.

The first and most important quality of a good leader is to be a good member.

"You can't lead others until you can lead yourself."

– Dr. Tim Lautzenheiser

Chain of Command

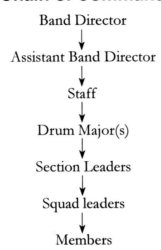

Band Director

↓

Assistant Band Director

↓

Staff

↓

Drum Major(s)

↓

Section Leaders

↓

Squad leaders

↓

Members

What should the student leaders be expected to do?

❖ Be a role model by being a great member

❖ Communicate to members - phone calls, emails, reminders, etc.

❖ Perform basic music check-off's

❖ Perform basic marching check-off's

❖ Give extra help to members

❖ Be supportive of members

❖ Plan small group informal social events

What should the student leaders not do?

❖ Be anything but supportive of the band program and staff

❖ See themselves in a position of power

❖ Do anything different than the instructional staff or contradict them

❖ Expect any special treatment for being a leader

❖ Be unprepared

❖ Be late

❖ Show a lack of respect

❖ Be anything but your best

With or without any actual rehearsal duties, the student leadership position is a large responsibility. This must be communicated to the potential student leaders *before* they make a commitment to assume the position.

The Leadership Team

The leadership team is the steering committee of the marching band.

The leadership team is comprised of all members who are in a leadership position and other members who are in charge of various work committees. The team should meet weekly during the season. Lunch periods in the band room often work well so no extra time is required of them. The purpose of these meetings is to address how to be a leader, small group teaching methods and what to do and not to do as a leader.

Using the leadership team as a steering committee or sounding board for the band director can be extremely helpful in maintaining a positive attitude in the band and a strong work ethic. It can also keep him/her informed of the overall attitude of the band on a weekly basis. Otherwise, knowing the "true pulse" of the band throughout a long season is difficult for the director. The director needs to know when to lighten up and relax and when to be more disciplined. For example, student leaders will usually not hesitate to say, "We need more discipline!" when that is the case.

The leadership team, if it is of sufficient size and instrumentation, can be used as a pep band. A pep band is frequently needed for various duties—pep assemblies, National Anthem at events, indoor parades, etc. Others see these extra duties as something special that they would like to do. They want to be a leader as they get older and therefore will strive to be good members.

Leadership Team Roles and Responsibilities

Drum Major(s) – The drum major or field commander is the conductor of the marching band in most groups. Their duties are conducting, helping with individual instruction in marching block, being a strong leader by example and serving as a liaison between the band members and the band director. (More drum major information follows.)

Section Leaders – There should be a section leader in charge of each major section—woodwinds, brass, percussion and color guard. They will serve as a squad leader (below) and coordinator of the other squad leaders. From time to time they will be required to informally lead sectional rehearsals.

Squad Leaders – If the sections are large enough, there should be a squad leader for every 4 to 6 members of the same instrument. They are the "work horses" of the leadership program and the ones that quietly keep the band running and rehearsing efficiently, making sure the members are doing what they are supposed to do at all times. Their two main responsibilities are assisting their squad members in learning the drill and managing the check-off system.

Work Crew Heads – Every band program needs student workers to run efficiently—music librarians, field set–up crew, band room clean-up crew, etc. The person in charge of each of these committees can be a senior who might not have strong leadership, music or marching skills, but is a dedicated member. If possible, it is best if every senior can be a member of the leadership team in one function or another.

The Leadership Team

Drum Major

Assistant Drum Major(s)

Section Leaders			
Woodwind	Brass	Percussion	Color Guard

Squad Leaders		
Flute	Clarinet	Saxophone
Trumpet	Mellophone	Trombone
Baritone	Tuba	

Percussion	
Snare -	Quads -
Bass -	Cymbals -
Front Ensemble -	

Color Guard

Work Crews				
	Woodwind	Brass	Percussion	Color Guard
*Attendance				
Field Set-up				
Room Clean-up				
+Equipment Box				
Librarian				

* The band director is responsible for attendance but a leader notates it in the book.
The director checks for accuracy.

\+ Each section has an equipment box for needed supplies – sticks, heads, reeds, crutch tips, etc.

The Selection Process

*Auditions for leadership positions begin on **the first day in band**.*

The qualifications for a leadership position should be defined on the application. It should be made clear that selection is not based on a brief tryout or application but on the student's entire participation in the total band program.

(A Sample)
Leadership Application
(Due Tuesday, April 30, 3 pm)

Name_____ Instrument_____ Grade next year_____

Qualifications
(For your own reference – do not fill out)

Positive attitude (10 points)	Energetic (10 points)	Good Listener (10 points)
Self-confident (10 points)	Sense of humor (10 points)	Sensitive to others (10 points)
Helping attitude (10 points)	Marching ability (10 points)	Performance ability (10 points)
Next year Concert Band/Wind Ensemble (or Winter Guard) (10 points)		

1. This year, were you in:

   Concert Band ____   Marching Band ____   Jazz Ensemble ____

   Wind Ensemble____   BB Pep Band ____   Winter Guard ____

   Squad Leader ____   Winter Percussion ____

2. Are you enrolled in Concert Band or Wind Ensemble for next year (Guard - Winter Guard)? _____ (If not, why not?)

3. Will you be able to attend and work Band Boosters Carnival - Tuesday, July 12?

4. Are you willing to work? _____ List two work crews that you are willing to work on:

   Field set-up ____   Attendance ____   Music Library ____

   Equipment ____   Truck ____   Band Room Clean-up ____

5. Are you willing to be responsible for your squad members' music & marching check-offs, transportation, phone calls, etc.? ____

6. Can you march in the Fourth of July Parade? ____

7. Will you have to miss any summer practices? ____ When? _____

8. Please write a paragraph or two (on the back) explaining why you should be selected.
   Has your entire participation in the total band program qualified you for a leadership position? Please include how "What can I do to help?" fits into your philosophy.

9. Will you help with April 29-30 Flower Fundraiser unloading?____
   Leadership Workshop, May 2?____ If not, why and how can you do make-up work?

10. Are you interested in Squad Leader or Drum Major?

The Drum Major

The drum major is the ambassador for the marching band on and off the field.

The drum major or field commander is not only the conductor, but the representative of the marching band in performances. The drum major's roles include starting rehearsals on time, leading stretching, supervising the work crews, getting the members back on the field after breaks and functioning like a quasi-assistant band director. Whatever needs to be done, the drum major should do it. It also includes the "not so glamorous" jobs like picking up trash that members left and setting up chairs and stands.

The number of drum majors depends on the size of the band, how spread the formations are and how many students are needed in the other sections. A small band can adequately have only one, and a large band might need four—three spread out in front and one on the backside to conduct when the band faces backfield.

The drum major should maintain a dignified bearing on the field in performances. One rule of thumb is the drum major should never run in uniform, because it is too distracting. If a drum major needs to move to various positions on the field, it should be done at a brisk walk or march.

A word of caution: the drum majors have traded their instruments or guard equipment for these duties, and although they are at the top of the student "chain of command," they are still band members. There is a tendency for drum majors to go on an ego trip, and this needs to be discouraged if it becomes a problem. The following procedure is recommended for tryouts. A detailed information sheet is online: www.dynamicband.com.

Drum Major Tryout Information

Desirable Qualities of a Drum Major

- Positive Attitude
- Leadership
- Dedication
- Musical Ability and Intelligence
- Commanding Voice
- Personality
- Dependability

Tryout Procedure

- Marching technique
- Vocal commands
- Conducting and showmanship to a recorded song
- Conducting a live band on the Fight Song
- Leadership application
- Tryouts will be in band uniforms

Leadership Meetings

Here are eight topics that can be used for weekly leadership team meetings to give the leaders the tools and guidelines they need to succeed and to act as a sounding board for the band. Keep in mind that it is equally important for the band director to receive information from the leaders as to give it. The band director needs to be careful not to get defensive, because there might be some perceived criticism. The only student ground rules are: tell the truth as you see it and don't get personal or state names. The purpose is to have an honest discussion and to be factual and not critical. The joint outcome needs to be: "How can we solve these problems?" (if there are any).

The following pages contain notes for the director to use at those meetings. The first and last topics of discussion for each session are always the same:

How is the band doing today? This is as important (or sometimes more so) than the main topic for the day. If this discussion takes up all of the allotted time, it is not a problem. In fact, it is very good! At first, student leaders may be reluctant to have an open discussion until they feel it is a safe environment and the band director is honestly interested in their opinions. Once they become comfortable, there is sometimes no stopping their open and honest discussion.

What do we need to do for next week? At the conclusion of the meeting, a few comments should be made on the goals for the week, both in terms of performance and the non-performance issues (i.e. attitude, rehearsal etiquette, etc.) that were discussed during the meeting.

Eight Outlines for Leadership Team Meetings

1. **SO YOU'RE A LEADER? WHAT DO YOU DO NOW?** – What are the characteristics of a great leader? What are the roles and duties of the student leader?

2. **WHAT DO YOU NEED TO DO BEFORE WE START?** – What should the student leader do before the first rehearsal to make things go smoothly?

3. **REHEARSAL PROCEDURES FOR LEADERS** – Basic teaching tips and guidelines to help the student leader work in small groups.

4. **DEVELOPING GOALS** – The student leadership team develops and writes goals for the marching band season.

5. **REHEARSAL PROCEDURE, PART TWO** – More rehearsal ideas and concepts for the student leader.

6. **LEADERSHIP QUALITIES ⟶ ACTION** – Changing leadership qualities and potential into action.

7. **PROBLEM SOLVING** – How to handle the inevitable problems that arise. Knowing what to do and when to seek assistance.

8. **CONGRATULATIONS ON A GREAT SEASON!** The season in review—what went well, what did not and looking ahead to next season.

So You're a Leader, What Do You Do Now?

Today's topic is roles and duties of the student leader.

How is the band doing today?

(Note to director: If this meeting is held before the season begins, and it should be, a discussion of the previous season would be a good starting place.)

You, as student leaders, have the best knowledge of what the band members are really doing and thinking. Together, as a leadership team, we can make the experience and the band's performance better and more enjoyable. Don't be shy in stating your opinion and don't feel you will be criticized for telling the truth. The only ground rules are: tell the truth as you see it and don't get personal or state names. Let's discuss how the band did last season in the following areas:

- **Performance** (What was good? What needs improvement?)
    - Music
    - Visual
- **Attitude**
    - Overall attitude and enthusiasm
    - Rehearsal etiquette
    - Preparation (memory, bringing drill books, etc.)
    - Stress level
    - Attitude in regards to recent performances and outcomes

Roles and duties of the student leader

First, leadership is not a "100% of the time" job. In fact it is maybe 10% of the time that a leader should act or speak any differently than any member. You were chosen because you are great member and now you have to become a great leader. You can't become a strong leader until you start doing it and get some training and guidance. Don't ever forget that your first job as a leader is to be a great member!

Secondly, the characteristics for leadership are:

- Positive attitude (first thing on the list)
- High energy
- Self-confidence
- Sense of humor
- Sensitivity for others (a good listener)
- Helping attitude
- Strong performance ability – Music and visual (last on the list)

You need to make sure that you display all of these characteristics all of the time. (Of course no one can achieve that 100% of the time, but Be Your Best at it.) How close can you come to 100%?

What should the student leaders be expected to do?
- ❖ Be a role model by being a great member
- ❖ Communicate to members - phone calls, emails, reminders, etc.
- ❖ Perform music check-off's
- ❖ Perform marching check-off's
- ❖ Give extra help to members
- ❖ Be supportive of members
- ❖ Plan small group informal social events

What should the student leaders not do?
- ❖ Be anything but supportive of the band program and staff
- ❖ See themselves in a position of power
- ❖ Do anything different than the instructional staff or contradict them
- ❖ Expect any special treatment for being a leader
- ❖ Be unprepared
- ❖ Be late
- ❖ Show a lack of respect
- ❖ Be anything but your best

What do we need to do when we begin rehearsals?

Based on our first discussion today, we all need to work with our section or squad members on:

1.

2.

3.

Here is some information on our new show and the staff goals for the coming season:

Music

1.

2.

Visual

1.

2.

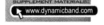

Leadership Meeting 2

What Do You Need To Do Before We Start?

Today's topic is things that need to be done before the first rehearsal.

At our first meeting we discussed roles and duties of the leaders. Today we will talk about some jobs that need to be done between now and our first rehearsal of the season.

How is the band doing today?

(Note to director: If this meeting is held before the season begins, and it should be, a conversation about the first meeting would be appropriate. Review concepts of group discussion as stated in Meeting 1 outline, if needed.) Are there any more comments pertinent to our first leadership meeting? Could someone summarize our discussions?

Things to do before the first rehearsal

We had our auditions for marching band, selected the leadership team and had our first leadership meeting. There are some things that the squad (or section) leaders should do between now and the first rehearsal. You can have a big impact on the initial impression that the rookies have at that first practice. If you can recall when you were a rookie, it can be an intimidating and uncomfortable experience. Here is what you need to do:

- Get an accurate phone and email list (the director has the rosters)
- Contact your squad members in the next two days and congratulate them for making the marching band.
  - See if they have any questions.
  - Do they know the schedule for the first rehearsals?
  - Do they have their music and know what to prepare for the first practice?
- Contact your squad members again one week before the first rehearsal.
  - Any questions about the first rehearsal or the marching band in general?
  - Remind them about what music (or guard skills) to have prepared.
  - Do they have transportation?
- At the first rehearsal, make everyone feel welcome (look for the "lost puppies") and have name tags for everyone in your squad.

If there are any problems, especially with someone who is thinking of dropping out or problems from a parent, you need to call the band director as soon as possible.

The drum major (or section leaders) will contact you to make sure this was completed and that there are no problems.

What do we need to do before the first rehearsal?

Here are the staff goals for the first few rehearsals:

Music

1.
2.

Visual

1.
2.

156

Leadership Meeting 3

Rehearsal Procedures for Leaders

The topic for today is how to teach in small group settings.

You cannot learn how to teach in a short meeting, but we can give you some basic suggestions and guidelines. Use what you know from how you are taught in this band and pay attention from a teacher's point of view. "Experience is the best teacher" so be aware and keep learning.

How is the band doing today?

Let's discuss how the band is doing in the following areas:

- Performance—Musical and Visual
- Attitude

Rehearsal procedures for leaders

(Pass out this outline to each leader - available online, www.dynamicband.com)

You will generally have a short block of time (15-20 minutes) to work with your squad members. Remember these concepts:

- Positive Attitude
  - At all times
  - "What can I do to help?"
  - "That was good (or better) now work on..."
  - Avoid negative comments as much as possible (they rarely improve things)
- Learn names ASAP, your squad first, then section, then all
- Talk less, play more (fix one thing at a time)
  - Say <u>one</u> sentence then play
  - Then say your second sentence or comment, then play, etc.
- Define goals ("today we are going to learn... and review...")
- Plan time allotments (5 minutes of Letter B, 10 minutes of Letter D, etc.)
- Everyone is always busy; no one sits and watches. If someone is done, let them help others one-on-one.
- Discipline
  - Attention–should be perfect (put them at-ease when you talk)
  - Silence–when you are talking to a group
  - Eye Contact–when you are talking to a group
- Music rehearsals
  - Rehearse in small segments—one measure, phrase, letter. It must be correct to continue.
  It is better to get one measure fixed correctly than the whole section at an average level.
  - Memory practice—same way
  - Demonstrate for good tone, style, volume (not rhythms)
- Visual rehearsals
  - Same concepts
  - Remember one sentence, then have them do it.

157

- Check-off system
  - Squad leaders should prepare, instruct and rehearse members—other leaders should check them off.
  - Report check-offs to drum majors promptly. They will mark charts quickly.
- Everyone can learn! ...but not at the same rate or method. Some take a long time. Some need to hear things in many different ways. Some need to see it. Some have to do it and then they understand.
- Don't hesitate to ask for help or suggestions from a staff member or veteran leader.
- You are responsible for your squad's performance—Music & Visual
- End the rehearsal with a compliment and what should be prepared for the next session.

"Patience is a virtue."

What do we need to do in the next week?

Based on our first discussion today, we all need to work with our section or squad members on:

1.

2.

Here are the staff goals for the coming week:

Music

1.

2.

Visual

1.

2.

Leadership Meeting 4

Developing Goals

The leadership team should develop goals for itself and the band.

The marching band has broad goals as stated in Chapter 1. The leadership team should make a list of specific action type goals to refer to as they mold the band's personality. The process of creating these goals helps the leaders take ownership for the marching band. They will be much more involved if they feel that they created the goals.

How is the band doing today?

Let's discuss how the band is doing in the following areas:

- Performance—Musical and Visual
- Attitude

Developing action goals

(There is no handout for today's activity. After the team creates their own "Leadership Team Goals," they should be printed and distributed to the entire band. This could be the basis for a full band Attitude Session.)

The activity for today is to create a list of action type goals in short phrases that we, as the Leadership Team, want to use with this year's band. We are looking for action phrases like "make friends" and "work hard." We will put them up on the board and see if a majority of you agrees to each phrase. One of you needs to copy them, and we will print and distribute them to the entire band.

(Note to director: The following lists were compiled by an actual marching band leadership team in two successive years. Notice the similarity of the two lists and how they compare to yours. You may want to suggest a few of these phrases if the students need some help getting started or something important to you is omitted. You are a member of the team and entitled to suggest goals!)

Leadership Team Goals

1. Make friends	1. Family atmosphere
2. Know names	2. Be your best
3. Be focused	3. Have fun
4. Work hard	4. Help other members
5. Persevere	5. Dedication
6. Be punctual	6. Improve section's skills
7. Be better than we thought we could be	7. Positive attitude
8. Always improve	8. Guard+Winds+Percussion = Band
9. Be a role model	9. Be responsible
10. Remember goals	10. Respect
11. Practice at home	11. Self-Discipline
12. Keep a positive attitude	12. Improve myself

13. Don't waste time
14. Help others improve
15. Be sensitive to others
16. Motivate
17. Develop teamwork
18. Show respect
19. Remember "What can I do to help?"

13. Work hard
14. Confidence

What do we need to do in the next week?

Based on our first discussion today, we all need to work with our section or squad members on:

1.

2.

Here are the staff goals for the coming week:

Music

1.

2.

Visual

1.

2.

Leadership Meeting 5

Rehearsal Procedures - Part Two

Today's discussion is on more ideas for leading small groups.

Leadership Meeting 3 was an introduction to teaching and working with small groups in marching band. This session repeats some of the information in a different form and adds some new concepts. Leaders should continue to re-evaluate themselves and look for new approaches.

How is the band doing today?

First, let's discuss how the band is doing in the following areas:

- Performance—Musical and Visual
- Attitude

More rehearsal thoughts for leaders

(Pass out this outline to each leader—available: www.dynamicband.com)

There are some repeated concepts here with new approaches and some new ideas.

1. Positive Attitude The atmosphere/attitude needs to be positive at all times. A few phrases (and the opposites) that are more specific are:

- Encouraging   (not critical/demeaning)
- Goal-oriented/organized   (not random)
- Patient   (not impatient)
- Serious   (not frivolous)
- Constructive   (not critical)
- "We" oriented   (not "I/me")
- Expecting/encouraging excellence   (not demanding it)
- Pleasant or business tone of voice   (not angry)

2. Some overall rehearsal concepts
- Relaxed focus—Students are relaxed (not tense) and focused (not inattentive).
- There is nothing easy or difficult, only familiar or not. It just takes repetitions.
- Approach problem solving in rehearsal as one would in a private lesson setting. Look for the right words and actions to improve the performance.

What do we need to do in the next week?

Based on our first discussion today, we all need to work with our section or squad members on:

1.
2.

Here are the staff goals for the coming week:

Music

1.

2.

Visual

1.

2.

Leadership Qualities ⟶ Action

You must take your leadership qualities and transform them into action.

All of you have the characteristics to be a great leader, but you only become a great leader when you turn those qualities into action.

How is the band doing today?

Let's discuss how the band is doing in the following areas:

- Performance—Musical and Visual
- Attitude

Changing qualities into action

(Pass out this outline to each leader —available: www.dynamicband.com)

We are the motivators of the band.
It is up to us to make things happen.

High energy   Whether you are tired or not, you must be energetic to be a great leader. Sometimes you have to *pretend* you are energetic.

Self-confidence   Approach your leadership job with confidence. Be prepared and organized. Sometimes you have to be a great *actor* to appear confident. (There is not much difference!)

Sense of humor   Don't take yourself too seriously. (But don't be a clown either!) Lighten up at times and relax.

Sensitivity   Be aware of the feelings of others around you and be a good listener.

Helping attitude   "What can I do to help?" is one of the band's mottos. Live it!

Empathy   Being a strong leader and a strong performer are not synonymous. You need to put yourself in the shoes of the members you are working with.

Positive attitude   You must be positive in everything you do.

Attitude is Everything!

Tact	*"Tact is the knack of making a point without making an enemy."* –Sir Isaac Newton. Avoid public conflicts and handle problems privately, out of rehearsal.
Support	This is a leadership *team*. Help and support each other.
Friendship	You don't have to be *friends* with everyone, but you do need to be *friendly* to everyone.
Appreciation	*Show* your appreciation to *everyone* for all they do.
Harmony	We are all in this together. We need to make "beautiful music" together, literally and figuratively.
Respect	Respect **yourself**
	Respect **each other**
	Respect **everything** you are given to use
	Respect the **traditions of the band**
Preparation	If you expect good preparation from the members, you must be prepared *first*.
Punctuality	To be early is to be on time. Set the example.

> # Be Your Best
> ## Strive for Excellence in All You Do.

What do we need to do in the next week?

Based on our first discussion today, we all need to work with our section or squad members on:

1.

2.

Here are the staff goals for the coming week:

Music

1.

2.

Visual

1.

2.

Leadership Meeting 7

Problem Solving

Inevitably, problems will arise in the leadership process.

Knowing how to handle problems that arise and when to seek assistance, is an important lesson in teaching and leadership.

How is the band doing today?

Let's discuss how the band is doing in the following areas:
- Performance—Musical and Visual
- Attitude

Problem solving

(Pass out this outline to each leader —available: www.dynamicband.com)

Problems come in all shapes and sizes when you are a leader or a teacher—the students just aren't getting it, the members are not behaving well, there is confusion regarding music or marching, an individual simply cannot do something, etc.

- If an individual is having a problem, have an experienced member work one-on-one to assist the student.
- Don't hesitate to ask for help from a staff member or drum major.
- Keep the group busy. Talk less—play more.
- Make sure you are accurate in your instructions, tempos, performance, etc.
- Individual behavior problem
  - Politely ask the student to cooperate. (i.e. "We need you to cooperate so we can all improve." or "Would you please stop talking during the instructions?")
  - Speak to the individual outside of the rehearsal (avoid confrontation)—identify the problem factually and ask for their cooperation.
  - Next problem, inform the nearest staff member.
- Group behavior problems (i.e. excessive talking, lack of effort)
  - Speak to group in a close setting about the problem and why it is interfering with a productive rehearsal
  - Next problem, inform the nearest staff member.

What do we need to do in the next week?

Based on our first discussion today, we all need to work with our section or squad members on:
1.
2.

Here are the staff goals for the coming week:

Music
1.

2.

Visual
1.

2.

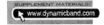

Leadership Meeting 8

Congratulations on a Great Season!

The leadership team made a big difference this year.

It is important about one week before the end of the season to do a review of the season. Did the leadership team and the band meet their goals for the year? Credit should be given to the leadership team for the positive effect they had on the band.

How is the band doing today?

Let's discuss how the band is doing in the following areas:

- Performance—Musical and Visual
- Attitude

The year in review

(Lead the discussion and put comments on the board under music, visual and the non-performance aspects of the marching band. Copies of the goals developed in Meeting 4 would be good to hand out again and use as the basis for discussion.)

You are to be congratulated for leading the band on a successful season. With one week left in the season, we do not need to wait for the final show and audience or judge reaction to decide if we were successful. Let's review the season looking at the goals we developed at Meeting 4 and break them into Music, Visual and Non-performance issues.

1. What aspects of the band and its season were good?

2. What facets of the band need to be improved for next season?

What do we need to do in the final week?

Based on our first discussion today, we all need to work with our section or squad members on:

1.

2.

Here are the staff goals for the coming week:

Music

1.

2.

Visual

1.

2.

Thank You for all you did to make it a great season!

Resources

There are many resources available in the area of student leadership.

Summer Camps - Drum majors should be required to attend a summer drum major camp and there are many available around the country. The conducting and leadership skills demanded for this position need a week of intensive study in a camp setting. Since it is a requirement, the band boosters should provide scholarships for tuition, room and board.

Bands of America hosts an excellent drum major camp at the Summer Symposium with a Leadership Weekend for students. There is an excellent curriculum on all phases of the band program for directors as well. (www.musicforall.org).

Clinics and workshops – There are many available for both students and directors. Music conventions will often have sessions on developing student leadership.

There are many speakers and clinicians in this field who run workshops for student leaders. Here are two highly recommended clinicians in the areas of attitude and leadership for band.

Dr. Tim Lautzenheiser - www.attitudeconcepts.com

Fran Kick - www.kickitin.com

Student Leadership Workshop with Dr. Tim Lautzenheiser

Books and DVD's – There are literally hundreds of books and other materials available on the topic of leadership. It is a good idea for the band director to read a new book on the subject once a year. A good assignment for student leaders is to read a book on leadership and turn in a book report at the first summer leadership meeting.

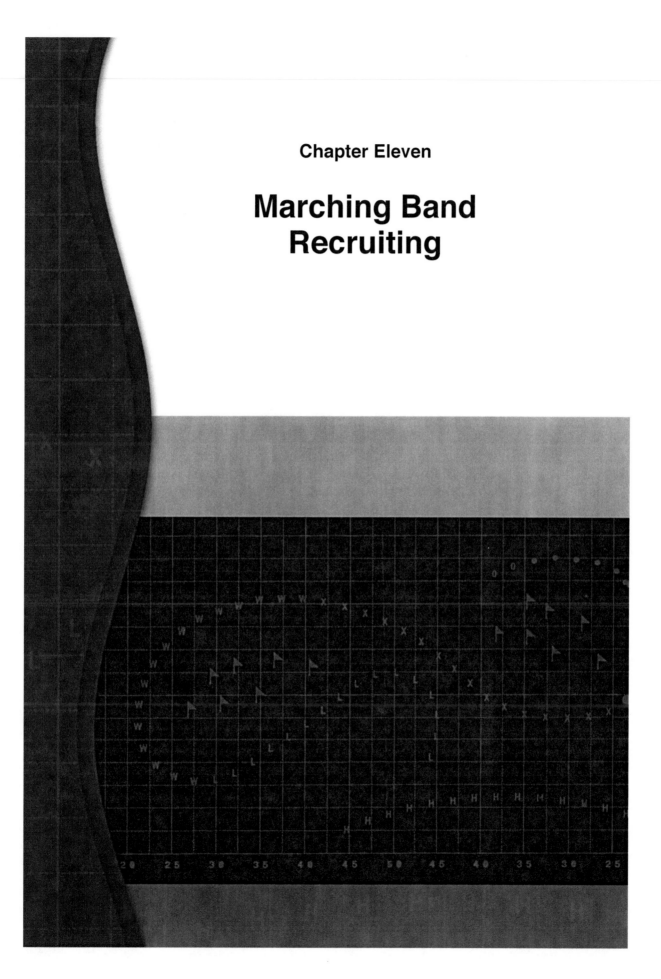

Chapter Eleven

Marching Band
Recruiting

Marching Band Recruiting

You are ALWAYS recruiting for the band program.

Participation in high school band is a voluntary activity. All band directors would like to think that *all* middle school band members will automatically enroll in the high school program, but that is generally not the case. Everything that any of the high school band ensembles do is an opportunity for recruiting the younger members and to influence those very young to sign up for band as soon as they are old enough. Performing well, acting with class and displaying a positive attitude on the part of the members and staff goes a long way towards making a favorable impression in the school and community.

The band director is very visible in the community and has the opportunity to recruit simply by being personable and professional. Speak at community service clubs, like the Rotary Club and bring a small ensemble to perform. These organizations are usually looking for people to make short presentations. For better or worse, the director is always making an impression.

In the school setting, the director should be cooperative, supportive and visible to the middle school director and students. If the high school director is the middle school director, he/she should approach the band program as a continuous fifth/sixth through twelfth grade program. When the students reach 9th grade they will naturally want to continue in the band. If there are separate directors, make frequent appearances at rehearsals, concerts and festivals. Offer to help with sectionals, ensembles, guest conduct or anything that could help the middle school director. It is *ideal* when the middle and high school directors are all involved at both levels.

Although some small schools march eighth graders to fill out the ranks, it should be avoided if possible. As the program develops in quality and numbers, it should move towards becoming a 9th through 12th grade marching band.

Fall Performance

To begin the actual recruiting "season," invite the middle school band(s) to join the high school marching band in a late fall performance. Many marching bands do a Fall Pops Concert late in the season to feature the marching band and the concert bands (if they function in the fall). Some marching bands invite the middle school members to a football game performance. This is successful if the middle school bands do some parade marching and will not be intimidated by performing for a large crowd. There is also the issue of controlling middle school students before they have been indoctrinated into the high school level of behavior. This can work well but for most situations, the indoor concert is a safer and more comfortable situation. The middle school band(s) can watch the high school bands perform and then join them for a massed band performance of the school song and perhaps a simple pop music arrangement. The high school members should be coached to be friendly and helpful and not intimidate the younger students. The important thing is that it is a positive, exciting and enjoyable experience for the middle school band members.

If the high school marching band sponsors a competition, invite the middle school members to attend and give them each a free ticket. They will get to see the high school band and other groups perform and feel the excitement of such an event. Hopefully, their parents will attend these performances as well.

Band Recruiting Schedule

Recruiting is an eight month process.

The band director should maintain and post a calendar of activities and deadlines for recruiting the incoming and current members for the next season. He/she should also keep Band Boosters up to date with these events and solicit their help when needed.

Early October – Marching Band Competition at HS—free tickets to all Eighth Grade Band members—distribute 7-10 days in advance

Late October – Fall Pops Concert with the Eighth Grade Band as special guests

January – Eighth Grade Band meeting/clinic at the high school band room during the school day—recruiting for the Total Band Program—concert band, marching band, jazz ensemble, winter groups—Have some of the groups do a mini-performance or rehearsal demo. See Eighth Grade Band Information Packet *

January – Parent letter home following meeting/clinic *

February – Eighth Graders sign up for high school courses

February – Winter Guard and Percussion Competition at HS—free tickets to all Eighth Grade Band members—distribute 7-10 days in advance

March – Show Preview Meetings—Kick off meeting for current members with tentative plans for the new year—show concept, contests and trips *

March – Packets delivered to eighth graders for April Clinic/Tryout with information and music—Color Guard info flyer mailed home to all 8th & 9th grade students and dance studios

April – Clinics/Tryouts for Woodwinds, Brass, Percussion, Color Guard—3 evening clinics to assess interest (most importantly) and teach some fundamentals—Easy Tryouts—(Anyone extremely weak musically or visually should be urged not to participate, offered to be a manager or not accepted. Usually the weaker members choose not to participate or make a three day commitment. If a student chooses not to be in marching band, it is best to know early rather than after a few days of Band Camp.) Post roster of new members in middle schools and on website. Commitment cards are due with *firm commitment* at tryout. The Band Boosters will have an informational meeting for all eighth grade band parents at the same time as the clinic/tryout.

May - Finalize numbers and send to drill writer.

May-July – In-coming transfer students and mini-camps by sections. Extra transfer student information packets should be left at main office and with the principal and counselors (whoever handles new students). Summer rehearsals in July and Band Camp late July or August

* More information on the following pages and at www.dynamicband.com

Eighth Grade Information Packet

This important packet is the introduction to the high school band program.

These papers should be distributed to all eighth grade band members at the January meeting/clinic. It should look professional and be organized since this is the first impression of the band. It should also be available on the band website. The Eighth Grade Information Packet should include the following information (on the following pages and available online: www.dynamicband.com):

1. **Eighth Grade Band Information**—complete information on the high school band program and what the options are for new freshmen.

2. **High School Band Program** circle graph to represent the concert bands as the foundation of the program and the other options throughout the year.

3. **High School Curricular and Co-curricular Band Offerings** from the HS Course of Studies booklet.

4. **Marching Band Information**—the complete information for the upcoming marching band season including tryouts, Band Camp, Summer and Fall schedules and Band Fees.

5. **Tentative Sign-up** form for eighth graders to state their intention. (Final sign-up for Concert Band and other classes is in February. Final commitment form for Marching Band is in April at Tryouts.) Available on web, www.msconcepts.com/dynamicband.html

Other Recruiting Materials

1. **The Show Preview Meeting** is the kick-off meeting for current members with tentative plans for the new year including show concept, contests and trips. These materials are handed out to current high school band members:

    a. **Show Preview Meeting Agenda**

    b. **Marching Band Information**—updated since the January eighth grade meeting with more current information

    c. **Tentative Sign-up Form**

2. **Letter to Eighth Grade Parents** 3 weeks prior to April Tryouts—to be sent with Marching Band Information, Attendance/Reserve Policies and Final Commitment Card.

3. **Final Commitment Card** form for April tryouts

Director's Roster

The director needs to keep an accurate roster with sign-up information for concert and marching programs indicating "yes," "no," "undecided," or "no form." Use this list to personally contact any "no," "undecided" and "no form" students to try to convince them to participate. A gentle "arm twisting" with the personal touch will often bring good results, but do not exert too much pressure. It is usually best, when students feel strongly against being in band, to let it be.

Eighth Grade Band Information

This packet includes information on the Total Band Program.

It's that time of the year to start thinking about plans for high school! *Welcome to the Central High School Band Program.* I would like to encourage you to continue your instrumental music study when you reach the high school. This paper explains your opportunities in the CHS Bands as an incoming freshman. There are two options for freshman students who play a band instrument: Concert Band and Marching Band.

Concert Band is the freshman curricular band which meets daily as a regularly scheduled class for one credit. This ensemble performs at concerts and other musical functions. Occasionally, if there is an opening, advanced students may audition for the Wind Ensemble. All incoming freshmen should register for **Concert Band** and changes, if any, will be made later. For those interested, see HS Web Courses in the Course of Studies Book for an opportunity that can help many music students with scheduling music classes into the school day.

CHS Marching Band (The Marching Tigers) is one of the most popular co-curricular activities at Central High School. The band performs at parades, football games, community events, and band competitions including the Regional Band Competition. The band practices after school or in the evening and performs on most Saturdays in the fall. It is not possible to participate in fall athletics since rehearsals and performances conflict. Summer practices include two evenings weekly in July, Band Camp at State University and CHS, and August practices in preparation for early performances. **The two weeks of Band Camp are required for all marching band members (July 24-28 & July 31-August 4).** A detailed schedule and the student fee structure will be printed in the *Tiger Beat.*

Some eighth graders are intimidated about going into the program because of the success and reputation of the CHS Bands. Please keep in mind that every year over 40 freshmen participate and do very well. A special program of instruction, help, and encouragement will prepare you for the skills you will need. Participating in the CHS Band Program is a great way to make friends and become comfortable in the high school setting.

We have been sending you the *Tiger Beat*—the CHS Band's newsletter to keep you up to date on information you will need to know and also to show you what goes on in the spring with the CHS Bands. You can also check the Band website - www.centralband.org. If you would like to receive the email news, send an e-mail to bandnews@centralband.org.

There are other opportunities that begin in the second quarter of the year such as jazz ensembles and small ensembles. In order to be in these groups you must be enrolled in the Concert Band or Wind Ensemble. We also have a very active Winter Guard and Percussion Ensemble and Basketball Pep Band.

We encourage you to continue your instrumental music study by signing up for both the Concert Band and the Marching Band.

Central High School Band Program

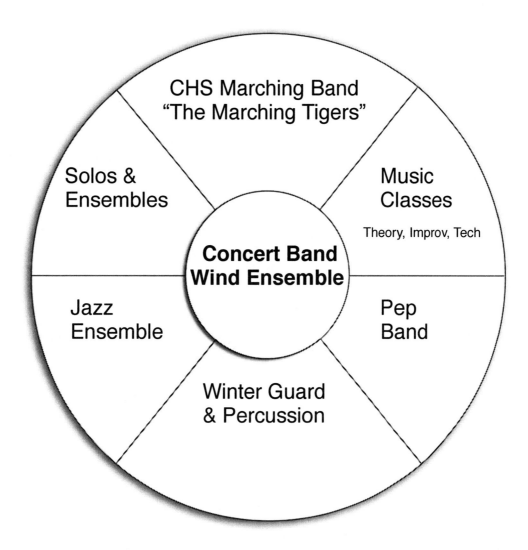

The concert ensembles—Concert Band and Wind Ensemble—are the foundation of the Central Band Program. The many co-curricular ensembles and music classes are offered to supplement the basic concert ensemble experience.

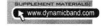

Curricular Offerings

Concert Band is open to 9th, 10th and 11th grade students who have achieved a reasonable degree of proficiency on a woodwind, brass, or percussion instrument. Emphasis will be placed on basic skills and theory. This ensemble will perform at concerts and other functions. A method book fee will be collected. Members of the Concert Band are eligible to participate in the marching band, which is a co-curricular activity meeting after school in the fall. *(Year course - 1 credit)*

Wind Ensemble is open to those 10th, 11th and 12th grade students who have achieved a high degree of proficiency on a woodwind, brass, or percussion instrument. A wide variety of music, individual skills, and theory will be covered in this course. This ensemble will perform at concerts and other functions. A method book fee will be collected. Members of the Wind Ensemble are eligible to participate in the marching band, which is a co-curricular activity meeting after school in the fall. Students must audition with the band director to be placed in this ensemble. *(Year course - 1 credit)*

Jazz-Rock Improvisation is for musicians who wish to begin or continue their skills in jazz improvisation. Improvisation is the creative art of playing and creating melodies based on the chord and scale structure of the song. Outside lab practice time will be required. Basic instrumental skills and knowledge of scales is a prerequisite. A method book fee will be collected. *(Semester course - 1/2 credit)*

Music Technology is a class designed to study and use computers and musical instruments to create music. MIDI technology, sequencers, sound modules, and music keyboards will be used to arrange, compose, sequence, and print music. Basic skill on an instrument and a desire to be creative are required, but no previous keyboard or composing experience is necessary. *(Semester course - 1/2 credit)*

Piano Class I is a beginning piano class designed for students who have never played piano before and for students who may have played for a year or two but have not played for several years. The class will meet in the Music Technology Lab and will use electronic keyboards and pianos. Some piano music software will be utilized to enhance the learning process. *(Semester course - 1/2 credit)*

Web Courses are an opportunity for students to take classes outside of the regular school day. This opens up time in the school day to take music courses of interest. Courses are taught by CHS teachers and are offered in English, Social Studies, Mathematics, Science, Business and Fine Arts. See the Course Description Book for full information.

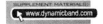

Co-Curricular Activities

Marching Band—The Central High School Marching Tigers is one of the school's largest co-curricular activities. This award winning band performs at parades, football games, community events, and band competitions and represents Central High School throughout the area, state and Mid West. (See "Marching Band Information" for complete information.)

Jazz Ensembles are offered as an important element of the total band program. Currently there are two jazz ensembles. The jazz groups perform at concerts and jazz festivals during the second semester. Rehearsals are after school two days a week following the Marching Band season. Students must be enrolled in Concert Band or Wind Ensemble to participate (except guitar, bass, keyboard). There is a uniform fee.

Winter Guard & Winter Percussion are extra-curricular activities for those students interested in indoor competition. There are several rehearsals weekly and competitions on weekends including several overnight trips. These groups compete at local, state, and regional events from December through early April. There is a participation fee and audition.

Solos and Ensembles are opportunities for band members to play in small groups to improve their skills. Much of the rehearsal is on an independent self-study basis. There are opportunities to perform such as the district Solo and Ensemble Competition and various community events.

Pep Bands are formed throughout the year as the needs arise. They perform for a variety of events such as school assemblies, sports activities, and community events. The Basketball Pep Band (BBPB) plays at most home basketball games. The BBPB rehearses one hour prior to game time.

Marching Band Information

Participation in Central High School's award winning marching band—**The Central Marching Tigers**—is an opportunity to become involved in one of the school's largest and most active extra-curricular activities. The band performs at parades, football games, community events, and band competitions including Regional Contests.

Schedule

Clinics & Tryouts for all members (including Eighth Graders)

Marching & Music (or Guard) skills will be taught

Brass & Woodwinds

Tuesday, Wednesday, Thursday—April 12, 13, 14—6:30-8:00 pm

Percussion & Color Guard

Monday, Tuesday, Wednesday—April 25, 26, 27—6:30-8:30 pm

Audition results will be one of three categories:

Regular Member
Full position member for competition show drill and performances. Members will be re-evaluated for regular and reserve positions in Band Camp as well as throughout the season.

Reserve Member
Reserve members are marching band members that will perform in parades and football pre-game shows but will not have a full time position in the competition show. They will attend all performances, trips, rehearsals, and band camp. Members will be re-evaluated for regular and reserve positions in Band Camp as well as throughout the season.

Not Accepted
It is anticipated that a small percentage of students will not be accepted into the marching band if there are deficiencies in basic playing and movement skills.

Band Camp

July 25-29   Band Camp (Monday at CHS / Tuesday-Saturday at State University)

August 1-5   Band Camp at CHS

Band Camp is Required for All Marching Band Members

This is the time the whole band works on fundamentals and the competition show. It is the most important activity in establishing a successful marching band in attitude and performance.

Other Summer Practices

(Attendance expected when you are in town. Send a note before absence.)

June 27, 28, 29	Percussion Mini-Camp (8-12, 1-4, 6-9)
June 30, July 1-2	Color Guard Mini-Camp (8-12, 1-4, 6-9)
July 3	Veterans only parade practice (6-8pm)
July 4	Fourth of July Parade (veterans only & all percussion) 8 am
July 6	First summer practice for all - "Rookie Night" - 6-9 pm
July 11, 13, 18, 20	Monday & Wednesday Practices for all 6-9 pm
August 8 until school	Monday thru Friday 8 am - noon plus Wednesday 1-4

P.E. Credit for Marching Band

Completion of Marching Band with 90% attendance and attendance at two PE Health classes in August will earn 1/4 credit which equates to one Physical Education course. See CHS student handbook for more information.

Fall/School Schedule

Mondays	No rehearsals except on Regional week	
Tuesdays	6-8:30	Color Guard & Rhythm Sections
	3:15-5:30	Woodwinds & Brass
Wednesdays	6-8:30 PM	Full Band rehearsal
Thursdays	6-8:30 PM	Full Band rehearsal
Fridays	6 PM	Football games
Saturdays	Marching Band rehearsals & competitions	

Confirmed Contest Dates

September 24	Botkins Band of Pride Invitational
October 15	Southeastern High School Invitational
October 29	Central High School Tiger Invitational
November 10-12	ABC Regional Championship

Fee Requirements
for The Central High School Marching Tigers

Marching Band fees are $____ (Color Guard $____) plus 15 calendars sold ($__). Calendar sales is the only required selling, however it is advisable for students to participate in the other projects. These projects are the easiest way for students to generate *all* of their required band fees. If students do not participate in fundraisers, the Band Boosters Budget will not meet the needs of the band program. Students receive a percentage of their total sales to apply to their band fees. Band fees are due in total one week prior to Band Camp. There can be no refunds on band fees or sales credits. Marching Band fee covers expenses for Band Camp, travel, Band Shirt, uniform rental & cleaning, additional staff and other operating expenses. The only other expenses will be for personal uniform items such as socks, marching shoes, etc. Guard fee includes extras such as dance shoes, gloves and make-up that the members will keep.

High School Pay to Participate Fee - $__ due in September. You will be billed through CHS.

Students will not be excluded from marching band because of financial need. If a student has made a reasonable effort to earn fees through the fundraising projects, a Band Booster support fund is available on a confidential basis. Contact the high school band director.

Read the monthly *Tiger Beat* newsletter for fund raising opportunities (or Band Website -www.centralband.org)

Regular Season Fee Projects
Opportunities to earn fees
(See website for more information if interested www.centralband.org)

January-February – Calendar Ad Sales

March – Spring Flowers

March-May – Marching Contest Book Ads

July – Calendar Sales (15 minimum)

The Marching Tigers
Show Preview Meeting

1. **Tentative Sign-up Form—Turn in today**

2. **Spring Flower Sales Info**
   - Help unload flowers on Saturday, April 30, 6:15-8:30 am
   - Sign-up on board
   - Delivery your flowers immediately!

3. **Next Year's Band Fees**
   - Musicians - $___ plus 15 calendars sold
   - Color Guard - $___ plus 15 calendars sold
   - CHS Pay to Participate Fee $__ is due in September

4. **Important Dates—Be There!**
   - April 12, 13, 14—6:30-8 pm—Woodwinds & Brass Tryouts
   - April 25, 26, 27, 28—6:30-8 pm—Color Guard & Percussion Tryouts
   - April 30—Spring Flowers
   - May 2—Leadership Workshop
   - May 5—Band Awards Evening
   - May 6—Drum Major Tryouts
   - May 9 & 10—Athletic Physicals - get info packet
   - May 22-27—Fine Arts Festival Concerts
   - June – **Everyone Get in Shape!**
   - June 20, 21, 22—Woodwinds & Brass Mini-Camp
   - June 27, 28, 29—Percussion Mini-Camp
   - June 30, July 1, 2—Color Guard Mini-Camp
   - July 3—Parade Practice - 6-8pm
   - July 4—Fourth of July Parade
   - July 6, 11, 13, 18, 20—Monday & Wednesday evening practices—6-9pm
   - July 7—Calendar Blitz
   - July 25-29—Band Camp at State University
   - August 1-5—Band Camp at CHS
   - August 8 until school—Monday thru Friday 8am-noon plus Wednesdays 1-4

5. **Show Schedule** (as of 3/1) Subject to change
   - September 24   Botkins Band of Pride Invitational
   - October 15   Southeastern High School Invitational
   - October 29   Central High School Tiger Invitational
   - November 10-12   ABC Regional Championship

6. **Next Year's Theme and Show Music**

Central High School Marching Tigers

Dear Band Parents,

We are very pleased that your child has expressed interest in The Central High School Band Program. Thank you for your support of your son or daughter's continuing music experiences.

The CHS Marching Band—The Marching Tigers is a great activity that helps develop confidence, positive attitude, self-esteem, cooperation, and self-discipline. It also gives members the thrill of performing in a great band in front of thousands of enthusiastic fans. It takes a large amount of time, discipline, and dedication but the rewards are equally great.

Tryouts for The Tiger Band are being held soon on the following dates:

Brass & Woodwinds
Tuesday, Wednesday, Thursday—April 12, 13, 14—6:30-8:00 pm

Percussion & Color Guard
Monday, Tuesday, Wednesday—April 25, 26, 27—6:30-8:30 pm

This will be an introduction to marching band, and some simple marching skills will be taught along with review of middle school music techniques. There will be an "Easy Tryout" consisting of the School Song and the Warm-up (#1-4) for memory plus the marching skills. We are mostly assessing interest and commitment in this three-day clinic.

We need Your Help Now. It is very important that we have a firm commitment so we can begin working on writing the competition music and drill. We need an accurate instrumentation count in order to do this. We also need to look at the need for large and percussion instruments, how many buses will be needed, how many rooms at band camp, how many uniforms, etc.

Learning to make choices and commitments is one of the first and most important lessons in being a part of the band program. It is time to make that commitment now. This is a firm commitment! We expect that if you sign up now, you will not change your mind. There is no quitting in band! Based on your decision, we will make commitments regarding instrumentation and numbers. We cannot go back and change.

Please read the enclosed information so you understand what the marching band is all about. There is a lot of information to help with your decision. The Tiger Beat monthly newsletter will continue to keep you up to date. If for some reason you are not receiving it, please send a note and address to me at CHS.

Please sign (either Yes or No) the enclosed post card and return it to me today or turn in at the Tryouts. If you have any questions, please email me at bandir@centralhs.k12.oh.us. or call me at 456-7890 (8:20-9:10 am).

Chapter Twelve

Band Camp

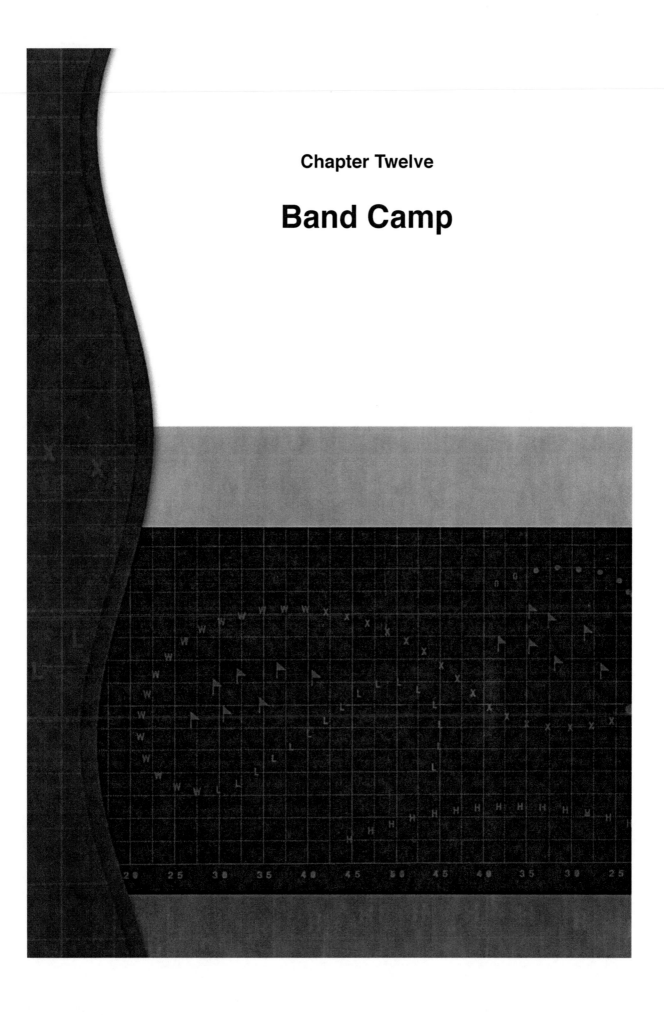

Purpose of Band Camp

Band Camp is the most important week of the marching band season.

Band Camp, whether at school or off-campus, is the most vital week of the year. It not only "sets the tone" for the marching season, but for the entire school year of band activities. Band Camp is the time to lay a solid foundation of the essential areas for a successful marching band: musical skills, social/attitude development, marching/visual skills and strength development.

Band Camp is an opportunity for extended rehearsals and in-depth focus. There are many approaches to how much time is allotted for Band Camp. The duration runs anywhere from a week of morning practices to two weeks of "three-a-days." What is needed depends on the situation and varies from school to school. If the incoming freshmen are not very strong, Band Camp (and other summer rehearsals) is the opportunity to catch up and be prepared for the level of high school music and marching skills required. The director needs to balance what is needed with what would be accepted by the students, parents, and school. It may take several years to gradually implement a full schedule of what is necessary for the students to achieve success. A balance of what is *really needed* and what is *too much* is important. Experience shows that students and parents will dedicate a huge amount of time and effort to anything that gives them a sense of enjoyment, belonging and success. The band members, especially the rookies, must feel that they *are part of and belong to* a great organization by the end of Band Camp.

Goals

The band director should have clearly defined and written goals for what to accomplish during Band Camp. Band members and staff need to know what to expect daily and for the entire camp. Many different approaches work here. Some possible goals could be:

- Fundamentals of music and movement
- Learn all of the show
- Learn all of the music and the opener drill
- Learn the school songs and basic marching

For most programs, the goal of Band Camp is to work on fundamentals of music and movement with a little bit of the show learned to keep it interesting and get it started. Establishing good *rehearsal etiquette* and *standards of excellence* are primary reasons for Band Camp as well. Add the school songs and National Anthem and the band will have a solid start to the season.

Social

Perhaps the strongest reason to have a Band Camp is for the social or non-performance aspects of the program. This is especially true of an off-campus Band Camp. Even with many hours of rehearsals, the band members have lots of time to get to know one another, develop friendships, gain a *sense of belonging* to the marching band and develop the *band family* atmosphere. This is most important for the rookies. It can be extremely intimidating and uncomfortable for a 13 or 14 year old, just out of middle school, to walk into an active band program. If they only show up for practice and leave immediately after, there is no time to develop the social connections that are so important.

Goals for Band Camp

Music	Marching
Levels I & II:	**Levels I & II:**
Daily Warm-up	Marching Basics
Fight Song	
Alma Mater	Contest Show Opener Drill
Parade song	
Star Spangled	Opener Drill with Music by
Contest Show Opener	the end of the week
Rehearse:	
Contest Show Ballad	
Contest Show Closer	

The *overall goals for Band Camp* are to lay a firm foundation of music and visual basics, establish rehearsal etiquette, learn the contest show opener and begin to develop the band family atmosphere.

Goals for Post Camp

Music	Marching
Week 1	
Level I :	
Ballad	Pre-Game Show Drill
Closer	
Week 2	
Level II:	
Ballad	Contest Show Ballad Drill with Music
Week 3	
Level II:	
Closer	Contest Show Closer Drill with Music

184

Organization

Organization and planning are most important in preparing for Band Camp.

At School versus Off-campus

There are pros and cons to each location and the decision needs to be weighed carefully with the cooperation of the Band Boosters and administration. A new band director will carry on the tradition he/she inherits. But if one is considering a change, here are some points to think about:

Band Camp at school

Pros: Familiar facilities   Cons: Students leave after practice
        No extra costs   Social time is minimum
        Easier to get part time staff   Absence for appointments, etc.
                                               Nutrition

Band Camp off-campus (college, band camp facility, church camp)

Pros: Esprit d'corps   Cons: Cost
        No disruptions for appointments   Extra staff needs to travel and have the time
        Facilities might be better   Chaperones & nurse needed
        Social activities easier to schedule   Transportation usually needed
        Nutrition

Get Organized!

"Organization is the key to success" especially at Band Camp. These rehearsals *set the standard* for how well, not only the marching band, but also the concert band will rehearse and perform. Habits, good or bad, are very hard to break.

Set up an attendance block the first day of camp as well as seating assignments for indoor and outdoor rehearsal forms.

Have these things ready to go several days *before* Band Camp:

- Printed schedules
  - *Everybody* gets a copy
  - *Every* minute is accounted for—recreation and down time is important, but it must be scheduled.
- *All* equipment needed at camp is ready to go several days beforehand
  - All instruments and equipment *in good repair*—get it repaired as soon as school ends.
  - Electric equipment—sound system, Dr. Beat, tuners, *batteries*, etc.
  - Copies of drill
  - Music parts and scores with extra parts
  - First Aid kit and medical forms
  - Field equipment—ladders, markers, paint (if painting drill sets), etc.
  - Drill teaching equipment
  - Videos/DVD's of band and DCI to show as motivation if facilities allow
  - *Sunscreen!*
  - *Water!*—very important that this is planned!

Communicate

- Send out information periodically throughout the previous school year—mailings, newsletters, email news, website, handouts, etc.
- Announce date and location of Band Camp as soon as it is confirmed—no later than January with reminders every month.
- Buses ordered—as soon as school ends
- The Band Boosters should make arrangements in the spring for chaperones and a nurse if camp is off-campus—make sure to communicate what is needed to them.
- Send list of "What You Need to Bring to Band Camp" a month before.
- Meet with freshmen and rookies and discuss what to expect at Band Camp.
- Spend some time each day at Band Camp with the full band in a meeting with no instruments just to talk about goals, traditions, attitudes, discipline, teamwork and other expectations. This does a great deal to establish the band as a family and create unity. Too often these things are addressed too casually or after problems are encountered. Often called "Attitude Sessions", these meetings should be continued periodically throughout the season. (See Chapter 9: Attitude)

Nutrition and Health

Regardless of whether band camp is away or at "home," serious consideration needs to be given to ensuring the students receive nutritious meals. If the camp is away, there is much more control over what the students eat. Only facilities that serve nutritious food should be considered. Chaperones should take attendance at all meals and insist that no ones skips. Before camp, it should be stressed how important good nutrition is when such physical exertion is being expended. You might want to ask the school health teacher or a band parent who is in the medical profession to give this talk. There is much less control with band camps at school and students are notorious for skipping breakfast and eating junk food for lunch. Some Band Booster groups provide some of the meals at school camps and this helps. Emphasize "Band Camp is not the time to be dieting!" They will get plenty of exercise throughout the week so they don't have to worry about dieting.

The importance of using sunscreen, wearing hats and light clothing and drinking plenty of water should be stressed at the same time good nutrition is discussed. The director and staff need to keep reminding the students throughout the week of the importance of their health. The staff also needs to be knowledgeable about heat related illnesses and what to do in an emergency.

Driving

Teenage driving is a concern to and from band practices and a very serious matter. On the first day of band camp discuss the importance of safe driving. Also be on the lookout and any unsafe driving should be immediately reported to the school administration. Let the students know that there is a zero tolerance policy for reckless driving. There are too many tragic stories of teenage driving to take any chances.

Parent Show

End Band Camp with a parent show, but don't feel it needs to be a polished performance. It is important that you talk to the crowd and welcome them and make them a part of the band program. Demonstrate what the band achieved during camp including basics, the school song and any part of the show that may be ready for a rough first viewing. The parents, alumni and friends are usually thrilled to see the start of the new season and certainly do not expect perfection.

Everyone (including the staff!) should enjoy Band Camp and the start of a new season.

Instructional Staff

Band Camp is the most important time to bring in instructional staff.

Band Camp is the most effective time to bring in outside help and it should be a very high priority. Even in a small program, it is not possible for a single band director to handle all of the many tasks to be accomplished. The following recommendations for staff is given as a guideline to insure a successful Band Camp for the students:

- Band Director (and Assistant Band Directors)
- Caption Heads for Woodwinds, Brass, Percussion and Color Guard with the director functioning as one of these
- Staff—One can often find young adults with a strong background in marching band and/or drum corps to work for a modest salary. College Music Education majors are often eager to do this just to gain experience. Ideally you should have staff, including caption heads, for each sub-section. This of course depends on the size of the band. (See chart below)
- Grad Staff—Try to get strong graduates of the program, especially if they are majoring in music, to work Band Camp after they have been out of high school for at least a year. They can function as assistant staff members and work with individual students and small sections, as well as serving as field techs. They are usually thrilled to work camp for room, board and a "Staff" shirt.
- Administration—Make sure all staff are approved by the administration and all policies are followed.
- Band Camp is the best time to give opportunities to the Student Leaders to work with small groups and individuals, help with memory work and do check-off's.

Minimum Band Camp Staff		
Small Band	**Medium Band**	**Large Band**
Woodwinds	**Woodwinds**	**Woodwinds**
	- Flute	- Flute
	- Clarinet	- Clarinet
	- Saxophone	- Alto Sax
		- Low Reeds
Brass	**Brass**	**Brass**
	- Trumpet	- Trumpet
	- Horn	- Horn
	- Low Brass	- Trombone
		- Baritone
		- Tuba
Percussion	**Percussion**	**Percussion**
- Battery	- Snare/Tenor	- Snare/Tenor (2)
- Front Ensemble	- Bass/Cymbals	- Bass/Cymbals (2)
	- Front Ensemble	- Front Ensemble
Color Guard	**Color Guard**	**Color Guard**
	- Flags	- Flags
	- Rifle/Sabre/Dance	- Rifle/Sabre
		- Dance
Marching Specialist	**Marching Specialist**	**Marching Specialist**
(All staff members assist with marching rehearsals.)		

Daily Schedules

Since there are so many types of rehearsal groupings, a detailed schedule needs to be planned and given to each member, chaperone and staff member.

Band Camp has been planned, organized, staffed. Now it needs a comprehensive schedule to take advantage of the instructional staff and achieve the goals. To get the most out of the available time and to keep it interesting for the students, a wide variety of groupings should be utilized. Segments never run more than an hour, so interest is easily maintained.

On the following pages are the daily schedules organized in two ways and specific goals for the camp defined. The Percussion and Color Guard are a little more flexible since they are smaller and more contained sections.

Types of sectional groupings and activities:

- Full Ensemble—Full Band (minus Guard sometimes)

- Section—large section—Woodwinds, Brass, Percussion or Color Guard

- Sub-section by instrument—homogeneous (e.g. Trumpets or Snares only)

- Squads—students are grouped into squads of 4-6 same instrument musicians or Guard with a squad leader. Squad rehearsals are run by the leaders (supervised by staff) and work on memory work, Level I music and marching check-off's and individual help when needed.

- Any combination of sections as it relates to the music—Low Brass, Upper Winds, etc.

- Tracking—Tracking is basically parade marching in short segments to solidify marching and playing together. It works best early in the season in small sections (10-20) but can be done in any grouping. Start with simple music—scales, School Song or simple rhythmic parts from the show. (Rule: Rookies never stand, march or sit next to other rookies. They need to model the veterans.)

  - Mark Time 8, Forward March 16, then play 8-16 measures (longer later) while moving, Forward March 16, Halt—Make corrections & suggestions. Continue until it starts to become easy for the rookies. Keep the music simple at the beginning.

  - Have a Drum Major or staff member hit a gok block to keep time.

  - Full Band tracking later in the season can solidify difficult tempos and other ensemble issues. It can be done on a "track", parking lot, campus, anywhere that there is level terrain and some distance.

  - This helps the rookies start marching and playing in small, simple segments without having to worry about drill considerations. Of course, it is an excellent review for the veterans as well.

The big rehearsal blocks of time (morning, afternoon, evening) start with a Full Band session. This is either Exercise/Marching Block or an Attitude Session. This helps with taking attendance and builds the Band Family feeling. It is motivating for the day to grow from small groups and segments and end with a Full Band "Run-Thru" even if it is only a small piece of the show. Band members and staff get to see the "fruits of their labor" and plan for the next day.

It is suggested that the printed schedule be distributed to all students when they arrive at camp to assure that they will all have a copy. Chaperones or student leaders can add social activities to the schedule.

Central High School
Marching Tigers
Band Camp Schedule

Time	Brass	Woodwinds	Percussion	Color Guard
8:00	--------------------------------- Exercise/Marching Block ---------------------------------			
9:15	------------------------ Warm-up ------------------------		Warm-up	Guard
9:45	Trp - Room 101 Low Brass - Tracking Mellos - Room 114	Woodwinds - Band Rm.	Sub-sections	Guard
10:30	--------------------------------- Break ---------------------------------			
10:45	Trp/Mello - Tracking Low Brass - Band Room	Flute - Tracking Clar. - Squads-outside Sax - Squads - by part	Sections	Guard
11:30	--------------------------------- Lunch ---------------------------------			
1:00	------------------------ Attitude Session - Band Room ------------------------			
1:45	1st,2nd,3rd Trp - Squads-out Mellos - Squads outside Low Brass - Squads outside	Flute - Squads-outside Clar. Tracking Sax - Band Room	Sub-sections	Guard
	Brass - Band Rm.	Flute - Room 101 Clarinet - Room 114 Sax - Tracking	Percussion Ensemble	Guard
3:15	--------------------------------- Break ---------------------------------			
3:30	-------------- Music - Full Ensemble - Band Room --------------			Guard
4:30	--------------------------------- Dinner ---------------------------------			
	--------------------------------- Evening - Full Band ---------------------------------			
6:30-Exercise/Marching	7:00-Drill	7:30-Break	7:45-Warm-up	
8:00-Drill & Play	9:30-Announcements	9:45-Activities	11:00-Lights Out	

Central High School
Marching Tigers
Woodwinds - Brass Schedule

Flute:

Staff

(Grad Staff)

Clarinet:

Staff

(Grad Staff)

Saxophone:

Staff

(Grad Staff)

Trumpet/Mellophone:

Staff

(Grad Staff)

Low Brass:

Staff

(Grad Staff)

Squad Time: Check-offs outside

Supervise - Students can either practice - in groups or single - or check-off

Squad Leaders do level I Check-offs & Level II School Songs, Staff does Level II

Flute:	**Clarinet:**	**Saxophone:**
9:45 Woodwinds - Band Room --		
10:45 Tracking	Squads - outside	Squads - outside - by part
1:45 Squads - outside	Tracking	Music - Band Room
2:30 Music - Rm. 101	Music - Rm. 114	Tracking
3:30 Full Band-Band Room ---- Observe your section, play along if you wish		
Trumpet/Mellophone:	**Low Brass:**	
9:45 Music - Room 101/ & 114	Tracking	
10:45 Tracking	Music - Band Room	
1:45 Squads - outside	Squads - outside	
2:30 Brass - Band Room ---------------------------		
3:30 Full Band-Band Room ---- Observe your section, play along if you wish		

Packing List for Camp

1. *All* equipment: instrument/sticks/reeds/ music/ flags/poles/rifles/etc.
2. Pencils/highlighters for your drill coordinates
3. Pillow and one set of sheets & blanket or sleeping bag. The camp gets cold at night.
4. Towels (beach & bath) and wash cloth
5. Deodorant (please!), soap, shampoo, toothbrush & toothpaste, other personal articles
6. Plenty of t-shirts (so you can change often), comfortable shorts, swimsuit, sweatshirt, underwear, jacket, long pants, etc.
7. Appropriate footwear: 2 pairs of gym shoes (an old pair for morning practices in the dew), flip-flops for the shower
8. Bring lots of athletic socks (enough to change into when they get wet). Athletic socks must be worn to prevent blisters. Bring enough to change often to keep your feet cool and clean. Veterans suggest twice as many as you think you'll need!
9. Band-Aids for those who do not wear proper socks or do not have comfortable shoes.
10. Bag for dirty clothes
11. Hat(s) to block sun exposure (wind players especially should wear one to avoid sunburned lips which will affect your playing)
12. Sunglasses and sunscreen
13. Insect repellant (definitely needed for night rehearsals). Don't forget the anti-itch lotion.
14. Gold Bond for guys (ask Mr. M.)
15. Water bottle/canteen for on-field practices
16. Games (cards, board games) for indoor free time and small pool toys.
17. Cabins can be hot. There are electrical outlets if you would like to bring a small fan. It might be a good idea to bring an extension cord too!
18. Snacks: You can bring your own cooler and ice is available in the kitchen. Individual plastic bottles of juice drinks are very refreshing.

Any food items should be sent in re-seal able plastic containers or Ziploc bags. Remember you are camping in cabins surrounded by woods filled with all of nature's critters, not to mention hungry band directors who like to scavenge for food from home.

How to Have A Safe & Happy Camp

- Please limit the use of hair dryers, curling irons, radio/CD players, etc. and shut off when not in use to avoid blown circuits/fus
- No refrigerators, TV's, or large stereo systems permitted.
- No rollerblading or skateboarding due to camp insurance liability.
- Label **everything** that you bring to camp.
- We are limited by space for transporting students, instruments, equipment, etc. via buses and our trucks.
- Each student is guaranteed transportation of 1 suitcase, sleeping bag/bed linens, their instrument, a carry-on bag (that means you carry it on with you on the bus), and fans. Other items will be loaded if space is available.
- Anything else must be transported by parents.
- If you have questions about bringing something to camp that is not covered in this newsletter, you must check with Mr. M. prior to camp for approval.
- **All property is brought to the camp at your own risk. The camp, CHS Band and staff assume no liability for lost, damaged, or missing items. Therefore, it is recommended that if you don't absolutely have to have it, don't bring it!**

Band Nurse Notes:

Medication—All medicine needed for camp must be in a sealed plastic bag in its original container. A completed Medication/ Procedure Request form (available on CHS Band Website) signed by your physician must accompany any medication. Mark your child's name clearly on the bag and bring it the parent meeting on July 22.

Special thanks to Mrs. C. who has volunteered to help our kids… call or email her if you have any concerns—123-4567 or mrs.c@abc.com.

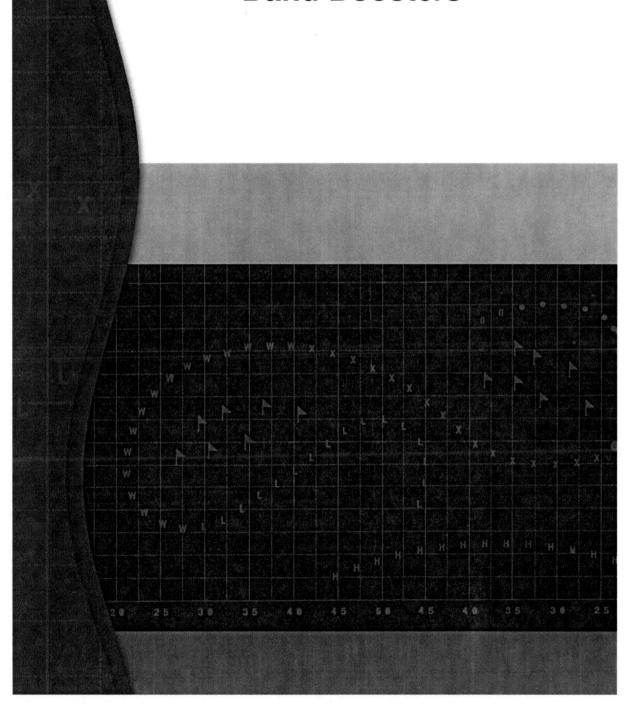

Chapter Thirteen

The
Band Boosters

Band Booster Organization

A supportive band booster organization is an essential element of a successful band program.

A strong and supportive band booster organization can be a tremendous help to the director, students and program when it is functioning properly. If the parents can see that band is having a positive influence on the students, they will want to be involved with the band program and boosters. The band booster organization is also one of the few areas where parents can truly get involved with their child's education. The band boosters are a vital part of the successful band program and the marching band in particular.

Unfortunately, the relationship between the band director and boosters in some schools is difficult at best. Trouble can arise when a parent/booster or group tries to exert undue influence on the program and director. If behavior like this is allowed to go unchecked, the band program could fall into chaos and dysfunction. Many a band director has left the position because of "out of control" band boosters. With a carefully prepared philosophy and purpose, and good *communication*, including the "line in the sand" agreement (next page), these problems can be minimized and avoided.

Philosophy

The philosophy of the Band Boosters Association is to act as a support group for the total band program. This includes the Concert Band, Wind Ensemble, Marching Band, Jazz Ensemble, Winter Guard, Winter Percussion Ensemble and all other ensembles and activities of the band program.

Purpose

The Band Boosters Association exists to provide moral, logistical and financial support for the total band program. The membership is open to all parents and guardians of band members. There are general meetings held four times a year and monthly board meetings, as required by the Constitution and By-laws. (See www.dynamicband.com for sample.)

Moral support – The most important function of the boosters is to provide encouragement to the band members individually at home and collectively at rehearsals and performances. Booster/parent attendance at concerts, competitions and events is very important to the band members.

Organizational support – The band program and the marching band, in particular, need a large amount of adult assistance for uniform management, chaperones, equipment, truck and transportation needs, food support on trips, communications, public relations and many other duties and functions.

Financial - The Boosters sponsor numerous fund raising events each year and provide substantial support to the band program.

The Line in the Sand

A guide to the roles and duties of the band boosters and band director

To communicate the roles and relationship of the band director and band boosters, it is important that the director make a clear statement several times a year. Several veteran directors call this "the line in the sand" speech. It should be given at the first board meeting and first general meeting with rookie parents and referred to later as the need arises. The message is mutually supportive of the director and boosters and outlines their respective roles and duties to alleviate problems before they arise.

In a nutshell, the "line in the sand" philosophy states that the band director is in charge of all **music and performance** related activities and decisions. The boosters are to provide **moral, logistical and financial** support to the band program. No one is to cross "the line."

How does this help the director?

The boosters are not involved in discussions about the band's performance. Things like flag colors, choices of music or soloists or comments regarding problems in the band are not appropriate for booster meetings. The budget, for example, is decided collectively, with the director giving input on needs of the program and the boosters working on income and booster expenses. It is the boosters' job to raise the funds and the director's job to stay within budget on his/her line items. These are clear expectations. The boosters' concern is the bottom line of the budget and not the priority or choice. Of course, the band director must not be excessive or extreme in decisions or the boosters do have the right and responsibility to question those choices.

Problems with individual students should not be discussed in booster meetings. If there is a concern regarding their own child, the parents are free to contact the director to discuss the matter, but not in the band booster setting. Further the director does not have to worry about the areas that are the responsibility of the boosters. For example, he/she should be minimally involved as far as fundraising goes other than being supportive and communicating to the students. The band director is free to concentrate on the band, the members and performances.

How does this help the band boosters?

Band boosters can "have a lot on their plates" for parents who are helping the band as part time volunteers. They greatly appreciate knowing what are their concerns and what are not. Booster board members are often approached by other parents about performance issues. They are relieved to be able to say "that is a performance issue, you should talk to the director." The boosters also appreciate the director not trying to micro-manage them. Many boosters are business professionals and they understand finances, fundraising, marketing or equipment management. They don't need to be told by a band director how to run what is basically a small business. The "line in the sand" also minimizes the otherwise inevitable topic of director's "politics."

Communicating the goals of the band program and everyone's roles is the key to a successful and pleasant relationship between the band director and the boosters. It can and should be an enjoyable association working for a common goal.

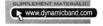

Board Members and Committee Chairs

A list of the Executive Board and Committees shows the depth of the organization.

The Executive Board consists of the four elected members, the band director, and the four appointed directors of the large committees. They meet monthly and conduct most of the booster's business in a small and manageable group. Other sub-committee chairs are invited, as their particular event is current. Four general booster meetings are held each year to communicate information. They are held in January (to approve the budget), at the end of the school year (Awards Night), prior to band camp and in December (to elect new officers).

The term of office and the fiscal year can be either the calendar year or the school year (June 1-May 31). *The calendar year is preferable* since it gives the newly elected members the winter and spring to get acclimated to their positions before the busy marching band season begins. Much of the planning for marching band happens in the winter and spring. Although the boosters exist to support the entire band program, most of the work is related to the marching band. For example, only a small amount of booster assistance is needed to put on a band concert.

It is also helpful that the elected positions be couples, when possible. This spreads the work-load and facilitates communication.

The list that follows shows the many positions and duties of the band boosters for a large and active band program. There are many positions "available" and it is best to get as many people involved as possible. This creates more parental interest and involvement. The workload varies with some positions being large commitments of time and some being very small. In that way, many people can get involved based on their time and availability. A small program should start with what is needed and build as the band program and boosters grow.

An exerted effort should be made to *delegate and involve* as many people as possible. Many booster organizations struggle with a handful of people doing all of the work. These groups often send a message of exclusivity and control although usually inadvertently. Parents usually have a very enjoyable time being involved in a worthwhile activity that helps their children. They like being "part of the action" with the marching band especially.

The boosters organization can become a real social outlet for many of the parents, and many of them make band parent friends that last long after their child graduates. Anything that can capitalize on this aspect should be used—a picnic or party to kick-off a meeting or work session, going out after the game, etc.

"What Can I Do to Help?" should be a motto for the band boosters. In requesting people to work, the boosters should use a phrase like "could you *help out the band* with a little bit of your time?"

The Band Boosters Association should seek not-for-profit status as a safeguard and to save funds by not being taxed on purchases. A Constitution and By-laws should be created if one does not exist with By-laws modified whenever needed to stay current. A sample is provided online; www.dynamicband. com.

Band Boosters Board and Committee Chairs
*(Board members in **Bold**)*

President   **Secretary**
1ˢᵗ Vice President   **Treasurer**
2ⁿᵈ Vice President (Band Director—permanent position)

Operations and Transportation
Director

Pit Crew   Truck Drivers
Props   Trip Coordinator
Event Parking   Trip Food

Student Activities
Director

Scholarship   Area Captain Coordinator
Nurse/Doctor   Color Guard
Flag Sewers   Winter Guard
Winter Percussion   Refreshments
Marching Band Uniforms   Water
Concert Band Uniforms   Volunteer Coordinator
Band Camp Coordinator   Rookie Liaison

Public Relations
Director

Publicity   Phone Chain (automated)
Newsletter   Email newsletter & news
Webmaster   Historian
Photographer   Tickets
Hospitality

Finance
Director

Budget   Audit
Concessions   Golf Outing
Garage Sale   Winter Guard & Percussion Show
Souvenirs   Marching Band Show
Commemorative Bricks Restaurant Events
Spring Flower Sale   Poinsettia Sale
Calendar Sale

Committees

Most of the positions and committees are obvious but a few comments will clarify. The President appoints the Directors of the four main committees with input from the rest of the board immediately following the election. They serve on the Executive Board and select sub-committee chairs for the various activities and events in their area. For any projects that are large and time-consuming, such as a marching band contest, it is a good idea to have a job shadow or understudy who will take over the following year. Some people prefer to co-chair an event and this works well because more people are involved and the workload is shared. Many of the sub-committees have several people involved with an activity. The following committee duties are available online; www.dynamicband.com.

The Operations and Transportation committee takes care of equipment and trip activities and "the always popular" pit crew. Many active bands have an equipment truck or trailer purchased by either the school or boosters for the safe transportation of instruments and equipment. The Pit Crew handles the equipment truck, sets up props and assists the front ensemble on the field for performances. Truck drivers drive the truck and must be CDL certified. Props are constructed as needed. The student trip coordinator handles itineraries with the band director and coordinates logistics. Trip food & housing handle either bringing food or finding places to go to eat and hotels if needed on the road. Event parking (often using the Pit Crew) takes care of on-site parking for sponsored contests.

The Student Activities committee is responsible for the various activities that directly involve or affect the student members. One important area is the scholarship committee. The Area Captain Coordinator assists the fundraiser events by putting students in teams, recruiting parent team leaders to collect money and coordinating the student groups. These groups remain constant for all fundraisers to keep it simple. It is ideal to have a Nurse or Doctor with the band at band camp, on trips and at competitions. Color Guard, Winter Guard and Winter Percussion have a parent coordinator to assist the Band, Guard and Percussion Director at shows and on trips. Flag Sewers obviously sew flags and save money for the budget. Refreshments and water are made available before and/or after performances. Uniforms for Marching Band and Concert Band (if used) are handled by the Band Boosters including fitting, assigning, cleaning, storing and collecting. The Band Director does not need to worry about any of those aspects of uniforms. It is recommended that uniforms do *not* go home with the students if it can be avoided. The Volunteer Coordinator keeps a roster of all Band Boosters and their participation in activities and assists chairs in recruiting. The Band Camp Coordinator handles all the arrangements for Band Camp including the facilities, food, grounds, arrival and check-in. Again, the Band Director need not worry about these details and can concentrate on teaching the band. The Rookie Liaison coordinates activities for helping the rookies get acclimated such as rookie night meeting for parents, rookie buddies (parent and student) and information sheets.

The Public Relations committee manages the publicity for band performances and the many communication vehicles utilized. These include a monthly newsletter (sent by email unless US Mail is requested), Email newsletter & news (short notes often weekly), the band website, the Phone Chain (a purchased service that contacts all listed members with one phone call regarding last minute updates, arrival times, etc.). The Historian and Photographer keep records and other historical data and make them available at events. Photos are available through the website. Tickets for large events are coordinated with bulk purchases to save parents time and to get blocks of seats together. Hospitality presents refreshments at meetings and some other events.

The Finance committee is responsible for the budget, yearly audit and coordinates all fundraisers with the collaboration of the treasurer. He/she makes reports to the Board regarding the progress of the various events. Good band fundraisers are Concessions at games, Spring Flower Sale, Poinsettia Sale, Golf Outing (plus it is a social event), Garage Sale, Winter Guard & Percussion Contest, Marching Band Contest and a Souvenir booth (T-shirts, buttons, etc.). Commemorative Bricks are partly a small fundraiser but also a nice memento for the band members and are placed in a location at the school. Restaurant Events coordinates the efforts of many businesses that sponsor "Band Nights" and donate part of the proceeds to the band. It is suggested that great care be taken in regards to the time commitment involved in fundraisers for both the students and parents. Avoid overburdening people with already busy schedules and avoid projects that do not generate substantial amounts of money. Some bands have opted to have the parents and not the students do all of the fundraising and there is merit to this.

In many situations, a percentage of money that is earned by an individual student or parent goes directly to offset the individual's fees. This needs to be within the guidelines of the overall school policies and rules and regulations of the IRS, especially in regards to not-for-profit status.

Student Band Fees
If student fees are necessary, they need to be as reasonable as possible.

It would seemingly be "ideal" if it were unnecessary to charge students extra fees to participate in band activities like marching band. In most high school situations a fee of some amount is necessary every year. The positive side to this is there is a commitment made when fees are involved, and participation often means more to the students who have worked hard to earn their fees. It also allows the marching band to do special events and include travel and go beyond what might be dictated if the school paid for the entire program. Many school districts require "pay to play" fees as in sports, and this needs to be communicated to the band members as early as possible.

Fees should be as reasonable as possible to achieve the budget and goals of the program. This depends greatly on the socio-economic level of the school and community and what has been required in the past. When the Band Booster Board sets the fees, careful comparison should be made to other school activities, athletics, community sponsored activities and other comparable school band programs. Once the fee has been established, it should be announced in all of the band communication outlets. This should be done in January for the coming marching band season. This gives everyone ample opportunity to prepare. A deadline should be set that is close to the start of marching band, but at least a week in advance to make sure the director knows what the exact (paid) enrollment will be.

Scholarships should be available for students in financial need. Any student who has made a strong effort to raise the money through fundraisers and outside jobs should not be eliminated from the band. However, this can be a difficult situation that should be handled confidentially. Other parents and students can be resentful if they think a student is receiving a "free ride" with no effort on their part. A scholarship fund that is separate from student-supported fundraisers might help the situation. Many school and service organizations also provide scholarships for such situations.

Band Booster Budget

The yearly budget should be created by a committee consisting of the Band Director, the Treasurer, the Finance Director and the Booster President. This should occur one to two months before the end of the fiscal year. The board then approves the budget before the end of their term at the end of the fiscal year. The entire membership in some booster groups then approves it depending on the process stated in the Constitution and By-laws. The newly elected board starts the year with a budget in-hand and can, if needed, alter the budget per the procedures in the Constitution and By-laws. The Band Director should state the needs of the band program, and the Boosters should do everything within reason to meet those needs. That is the purpose of this support group. The budget formation is always a "give and take" and making an overly ambitious jump in income and expenses is not in the best interest of the band and organization. It is better to set modest and attainable goals and if the income exceeds expenses, extra purchases can be made at the end of the fiscal year. Most guidelines do not permit carry-over funding into the next year. It is important that the Band Director and all Booster Board members do not go over budget. Many directors and organizations have had great difficulties caused by overspending.

Sample Band Booster Budget Allocations

INCOME

Account	Description	%
501 - Calendars	Community/School Calendar Sales & Ads	13%
502 - Spring Flowers	Spring flower sale	15%
503 - Concessions	Basketball concessions	6%
504 - Poinsettia Sales	December Poinsettia sales	8%
505 - MB Contest	Marching Band contest—October	10%
506 - Winter Contests	Winter Contest(s)	14%
507 - Golf Outing	Golf outing earmarked for Scholarships	2%
508 - Garage Sale	Garage Sale—June	1%
509 - Souvenir	Souvenir booth—T-shirts, etc.	1%
510 - Student fees	Student fees	21%
511 - Misc. Income	Income from small projects	9%

EXPENSES

Account	Description	%
601 - Equipment	Instruments, equipment, music	13%
602 - Band Camp	Band camp expenses	10%
603 - Specialty Staff	Instructional staff, drills, arrangements	20%
604 - Awards Program	End of the year awards	3%
605 - Color Guard	MB Color Guard equipment, costumes, etc.	6%
606 - Winter Guard	Winter Guard equipment, costumes, etc.	5%
607 - Winter Percussion	Winter Percussion equipment, costumes, etc.	8%
608 - Scholarships	Scholarships for lessons, camps, workshops	2%
609 - Uniform extras	Uniform annual expenses, repairs, parts, etc.	3%
610 - Transportation	Transportation for all groups, truck, charters	11%
611 - Food	Food for trips all groups	6%
612 - Long Term Projects	Restricted funds for Multi-year projects: Uniforms (6-7 yrs.), Big Trip (4 yrs.), Emergency	6%
616 - Misc. Expenses	Misc. expenses-Mailing, office, printing, Bank	7%

Band Travel

Band Trips are an important part of the band experience.

Whether it is a trip across town for a football game, or traveling across country on a big trip, band travel is an important aspect of the band experience for the members. The Band Booster organization is a key element of successful traveling starting with careful planning and organization. This should begin at the earliest possible time especially in the case of overnight trips. Trips for contests should be in keeping with the goals of the band. Many bands take a "Big Trip" every four years to give each member one opportunity to participate. This is often a three to seven day trip to a resort area like Florida or a big city and should include some special performance opportunities. Making the trip every four years also makes it a reasonable financial obligation for the families and community. Housing, plans for feeding the band and travel arrangements must be made early. Chaperone volunteers must be lined up and travel rules prepared and communicated.

Each school has policies regarding transportation via buses. Some use school buses for all trips and some use charter buses. Typically shorter trips are made on school buses, and longer trips are made on charters often funded by the Band Boosters. The band director needs to be aware of these policies and procedures and make arrangements for the school buses at the earliest possible time. The booster Operations and Transportation Director, the Band Director and the Trip Coordinator should meet to discuss and organize the trips in January or February. Plans should then be communicated and approved by the Executive Board. Charter buses, if used, should be contracted by the boosters.

A Band Booster nurse or doctor should accompany the marching band on all trips bringing the required paperwork for Emergency Medical Authorization and Medication Policy for each student. A list of significant medical information (i.e. severe allergies, diabetes, etc.) should be compiled and given to the band director for trips and daily rehearsals.

Housing

The booster Operations and Transportation Director should make overnight accommodations. Other bands, travel agents and the contest or trip sponsor should be consulted for recommendations regarding the appropriateness of the site for a band group. *Cheaper is not necessarily better!* Checking-in a band of teenagers in a hotel, especially late at night, can be a chaotic event unless it is well organized. It is suggested that a band booster check-in at least an hour early and arrange the room keys for easy distribution to one band member per room. While staying in a hotel, students need to be considerate of other guests and rooms should be left neat and orderly.

Feeding the Band

The same care should be taken in arranging for restaurants, caterers and locations that are appropriate for the marching band. Again, seek references as above. Consideration should be taken, depending on the size of the group, to the time needed to feed many students. *Nutrition should be a major consideration.* Although an occasional fast food is okay, especially if it is during travel time, band members need good nourishment to perform well and for their health.

Chaperones

Chaperones are a tremendous support to the band director and staff on trips.

The band director is responsible for the students during every minute of every band rehearsal, event or trip, especially in terms of liability. The Band Booster Chaperones are "in charge" and assist the director on trips during non-performance times. This allows the director and staff to have some "time off" to relax. This is especially important on longer trips.

Chaperone Guidelines

Your help is greatly appreciated by the directors, staff and boosters. You are an important part of the band team and we truly could not make trips without your support.

- Please arrive 15 minutes before the assigned student arrival time. Report to the Head Chaperone for bus assignment and any other duties. Get the bus list at this time.

- You are in charge of the band members at all times except when the band is in rehearsal, in uniform or otherwise with the staff. At those times you are free to go and relax, although make sure you are available should something arise.

- Students should wait outside the bus until told when to enter. Generally seniors load first, juniors next, etc. Take attendance from the bus list as they enter. This will also give you a chance to meet the students. Count the number of students on your bus.

- Once the trip begins, future attendance will usually be taken on the bus. A head count will suffice, if you are sure that all the students on your bus are assigned to your bus.

- The Head Chaperone will check with all buses to make sure that all students are accounted for and ready to leave.

- Everyone has a different approach to handling behavior and discipline but we would like to keep some uniformity in the chaperones approach. Please take a positive approach in working with the students. They are basically good kids and usually respond well to a polite but firm directive.

- The Rules for Band Trips are on the next page. Please insist that they are followed. Bus Rules are usually posted and include staying seated and keeping arms inside windows if open. Seek the assistance of the older students and leaders in setting a good example.

- Chaperones of course must follow the same rules as students including no smoking or drinking, even if out of sight.

- Please do not hesitate to contact the Head Chaperone or band director if you have any questions.

- Thank you so much for helping!

Rules for Band Trips

Be Your Best
Show Respect
Be Prepared
Be on Time

- The basic band rules address all situations and will eliminate any problems. A few policies and reminders are needed in regards to band trips.
- All school policies are in effect at all band functions including trips. Any problems will be referred to the administration as outlined in the policy. Band directors will enforce these policies at all band functions. No alcohol, controlled substances including tobacco are to be taken, bought or consumed. Public display of affection (PDA) is not acceptable.
- The chaperones are in charge and are to be treated with courtesy and respect. They are volunteering their time to help you and the band. Any problems will be reported to the band director. Follow all of their instructions. If you do not understand—ask. If you have a problem with a request, see the band director at the appropriate time. In the meantime, follow all of their instructions.
- All prescription and non-prescription medications must be handled by the nurse/doctor per the school's medical policy as stated on that form.
- Do not bring unnecessary, expensive valuables on the trip. The band is not responsible for lost or stolen items.
- All bus rules apply including no profanity, singing, chanting, horseplay or screaming. Any listening devices such as CD or MP3 players must be used with headphones on.
- Wait to board the bus until told when and how. Be quiet and helpful during roll calls.
- Be considerate of others and use charter bus restrooms as little as possible.
- If there are any concerns including medical ones, contact the chaperone as soon as possible. Each bus will have a first aid kit and the chaperones can contact the nurse or director if necessary.
- Buses and rooms will be assigned and no changes are to be made without the permission of the band director. Clean up your bus area.
- When using a hotel or dorm, no boys in girls rooms and no girls in boys rooms unless you are given specific permission. No exceptions.
- Do not leave your room unlocked.
- Know your chaperone and where their room is.
- You are responsible for the condition of your room and any possible damage.
- Take no souvenirs from your room or restaurants.
- You must be in your room and have lights out at the assigned times—you will need your rest. Don't be foolish and stay up all night! Use the phones only for serious calls and no long distance calls.
- All students must travel to and from performances on the bus. A student may leave only with their own parent or guardian with a written permission note given to the director. The parent or guardian must check in with the director or head chaperone when picking up the student.
- Remember that you are always representing the band and school.

Uniforms

A marching band in a sharp and well-fitted uniform is an impressive sight.

It is the Band Boosters' job to maintain, store, fit and assign the band uniforms. The band director's job is to select the design of the uniform and make sure the band follows the uniform rules. This is a good example of "the line in the sand" approach.

Purchasing

Funding for uniforms varies by district with some schools paying, some boosters and sometimes a combination. If boosters are the main source of funding, it is important to make yearly contributions to the fund (see Budget) in order to avoid a huge uniform fundraising drive. Uniforms last a long time; therefore they must be selected carefully. School districts have policies regarding large purchases that may include receiving several bids and samples.

Band uniforms generally last for 6–8 years depending on the quality, fabrics used and frequency of wear. A committee of four to six members, including the band director and a visual staff member, should study uniforms beginning in October or November. Uniforms generally need to be ordered with a firm commitment and all the details worked out *no later than* May 1 for delivery by fall. There are several good companies and they will provide design help (highly recommended) and all of the information needed to begin the process. A study should be made of preferred band and drum corps uniforms and the companies that make them. Companies will make samples for the committee to study. The boosters should concentrate on the construction and quality of the company, and the staff should concentrate on the design and how it affects the band's look.

Fitting

To get a crisp look that accentuates the marching style of the band, the uniform pants should be fit tightly and not too long (or short). There is nothing that looks as sloppy as baggy pants in a band uniform. The pants should be adjusted and altered if needed so they are tight in the hips and buttocks. Many pants come with an elastic stirrup that goes over the sock and inside the shoe, or they can easily be added. This gives a very sharp look in the leg extension of the marching style.

Cleaning

Uniforms used to be made of wool fabrics requiring dry cleaning. Today's uniforms are primarily synthetic fabrics that are machine washable either at home or laundromat. These uniforms are much more comfortable, flexible and cooler. The boosters should have a system to wash all of the uniforms at the same time following the company's instructions for cleaning.

Storage

It is best if uniforms can always be stored at the school and never taken home by the students. (They always wind up in the bottom of the guys' closets!) If facilities do not allow, inspections should be held regularly to check on the condition of the uniforms.

Drum Major Uniforms

Drum Major uniforms should be similar in style to the regular band style. Most bands choose all black, so when they are conducting on a ladder or podium, they will not be too distracting. It gives a dignified and strong appearance also. If this is an expense issue, a regular uniform or tuxedo can be used.

Maintenance

When uniforms are turned in at the end of the season, they should be carefully inspected for any needed repairs. Skilled boosters or a professional should make the repairs immediately. Extra uniforms are needed from time to time for extra small or large students or as the band grows in size. Most companies have a policy for these add-ons with timelines to observe.

Selling

When it is time to purchase new uniforms, the olds ones can be sold. Several national music magazines will run ads in the back of their publication. Recently a few uniform consignment businesses have appeared. One reputable company is The Guardroom.com, a web-based company (www.theguardroom. com). They service the seller and buyer and also handle flags, props and equipment.

Uniform Committee

There needs to be a Band Booster uniform committee and chairperson that handles all aspects of the band uniforms, including distributing and collecting uniforms for performances, assigning and fitting and maintenance. Ideally this should be a separate group from the chaperones.

Color Guard Costumes

Most competitive bands utilize a costume for their show that is new each year and in the style of the show concept. These can be purchased from the uniform companies including design services or can be sewn by skilled boosters. The consignment services mentioned above are a good resource for a developing program. The Winter Guard and Percussion groups also use yearly costumes. If budgets are not developed to accommodate this, costumes could be utilized for two–three years or a "permanent" guard uniform could be used that complements the band uniform.

Uniform Guidelines

In order to present a "uniform" look and make a great impression, it is important that uniform guidelines be *strictly* adhered to. The uniform is to be worn *completely* at all times in public view. Looking "First Class" at all times is part of the band's tradition.

- **Hats**—All hair must be tucked inside hat. The hat should sit just above the ears and not cover any part of the ears. The front of the hat should sit two fingers above the eyebrows. Baseball caps are not part of the band uniform and not to be worn at any time in uniform.

- **Jacket**—A T-shirt or similar shirt must be worn under the uniform. Jacket remains zipped at all times in public unless told otherwise by the staff.

- **Pants**—Shorts or leotard must be worn under the pants.

- **Shoes**—Shoes should only be the designated shoe style and must be cleaned for each performance.

- **Socks**—Black socks that go several inches above the ankle must be worn in uniform.

- **Parkas**—Parkas (or raingear) in a parka bag must be brought to each performance. Listen to directions as to where they will be stored.

- **Plumes**—Plumes will be handed out at the appropriate time —handle with care.

- **Jewelry**—There should be no jewelry worn that is visible in uniform.

- **Storage**—When returning uniform to storage, all items must be neat and properly presented.

Equipment

The Band Boosters are responsible for transporting instruments and equipment.

In most high schools, the Band Boosters handle the moving of instruments and equipment to off-campus performance sites. Some schools provide trucks, an extra bus or a converted bus and a driver. Many boosters now own equipment trucks, especially if they make frequent performance trips with the various ensembles. These can be outfitted with shelves and racks in order to best protect the instruments and utilize space. In any situation, the Band Boosters should provide the people power to unload, set-up, move and reload the equipment. The "Pit Crew" usually performs this job. The band director should give them careful instructions about what instruments are more fragile and how they should be transported. An efficient method for student loading and unloading should be devised.

Props

Props are used by many marching bands and winter groups and are generally built, transported and set-up by the Pit Crew. The director and staff should plan what they need to visually enhance the show, keeping in mind budget constraints, logistics and practicality. The director needs to constantly ask himself and the staff "Is this worth the expense and hassle for the results?" The director then needs to meet with the booster chair of the Pit Crew and discuss the feasibility of the ideas. Directors and visual staff are often creative but not very practical, and perhaps that is a good thing. The boosters will sometimes have to say what can or cannot be done logistically.

Props go in and out of fashion in the marching activity and are certainly not a requirement. The staff should carefully observe the best marching groups and shows in the activity and decide if props are an enhancement to the show. They can add a great visual dimension to a show or can be totally unnecessary.

Communications

Good communication is essential to any successful program and with today's high tech society, the band must communicate with all of the resources available. It seems that the more ways the information is sent, the more likely it will be read and understood by parents and students. The band director should take advantage of these methods to keep everyone informed:

- Band Program Website – The band's website features information on the total band program including calendars, announcements, staff info and the monthly newsletter.
- Monthly Newsletter – The monthly newsletter is published on the website as a PDF file and a hardcopy will be mailed home if requested. Current information and upcoming news is highlighted with the monthly calendar and reports on current booster projects.
- BANDNEWS Broadcast E-mail – This service is for anyone requesting it and sends out reminders of important events and deadlines as well as late breaking news. Boosters and alumni can sign up by sending name, e-mail address and year of graduation to BANDNEWS@ centralband.org.
- Phone Chain - This automated phone calling system contacts one phone number per band family and provides up-to-date information about last minute changes, arrival times and other emergency information as needed. It will only be activated by the Band Director or Band Booster Officers. Everyone is encouraged to sign up for this service.
- Wednesday Sheet - The Wednesday Sheet is distributed to marching band members each Wednesday at the end of practice with information and times of events and rehearsals for the following week and a half. This information can also be found on the band website.

Publicity

Good PR is important to the total band program.

A good public relations program promotes and advertises the total band program to the school and community. It is important for generating interest in concerts and marching performances and for advertising fundraisers. Local news media are often interested in human-interest stories and the band always has good stories to tell. A booster publicity chair under the Public Relations Director should establish contacts with the local and area newspapers, the school newspaper and radio and TV stations. They should use a Press Release format (sample available: www.dynamicband.com) and submit information in a timely manner for concerts, contest results, fundraisers and other interesting stories. The band program is *always recruiting*, and seeing band information in the news helps the middle school band members maintain interest. Further, band members work as hard as anyone in the school and they deserve to be recognized for their efforts. Emphasize participation, hard work and improvement more than awards and trophies and remember to include photos.

There are many mediums for communicating the efforts of the band members and program in the community. Here are a few items and projects that promote the band and build esprit de corps:

T-Shirts

It is common for marching band members to have an annual "tour shirt" as a souvenir of the season and to show band spirit. They are typically worn at competitions when the band is out of uniform. The cost of the tour shirt can be built into the band fees to insure that every member gets a shirt. Parents, staff and alumni typically are interested in getting and wearing the tour shirt.

Band Decals

Many bands have a decal made with the band's name and logo to put on car windshields, notebooks, etc. They demonstrate band spirit and also advertise the band around the community. The more the public sees the band name, the more common and accepted it will become. This is helpful in a long-term way to recruit young students to play a band instrument.

Band Calendars

Many bands sell a school events calendar as a fundraiser that includes important school activities for all of the schools in a district. It should include pictures of the band from the previous marching season as well as concert band, jazz ensemble and winter group photos. Some pictures of athletics should be included to promote good will in the school (and sell more calendars). With advertising space sold, this is an excellent fundraiser as well as PR tool for the band.

Marching Band Poster

Most school athletic teams have an annual poster distributed in the community. Why not the marching band? The photographer that takes the band photos can produce them.

Band Handbook

The Band Handbook is given to members of all ensembles in the band program.

This is a sample of a cover page for the Band Handbook Table of Contents with notes. A "clean" copy is available online, www.dynamicband.com.

Contents

Band Program Information

Marching Band Information

Band Boosters Information

Helpful Forms

CHS Band Roster

Dealing with Parents

Band directors and parents must work as a team for the success of the band and the individual students.

A healthy relationship between the director and parents is important to the successful band program. The marching band is one of the few areas in school where parents have the opportunity to be actively involved with the students and teachers in a positive and supportive way. However, every teacher in every school must deal with parents who are unhappy from time to time. It is an unfortunate facet of today's society. The young music educator is often uncomfortable in this role and needs to be as prepared as possible for these inevitable situations.

Pro-active approach

Establishing a rapport with parents is very important and establishes a pro-active stance before problems arise. This should begin as soon as the new band director first interacts with parents in either a private or band booster setting. The young educator needs to display positive personal and professional qualities starting with the first impression. A periodic review of "Characteristics of Great Band Directors" in Chapter 1 might be helpful. If the parents perceive that the director is confident, open-minded, energetic and humble, they will be supportive. Always show appreciation. Nothing compares to a sincere "Thank you for your help."

Establishing the "Line in the Sand" philosophy will avoid many problems before they occur. The director should make it clear that he/she is happy to discuss any concerns regarding the parents' child, but that Band Booster concerns should be handled through the president.

Communicate everything possible in writing and announcements with plenty of advance notice. Do not change schedules, rules, procedures unless absolutely necessary, and then explain why. Be *consistent* with the enforcement of rules and regulations and have fair consequences. Adults do not like changes or perceived changes.

The book *How to Win Friends and Influence People* by Dale Carnegie is a very helpful resource in developing positive people skills. It should be required reading for every young person entering the education profession.

Problems

When parents are upset about something, a few concepts will help defuse or at least minimize the conflict.

- A meeting is usually preferable to a phone conversation.

- Meet in your office and not in the hallway or side of the practice field.

- If a hostile attitude is displayed or expected, have a witness in the meeting. Give the principal a "heads up" and ask for support if a serious problem is expected.

- Be respectful ("I appreciate you coming in to discuss this situation.")

- Be a good listener and let them have their say without interruption. (Use phrases like "I understand what you are saying" and "I understand why your daughter might be upset.")

In regards to discussions of the child's ability or progress, tell the truth diplomatically and do not "sugar coat" how the student performs. It only aggravates the parents' discontent when the director uses phrases like "Suzy plays well but…" or "It was extremely close between your son and another trumpeter for the solo." It is better to say "John really did not play very well at his audition" or "He was very inconsistent, sometimes sounding good and sometimes not good at all. We are looking for consistency from our first chair players." Visual topics should be addressed with the same honesty. "Jim is still having a lot of trouble keeping his feet on the beat and in step." Always be specific about what the problems are musically or visually.

Once the parents have stated their position and concerns, the director should give a thoughtful response. He/she should explain what the background or process was in reaching a decision or in taking action. Problems often arise concerning rules, attendance policies and consequences. When everything is in writing in the Band Handbook that was distributed to parents and students at the start of the season, the director has a solid foundation and should refer the discussion to these documents in print. "Here is our policy and here is why we have it" is a good response.

The band director should be confident in decisions and not back down against his/her own feelings of right and wrong. However, the band director does not always have to be right. It is not a win-lose situation. Parents respect someone who can say, "Maybe I over-reacted and I will give it some serious thought." Sometimes the parents are totally correct and the director is wrong. Admitting a mistake and taking corrective measures is a sign of strength and not weakness.

If an impasse is reached or the comments begin to get repetitive, it is time to end the discussion. A polite but firm statement is in order such as "I think I understand the situation and we have covered the matter quite thoroughly. Thank you for meeting with me and I appreciate hearing your perspective. I will take a serious look into the situation."

When the situation is at a stalemate, it is good to refer the parents to the director's administrative superior. "If you still have concerns, you should contact the principal—Mrs. Smith."

Helpful phrases
Some phrases that will help develop a cooperative attitude in parents:

❖ "What can I do to help you?"

❖ "How can *we* improve the situation with your child."

❖ "Have their been similar problems in other areas of school or home."

❖ "I think if we work together with your child, we will have a positive outcome."

❖ "What specifically are you suggesting I do in this situation?"

❖ "Thank you for your input."

❖ "Let's communicate again regarding the situation."

Communication with parents, especially dealing with a negative situation, is difficult and uncomfortable for all young educators. It does get easier and less upsetting as experience and confidence is gained in the profession.

Chapter Fourteen

Marching Band
Evaluation

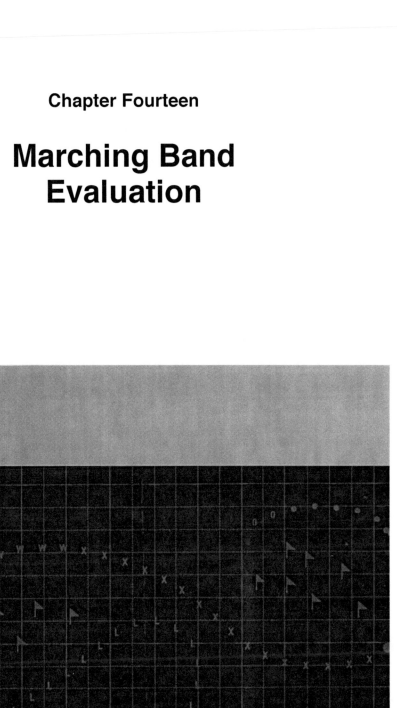

Band Evaluations
Purpose
Students should have the opportunity to evaluate their band program.

Near the conclusion of the marching band season, the members should be given the chance to review the year and give their opinions. As stated in the Band Goals, Rehearsal Techniques and Attitude sections of this book, the band members must think it is *their* band and feel ownership. The sense of ownership improves attitude, hard work and overall performance of the band.

Take ten or fifteen minutes of rehearsal time a week or two before the end of the season to do this activity. A rainy day is the perfect time. ("We don't have enough time" is not a valid excuse. In the big picture, "you don't have enough time" to omit this opportunity!) Don't wait until the season is over, because too many students evaluate the season based on final competition results and not on the real values of the marching band program.

It should be stressed that the staff takes these evaluations very seriously as they plan for the next season. That does not mean that every student idea will be implemented, but that it will be given careful consideration. Evaluations are anonymous so the students feel free to express their opinions.

The most important purpose of this exercise is to give members a *sense of value and ownership* of the band. After all, you have just spent many months expecting the students to do everything you request, put in countless hours of "blood, sweat and tears" and rehearsed in all sorts of weather. The *least* you should do is give them a few minutes to express their thoughts on the season.

Secondly, the director *needs to know* what the students think. Too many directors are afraid to allow the students a voice or think they "know it all" and it doesn't matter what the students say. The second quality mentioned in "Characteristics of Great Band Directors" in Chapter 1 is having an open mind and learning attitude. Every successful, veteran band director will state how much they learn about teaching from their students.

What often results in these surveys is that the students did not have a good understanding of *why* something was being done. When students are critical of something, the solution is often that better explanations are needed *rather than changing the content*. For example, students often have a hard time buying into spending a lot of time on fundamentals, but accept it when they understand that it will increase their music or visual performance. It needs to be explained and frequently reinforced. ("You are starting to sound great on the ballad because of all the time we have spent on long tones.") This improved understanding and teaching can be the result of student evaluations of the program.

Member evaluations should be done in all ensembles throughout the year. Another example of the importance of evaluations relates to concert band. One director, who emphasized music theory paperwork, found the students critical about this. They did not like it and had trouble understanding it. The next year he frequently explained the purpose and relativity to music performance, and students not only responded better, but did better on their theory assignments.

The Marching Band and Director Evaluation forms can be tailored to each situation and are available online, www. dynamicband.com.

215

Marching Band Evaluation

No name—Please give us your honest answers—Feel free to add comments

1. What section are you in?   A. Woodwinds   B. Brass   C. Color Guard   D. Percussion

Answers for the following:

A-Positive B-Somewhat Positive C-Neutral or No opinion D-Somewhat Negative E-Negative

2. *Overall*, did you enjoy the marching season? _____
3. *Overall*, is the band friendly? _____
4. *Overall*, are you proud to be in the band? _____
5. *Overall*, does the band have a family feeling? _____
6. What is the attitude of the total staff *overall*? _____
7. What is the attitude of the *your* section's staff *overall*? _____
8. What do you think of the Attitude Sessions? _____
9. Were the summer evening rehearsals valuable? _____
10. Was band camp at State University valuable? _____
11. Was band camp at CHS valuable? _____
12. What do you think of the marching basics program? _____
13. What do you think of the band's discipline/rehearsal etiquette? _____
14. What do you think of the after school/evening rehearsal schedule? _____
15. What do you think of rehearsals as to difficulty/fatigue? _____
16. What do you think of rehearsals as to present length? _____
17. What is your opinion of the competition show music? _____
18. What is your opinion of the competition show drill? _____
19. What is your opinion of the competition show music or guard work difficulty? _____
20. What is your opinion of the competition show marching difficulty? _____
21. What is your opinion of performing at home football games? _____
22. What is your opinion of performing at away football games? _____
23. Do you prefer after school or evening rehearsals?   **A.** after school   **B.** evening

GOLDEN OPPORTUNITY!
Please give us comments & suggestions for improvement on back.

Ideas for Next Year's Marching Band

(Fill this out only if you plan on participating next year)

1. How many contests should we attend next year?

    0   1   2   3   4   5   6

2. Which ones should we return to?

3. Any others you would like to attend?

4. How much should we practice next summer?

    ☐ Much less   ☐ Less   ☐ The same   ☐ More   ☐ Much more

5. Do you prefer after school or evening practices?   ☐ After school   ☐ Evening

GOLDEN OPPORTUNITY #2 !! What ideas do you have for next season? Your ideas are very important in our planning. This is **your** band. Consider: music, marching basics, attitude, rehearsals, trips, everything & anything. (As always, don't complain unless you have a positive suggestion for improvement.) Use the other side if you need more room.

Thank you! We really value and use your input.

217

Director Evaluation

DO NOT PUT YOUR NAME ON THIS FORM.

This is called a **Semantic Differential Test**. Look at the two words on the right and left on each line. Circle "Very…" or "Somewhat…" closest to the word on the right **or** left that describes how you feel. Circle "Neutral or No opinion" if that is how you feel. Questions refer to your overall impression during the whole year. Answers are only how you see it and not necessarily good or bad.

*Circle **one word only** per line.*

Fair	Very	Somewhat	Neutral or No opinion	Somewhat	Very	**Unfair**
Firm	Very	Somewhat	Neutral or No opinion	Somewhat	Very	**Not firm**
Unfriendly	Very	Somewhat	Neutral or No opinion	Somewhat	Very	**Friendly**
Available for help	Very	Somewhat	Neutral or No opinion	Somewhat	Very	**Unavailable**
Listens	Very	Somewhat	Neutral or No opinion	Somewhat	Very	**Doesn't listen**
Unpredictable	Very	Somewhat	Neutral or No opinion	Somewhat	Very	**Predictable**
Relaxed	Very	Somewhat	Neutral or No opinion	Somewhat	Very	**Tense**
Emotional	Very	Somewhat	Neutral or No opinion	Somewhat	Very	**Unemotional**
Inconsistent	Very	Somewhat	Neutral or No opinion	Somewhat	Very	**Consistent**
Not understanding	Very	Somewhat	Neutral or No opinion	Somewhat	Very	**Understanding**
Likes me	Very	Somewhat	Neutral or No opinion	Somewhat	Very	**Doesn't like me**
Stubborn	Very	Somewhat	Neutral or No opinion	Somewhat	Very	**Changeable**
Good discipline	Very	Somewhat	Neutral or No opinion	Somewhat	Very	**Bad discipline**
Action delayed	Very	Somewhat	Neutral or No opinion	Somewhat	Very	**Takes action**
Gives clear directions	Very	Somewhat	Neutral or No opinion	Somewhat	Very	**Gives Unclear directions**
Wastes time	Very	Somewhat	Neutral or No opinion	Somewhat	Very	**Uses time well**
Sense of humor	Very	Somewhat	Neutral or No opinion	Somewhat	Very	**No sense of humor**
Prepared for rehearsals	Very	Somewhat	Neutral or No opinion	Somewhat	Very	**Not prepared for rehearsals**

Chapter Fifteen

Band Director
Band/Life Balance

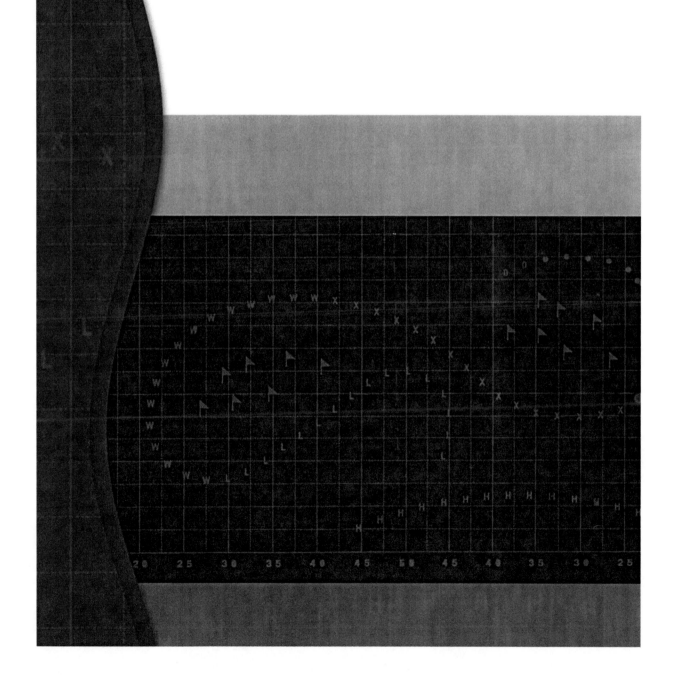

Band Director Band/Life Balance

Band directing would be fun if it only involved directing the band.

Any book on the marching band activity would not be complete without addressing the very important issue of maintaining a balance in the life of the band director. Many directors who start out young and enthusiastic get discouraged, have personal and family problems, lose their patience and eventually burn out and leave the profession. They become consumed by the seemingly overwhelming nature of the job. Every band director at least occasionally feels the effects of burnout. Here is a typical path that band directors take:

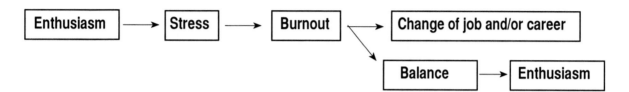

Enthusiasm

Enthusiasm is one of the first and most important qualities of a band director (see Chapter 1). Most young people going into the profession have this quality, and it will get them started on a successful path.

How long does the enthusiasm last?

- ❖ Until the first rehearsal and you realize this band is not what you expected.

- ❖ Until the first performance or competition and you realize it was not very good.

- ❖ Until either of the above and you realize this band is better than you thought and you don't know enough to handle it.

- ❖ Until you realize that college was easy (although at the time you thought it was hard) and this band director job is very difficult, demanding, stressful and exhausting.

- ❖ Or maybe you are lucky and the enthusiasm lasts forever. If so, you are fortunate.

The workload of a band director is enormous and overwhelming at times. ("Why didn't anyone tell me this before?") Your high school or college director may have told you, but you did not want to hear it anyway.

You became a band director because you love music and enjoy working with young people, so why can't you do just that? You did not expect the other duties to be so time consuming:

• Student complaints	• The band room is a mess	• There is not enough rehearsal time
• Parent complaints	• There is not enough money in the budget	• Principal is a pain
• Paperwork	• 1st trumpet moved	• You are always tired
• And on and on …		

Stress

Stress is a very common cause of illness in our society underlying as much as 70% of all visits to the doctor. It affects everyone and certainly includes band directors. Stress is *our reaction* to factors in our lives like anxiety, overwork and unrealistic expectations. These factors are often called "triggers." Since stress is our reaction to triggers, we can learn to control much of the stress that affects us.

Symptoms of stress could be just about any ailment, but frequently appear as anger, depression, high blood pressure, stomach ailments, insomnia, heart disease and stroke. The symptoms can be physical, mental, emotional or behavioral.

Stress Management

This frequently heard phrase is not "Stress Disappearance" because that is not going to happen, but one can learn to *manage* and reduce it. A stressed individual *must change* to manage their stress.

- Change your behavior & thinking—how do you react to a stress trigger?
- Change your daily lifestyle—choose a healthier lifestyle.
- Change the circumstances—what can you change, reduce or eliminate?

Tips for reducing stress:

1. Decrease or eliminate caffeine—that is almost heresy for band directors but will make a huge difference in your life. One of the biggest parts of drinking coffee is the ritual of the mug in your hand and drinking warm liquid. So switch to decaffeinated coffee or tea.
2. Get regular exercise—30 minutes, 3 times a week minimum.
3. Eat healthy meals and maintain an ideal weight.
4. Get a good night's sleep—7-8 hours.
5. Use relaxation/meditation techniques.
6. Take a break—band directors often work non-stop. Take a break and get away from it, even for 5 minutes.
7. Change the way you react to problems or triggers. See it as a challenge.
8. Share your feelings with spouse, friends or colleagues. Everyone needs a support system.
9. Keep humor in your life and job. Allow yourself to laugh at a funny event in class or make a joke. When you feel stressed or anger creeping in, stop, breath and think of a pleasant event.
10. Make time for leisure activities every day. Go on vacations yearly.
11. Leave it all at the office when you go home—leave the problems, the worries and your briefcase.

Band directors should set realistic expectations for themselves and the ensembles. Too many young educators expect and demand perfection and that simply sets them up for frustration. Teachers need to remember the spiral learning theory—tone, rhythm, technique and most other facets of music cannot be mastered in a day. It takes weeks, months and even years to become proficient. "Rome was not built in a day."

Band Director Burnout

Stress in moderation gives you energy, motivation and excitement. When stress becomes overwhelming, it leads to burnout. Once it reaches the point where you start slowing down, rather than being invigorated and attacking the problems, you begin to feel burned out. The symptoms are exhaustion, losss of energy, depression, feelings of failure, cynicism and loss of interest in working. Some teachers experiencing burnout are glad when they are actually sick enough to stay home from school. This is not a good situation!

These people often blame *their burnout* on everything and everybody except themselves. They get angry at the band and complain to anyone who will listen. (This is not the same as having a support group to share your concerns.) They go to work every morning dreading the approaching day. This is a long way from those first days of enthusiasm as a new teacher.

What can be done? Is it too late when you start feeling burned out?

Being aware of band director burnout as you enter the profession can help you watch for the warning signs and avoid these problems. Try to "nip it in the bud." Don't wait until stress leads to burnout, and leaving the profession or job is the only alternative.

Having realistic expectations, as mentioned under stress management, is a key to successful teaching. "Patience is a virtue." If your ensembles are getting better almost every day, then you cannot ask or expect more than that. That is the name of the game. Be happy!

A good understanding of everything the job entails, not just making music, will give you more realistic expectations. For a band director, often the least amount of time is rehearsing the band and the most amount of time is paperwork, meetings, parent phone calls, grading papers, etc. Get organized! Give yourself a set amount of time each day to handle paperwork, phone calls, etc. When the time is done, *let it go* and start in on the list tomorrow.

Don't feel sorry for yourself. Many adult jobs involve long hours and sometimes much travel and time away from home. To be a successful band director, you cannot work the same hours as some other teachers in the school. You can't go home at 3:00 every day! Neither can most professional workers. Give yourself a set routine—for example, work from 7:30 a.m. until 5:00 p.m. every day. If school is over at 3:00 and you have sectionals or jazz ensemble a couple of days a week after school, the other days you do office work. At 5:00, go home and leave it all at the office!

Do your best each day and then let it go until tomorrow.

What do you do if you can't escape burnout?

A job and/or career job change is a solution for many people. Someone who has made a great effort to get back to a balanced situation and can't shake the overwhelming feelings of being burned out, may need to find a new job. There is no question that some teaching positions are doomed for failure when you begin. If that is the case, get out as soon as you can. However, many positions that seem desperate will work given enough time. Too often a burned out teacher leaves a job and the same problems arise in the new job. He/she just took the burnout with them. The problem was not the situation but the teacher.

Life Balance

Life is always a balancing act—between necessities and desires, between duty and pleasure, between chocolate fudge sundae (name your favorite food here) and a healthy diet and so forth. Band directors, in particular, need to work on this aspect of their lives, because it is often too late by the time distress and burnout have arrived.

There needs to be clearly delineated "Band Time" and "Your (insert name) Time." Draw the line where band ends and your other life begins. Don't be afraid to say to people that you cannot do something tonight because you already have a commitment. That commitment (you don't have to announce) is your home life. Of course, you need to know what is *essential* for your job and what can wait until another time.

The controlling-type of individual will feel the need to be at every meeting, even small ones that would do very well without a band director present. The candy sale committee meeting would be a good example. Don't misread this to mean that the director can shirk his/her responsibilities. Know where to draw the line.

Learn to *delegate* work. The band director that insists on doing everything himself/herself will be overworked and overwhelmed. The director does not need to do fundraising, uniforms, cleaning the band room, filing music, refreshments, etc. Ask the question, "Do they really need my professional help as a music educator for this project or event?" And just because you have done it in the past, or your predecessor did, does not mean that you need to continue.

Learn how to say "I need some help with this project. Can we get some boosters or students to work on it?"

Let student leaders do some of the work around the band room. Not only does it help the director, it also teaches them responsibility and develops ownership. Responsible students should handle jobs like music librarian. Teach them how to file music in score order, how to pass out parts, give them time and then let them do it.

If you are fortunate enough to have a band staff, delegate jobs to them. Most people are reluctant to jump in and do something, even though they would be happy to do so if asked. The band staff functions better if it is truly a team effort. The director should step down and let another staff member run the rehearsal from time to time. Be a mentor to the other staff members. Often you discover that someone else does a particular job as well or better than you. You get a chance to watch and listen or even be a field tech. By so doing, you get a chance to relax from the pressure of always running the rehearsal. You also get a new perspective that helps understand the big, or sometimes small, picture better. It reduces stress when the marching band director has someone else who is qualified to run visual basics or visual ensemble rehearsals, while he/she runs the music rehearsals.

In balancing home and school time, many directors think that it is important to live relatively close to the school. They can therefore go home between school and the game for example.

Health

An important part of reducing stress and avoiding burnout is maintaining a healthy lifestyle. Band directors need to be conscious of their physical and mental well-being. Unfortunately, leading a stressful life makes a person ignore their health until a serious problem arises. The difficulty is that health problems begin so gradually that most people ignore them.

The many stress related illnesses were mentioned earlier. An upset stomach can lead to an ulcer before the person realizes. Some other health problems typical of all people as they age, should be a concern to band directors.

❖ Hearing loss is a concern for all musicians and music teachers, especially marching band directors and percussion teachers. Recently, much has been written concerning this problem. The band director needs to take a lead role in educating and insisting that ear protection is worn by students in loud environments. This applies most frequently to percussionists and instructors. Buy a large jar of foam ear plugs, have a 25 cent cup next to it and insist they are used.

❖ Back problems often occur in active adults. Many band directors go to a chiropractor or massage therapist at the first hint of back or muscle problems and this is a wise health decision.

❖ Foot problems are typical the older one becomes. The problems often begin when young but don't become persistent until later. Always wear quality shoes with good support that are not too tight or too old. It is worth the expense to buy quality shoes.

As mentioned earlier, it is most important to always be aware of good nutrition, exercise and relaxation.

Family

The most important topic has been left for last and that is the family. Sadly, many band directors get divorced or relationships fail because a balance of family and work was not a priority. Most directors who have maintained a healthy balance in their lives have very understanding partners, many of which are or were involved with band as students or staff members. At a minimum, they understand and appreciate the band activity.

Children need to be given the same attention that a parent in any occupation would do. Take time to go to the child's events and don't always drag them to band events unless they truly want to go.

Family vacations are important and should be scheduled, budgeted and planned in advance. It is too easy to put it off if not planned. If the marching band is busy on Saturdays, make Sundays the family day. Plan short trips, picnics or anything that is special to the family.

Keeping the family a priority will not only be good for the family but will help the director maintain a healthy band/life balance.

Chapter Sixteen

Methods Class
Materials

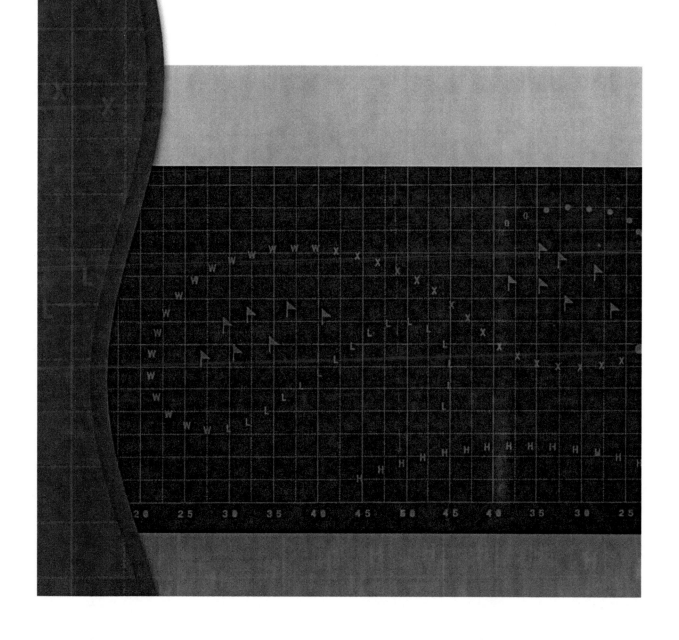

Methods Class Materials
Materials are provided for students and instructors to facilitate the learning and instruction of the marching band subject.

As stated in the Preface, this book was written as a textbook for the college music education major preparing to be a band director as well as for directors already "in the field." Sample class materials are provided online, (www.dynamicband.com), under Chapter 16 for the use of the students and teacher. This will give the students an understanding of what is expected of them by studying sample quizzes and exam questions. The teacher will have materials to use "as is" or to augment with other pertinent materials from their class lessons. Since files are in Word® format, changes and additions can easily be made.

A syllabus for a marching band methods course is presented including a weekly lesson format for a ten-week course. Some important components of a comprehensive, contemporary marching band methods class are suggested.

Observations of high school marching band rehearsals and competitions are essential for the young music educator. Studying a book and in-class discussions become relevant and meaningful when actual rehearsals and performances are experienced. During the early years of their careers, band directors should continue to take advantage of observing the most successful band programs possible. There is no greater motivator for directors (and their students) than to watch a great band in action.

Video/DVD presentations of marching band shows, preferably utilizing a big screen and a quality sound system, should be a regular part of the methods class. Having the students write comments on marching band adjudication sheets is a practical exercise that focuses their attention on specific areas. For example, during the discussion of Chapter 5: The Marching Program, students can use the various Marching Performance sheets. While studying Chapter 7: Show Planning, students can use the Music and/or Visual General Effect sheets. This can be a focal point for class discussion following the viewing. Using the judging sheets will also help the students become familiar with judging systems and terminology that they will encounter in competitive arenas.

It is highly recommended that an ample amount of time be devoted to drill writing. Not every director needs to be a drill writer, but every director needs to understand the concepts in order to teach drill effectively. He/she also needs to know how to evaluate the quality of a purchased drill. Many beginning directors will need, of necessity, to write basic drill in their first teaching position.

Assignments are available for many of the topics in the book. Of particular relevance are the drill writing exercises. These will be very helpful for the young director either writing drill or teaching and understanding a professional writer's drill.

Quizzes are available as samples for each chapter of The Dynamic Marching Band textbook. Since these are in a Word® format, they can easily be revised or added to creating a valuable resource for the instructor.

A sample Final Exam is available online, www.dynamicband.com This can be used as a study guide for students or as the actual test for with or without editing. There is nothing wrong with students knowing exactly what they are expected to know for quizzes and the final exam, eliminating "the guessing game."

Chapter Seventeen

Supplementary
Materials

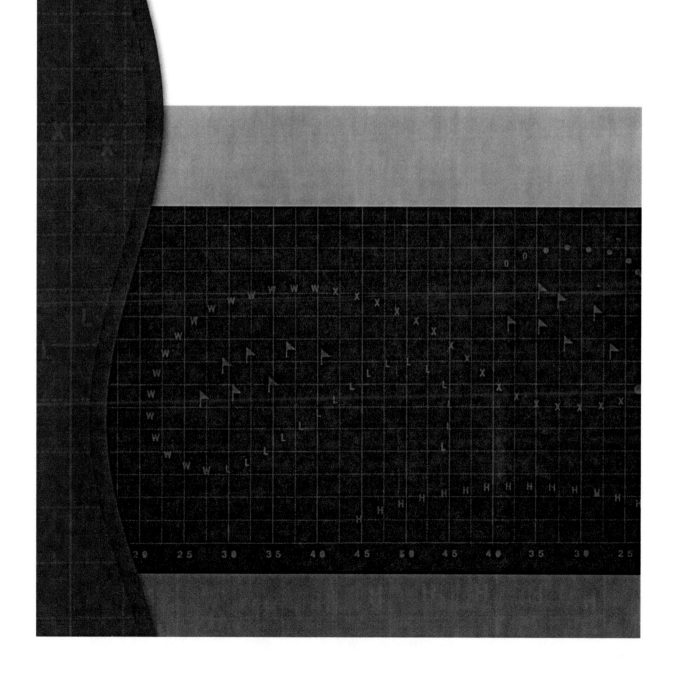

Supplementary Materials

www.dynamicband.com

The Dynamic Marching Band will be a timesaving resource for the young band director.

All successful band directors develop and adjust materials over a period of many years to save time and communicate effectively with the band students, staff, parents and administration. One of the key ingredients of The Dynamic Marching Band is the exclusive supplemental materials available for download including sample schedules, policies, recruiting tools, show plan guides and many other useful tools that can be adapted to fit the band director's situation. These files are in Word® and Excel® formats that can be altered as much or little as the director chooses. The intent is to save the young director countless hours of trial and error building up a library of usable materials.

Available materials are indicated on the text pages. Materials are accessible at www.dynamicband.com

Permission—What is allowed:

The purchaser of *The Dynamic Marching Band* is given permission to utilize the materials for his/her school only. Permission is also granted to edit the materials in any manner as is photocopying of these materials for the students of the school.

What is prohibited:

Copying of the supplementary materials available online is strictly prohibited as is sharing materials with other schools or individuals. This includes *The Dynamic Marching Band* materials that have been altered by the owner of the book.

The high school marching band is a positive, life-changing activity for students.

Make it a great experience for them and for yourself.

Enjoy!

About the Author

Wayne Markworth was Director of Bands at Centerville High School in Ohio for 35 years. He also served as Fine Arts Coordinator for the Centerville City Schools for five years and High School Music Department Chair for twenty years.

During his tenure the Centerville Band program involved over 250 students including three concert bands, three jazz ensembles, marching band, and two winter guards and two percussion ensembles. They received consistent superior ratings and awards and the Symphonic Band, Jazz Ensembles, and Marching Band performed at OMEA state conventions. Wayne developed the marching band, known as "The Centerville Jazz Band", into a unique and entertaining ensemble of 200 members that performed an all-jazz format on the field. They were finalists in Bands of America Regionals and Grand Nationals 57 times, with fourteen regional championships and the 1992 Grand Nationals Championship.

Wayne has been a consultant, arranger, and instructor for many bands and drum corps. His articles have appeared in several national music publications. He also performed for four years as principal trumpet with the Dayton Philharmonic Orchestra and studied trumpet with Vincent Cichowicz of the Chicago Symphony. Wayne received a Bachelor of Music Education degree from Indiana University and a Master of Music degree from Northwestern University.

Wayne has presented many clinics and workshops for students, directors and adjudicators on such topics as brass performance, the total band program, stress and performance, contemporary music and general effect in the marching band. He has taught music classes and workshops at the college level as well, including Miami University, Wright State University and the University of Dayton. In 1992, he received an Excellence in Teaching Award from the Dayton-Montgomery County Public Education Foundation and in 2000 received the Centerville Education Foundation Teacher of the Year Award. In recognition of his 35 years of service, Wayne was selected the Grand Marshall of the 2005 Centerville Americana Parade. In 2007, he was inducted into the Bands of America Hall of Fame. Wayne is an active clinician, adjudicator, arranger and trumpet performer and President of the music & consulting business Shadow Lake Music. He is currently teaching at Wright State University and is author of *The Dynamic Marching Band*, a textbook on Marching Band Methods.

Wayne Markworth
6321 Shadow Lake Trail
Centerville, Ohio 45459
937-434-4628
email: wmark@woh.rr.com

revised 9/04/07

—Notes—